ORIGINAL LOCAL

ORIGINAL LOCAL

INDIGENOUS FOODS, STORIES,

AND RECIPES

FROM THE UPPER MIDWEST

HEID E. ERDRICH

Minnesota Historical
Society Press

CLEAN
WATER
LAND &
LEGACY
AMENDMENT

www.mhspress.org

The Minnesota Historical Society Press is a member of the Association of American University Presses.

Manufactured in the United States of America

10 9 8 7 6 5 4

∞ The paper used in this publication meets the minimum requirements of the American National Standard for Information Sciences—Permanence for Printed Library Materials, ANSI Z39.48-1984.

International Standard Book Number
ISBN: 978-0-87351-894-9 (paper)

Illustrations by Aza Erdrich.
Photographs on pages ii-iii, 54, 92, 95, 166, 196, 203, 224, 244 by Kate N. G. Sommers.
Photographs on pages 2, 18, 107, 123, 166, 193, 222, 247 by Angie Erdrich.

Library of Congress Cataloging-in-Publication Data

Erdrich, Heid E. (Heid Ellen)
Original local : indigenous foods, stories, and recipes from the Upper Midwest / Heid E. Erdrich.
pages cm
Summary: "Indigenous peoples have always made the most of nature's gifts. Their menus were truly the 'original local,' celebrated here in 135 home-tested recipes paired with stories from tribal activists, food researchers, families, and chefs"—Provided by publisher.
Includes bibliographical references and index.
ISBN 978-0-87351-894-9 (pbk.)
1. Indians of North America—Food—Northwest, Old. 2. Indian cooking.
3. Local foods—Northwest, Old. I. Title.
E98.F7E735 2013
641.59′297—dc23

2013029114

Original Local was designed and set in type by Cathy Spengler.
The typefaces are Malaga and Ideal Sans.

For John Burke and to all our relatives,
in the spirit of manoomin
and all the good seeds

··· CONTENTS ···

MAPLE AND BERRIES

••• **197** •••

Maple Coffee 198

Berry Mistaken Ideas and Bear Nature 206

HERBS AND TEA

••• **225** •••

The Great Milkweed Caper 226

GOOD SEEDS

••• **246** •••

ACKNOWLEDGMENTS

••• **247** •••

RESOURCES

••• **249** •••

INDEX

••• **252** •••

ORIGINAL LOCAL

··· FOODS OF THIS

The foods of this earth, foods of this place where our ancestors lived near the Great Lakes and Great Plains, have long been a core of knowledge in my family. Living in North Dakota and in Minnesota, there was never a time when we—my parents, grandparents, relatives, and siblings—did not grow, gather, and hunt part of our own food each year. We learned early about cultivating our own plants, gathering wild foods, and respecting the animals whose lives we took. We learned a balance

EARTH •••

of the natural world and our human place in that balance. We have been relearning that lesson all our lives.

Our parents, Ralph and Rita Erdrich, were teachers who tended a large garden on their double lot in our small town in the Red River Valley. My early memories revolve around playing in or near my parents' garden, which was planted with strawberries, asparagus, squash, cucumbers, beans, peas, raspberries, currants, and dozens of other tasty, living, growing green things. We learned about wild plants, too, gathering Juneberries, wild plums, and other fruits. Many edible green plants, such as lamb's-quarters and sorrel, I've been able to identify practically all my life. In my childhood eye my mother is always "putting up" quart or pint jars of fruit or tomatoes in her speckled enamel canner, my father is always coming in the screen door with the day's garden offerings or with asparagus sprung from the seeds he scattered along the river that makes the North Dakota–South Dakota–Minnesota border of my family's homeland.

Even as a child, I knew that some plants were indigenous to our area and some were not, although I do not recall being given specific lessons in the subject. I knew that people living in the middle of North Dakota, the indigenous groups called the Hidatsa, Arikara, and Mandan, were great gardeners who grew corn, squash, and beans—the Three Sisters—as well as sunflowers. And I knew our Plains Ojibwe and Métis ancestors hunted bison. My own grandfather, Patrick Gourneau, had been a truck farmer whose enormous cabbages nourished many a farm family near the Turtle Mountain Reservation where my mother grew up and where my father taught before they were married.

I remember Grandpa's garden, too, but a later version, from the days when he was done with work as a farmer and grew only what he needed—a few rows of potatoes, beets, corn, melons, and cabbages of a hearty, but not gigantic, size. He also grew rhubarb, a plant I was disappointed to learn was not indigenous to North America. Tribal people all over seem to have an affinity for rhubarb, so I had just assumed it was always here. I remember that Grandpa let us munch the stalks as we walked between the rows of vegetables, and once he showed me that throwing the big rhubarb leaves down over the weeds makes handy mulch. That lesson I forgot until years later when my mother did the very same thing in one of my earliest gardens in Minnesota, and the memory of my grandpa Pat came flooding back to me. I've taught my own kids to mulch with large leaves, and I feel the garden path laid out for them through their ancestors' ways.

When I decided to write this book, I thought of my kids and what they might learn about the living world. I wish for them a childhood like my own, but that seems impossible—you can't let kids run around eating right off the vine in the cities these days—and yet what is more important than giving them a sense of how the earth where they live has nourished those who came before and can sustain them now, too?

Sometimes I tell my kids how we spent most of the year outside with our neighbors, who, it happens, were mostly Ojibwe and Dakota kids. We sometimes played at village making—gathering piles of "firewood," picking greens, snagging crab apples, and sampling berries we knew were edible. Perhaps we had some collective knowledge that came of culture, but I cannot be sure. Did other kids play this game as "camping" or some kind of back-to-nature fun in the 1970s? I do not know. But I can say our play gave us confidence. We knew we could make a raw and sour meal if circumstances required. But although my family was relatively self-sufficient in terms of produce, we did not push the envelope when it came to traditional methods of cooking or preserving foods. We did not eat a food just because it was available and something our ancestors ate.

When I was a child, if you had asked me if my mother served "Indian" food, I might have been baffled, but eventually I would have said yes and cited as my example Bullets and Bangs, which was meatball and potato soup served with small pieces of fry bread made from white flour and deep-fried. Now I know that the only thing indigenous about that traditional meal is the potato, a cousin food that came up from South America and is not officially indigenous to the Upper Midwest. But food ways are sometimes transparent: our way with food washes over us and we see through it because it is normal to us, the way we live that we

Patrick and Mary Gourneau farm, 1934

do not know is different from the way others live. In collecting these recipes, I learned that much of what I ate growing up, and much of what I eat now, is based in indigenous practice. And I learned to appreciate my eating as an enormous privilege indebted to the passions of indigenous people who protect these foods and seek to change the spiritual and physical health of their people by returning to an awareness of a way that makes us, and now the world, strong.

Indigenous foods evolved over many thousands of years to suit themselves to our climate. In the case of manoomin (wild rice), several genetically diverse types of the grass grew to suit specific lakes and rivers. Any change in the water's purity and, most distressingly, the water level itself threatens that specific variety of manoomin with extinction. Sometimes writing about and even cooking these foods seems like the band playing on the deck of the doomed ship *Titanic.* And yet, if we do not focus on them, who will want to save them? Gary Paul Nabhan, author of *Renewing America's Food Traditions,* had just such a notion when he created a book that urges folks to eat heirloom turkey, hand-harvested manoomin, and real Jerusalem artichokes.

Foods that indigenous people grew in the Great Lakes and Great Plains regions and the naturalized foods that came from other areas of North America are less at risk than manoomin, but they too respond to climate change and pollution. As I was writing this book, the unheard of took place: several food harvests were complete misses. On my annual visit to my home reservation (conveniently timed to coincide with when we usually pick chokecherries), I was dismayed to discover a late frost had killed the buds, along with the Juneberries and puckons, or wild hazelnuts. To tell you the truth, I was more than dismayed: I was full-on freaked. Such a thing had never happened to me or to my fellow berry pickers. We did not even have to say the phrase *climate change;* the freakiness of the occurrence said it for us.

That same September, the folks I planned to process wild rice with had no manoomin to harvest due to water level changes. Many lakes did not freeze well enough for an ice fishing season that winter, and there was no sugar bush because the maple trees had woken up too often and too early in the mild winter, and then a drought summer made for a second year with no sugar bush for my friends. These disasters speak ominously, but no one is giving up hope. Folks involved with indigenous food production, food independence and healthy food programs, and food sovereignty movements—efforts to maintain control of

Rita Gourneau Erdrich with her seven children, 1966

foods tribes developed—are remarkably full of wonder and hope. Many point to the rise of indigenous gardening programs, tribal efforts to protect corn, manoomin, and other sacred plants, and the increasing number of indigenous farmers as signs that the struggle has growing energy. We will retain our food ways into the new century.

*J*ust as these indigenous foods movements are growing, my awareness of indigenous foods and the issues surrounding them has grown over my lifetime. I do not consider myself a cook or even a foodie. And though my parents shared much knowledge of gardening and gathering with us, it was living in the Native American House at my college that really got me interested in cooking. At some point I began to buy cookbooks that I read as much for the history and culture they offered as for the recipes. Eventually I began cooking for crowds for special occasions, but I did not really cook for myself until after college.

After graduation, I found myself living in Paris. You would not think a person could just happen into life in Paris, but I did. For six months. Unexpectedly, and just as I was arriving in the city totally unprepared and broke, the French government instated a visa system that made it impossible for me to work. Instead, I cooked. I had a place to live, just a little money for emergencies, and no capacity with the language. What else was I to do? I cooked for myself, for the few friends I met there, and for an easygoing boyfriend who paid the rent. Cooking in France was a little tricky at first. There was the whole metric thing, for one. Plus I had been vegetarian for years, while those I was cooking for were passionate meat eaters. And the only cookbook I brought with me was for macrobiotic cooking. Yet I soon learned the way of the *lardon* and the *moule*, of pâté and mutton. In college I had watched my sheep-herding Diné (Navajo) friends not only cook mutton stew, a tribal favorite, but bring home a whole sheep and roast it in a pit. In Paris, when I saw mutton in the markets of a nearby neighborhood of Moroccan immigrants, I decided to learn to cook it. In other markets I discovered a half dozen new mushrooms, a hundred wonderful cheeses, the worth of crème fraîche, and more. I hope always to recall, with vivid scent memory, the first time I smelled grated whole nutmeg blooming in the heat of freshly sautéed summer squash.

Ironically, it was in France that I became distinctly aware of indigenous foods of the Americas, mostly because I missed them so much. I missed peanuts and peanut butter. I missed seeing pumpkins in the autumn—I missed pie. Chilies were hard to come by. And I had a hankering for maple the entire time. Most of all, I yearned for corn in any form: at the time, very little corn was available to cook with in Europe. A world without tortillas and tortilla chips was unimaginable to me, an ardent maker of salsa and enchiladas. Around the time of American Thanksgiving, and in desperation, I bought a can of baby corns, a food I've never enjoyed, anywhere. Those limp, sad, fetal corns just did not do the trick. Then we found popcorn, somewhere, and I knew I could endure.

It was also in France that I learned to suck it up, culinarily speaking, by reading my one cookbook, *Zen Macrobiotic Cooking* by Michel Abehsera. Turns out he was French. And he was a sympathetic soul, inscribing his cookbook "To my fellow man—for whom I worry and dedicate my life." I had expected the book to be vegetarian, but the food way Abehsera promoted included fish and fowl as secondary food sources. The author shared my feelings about beef and pork, so those were out. But his attitude was open, easy, and aware of human nature in a way that matched my own leanings: "Meat finds its way into Zen macrobiotics, quite simply, as a concession to man's sensual desires." Abehsera's teacher was George Ohaswa, whom he never failed to describe in a manner that let the reader know the master was constantly smoking. Perhaps another concession to man's sensual desires?

Although I read that book repeatedly and with intense interest, I never got the art of knowing which foods were yin and which yang. But I do remember balking at the detail that potatoes, tomatoes, and eggplant were considered "too yang for human consumption." I ignored all that, since those were among my favorite foods and mostly indigenous to the Americas. I figured Abehsera was just not thinking of Native Americans—perhaps we simply needed more yang foods. I also ignored the Zen master's advice to "eliminate coffee" and to avoid drinking liquids while eating. And he suggested a Zen approach to chewing I could not get the hang of, or I never really tried. Yet he taught me to make pumpkin and zucchini tempura, and looking back at Abehsera's recipes now, I realize I came to love cooking with toasted sesame oil, couscous, and watercress because of his book. He also brought me to a lifelong appreciation of the Japanese knife as well as the habit of avoiding "industrialized foods." Most importantly, I took to heart Abehsera's advice to eat locally, although he did not phrase it that way when he said, "Try not to eat food that is grown in a climate very far away from your country." He also encouraged readers to eat organically, to eat wild birds and fish. He sounded indigenous to me.

While I could not incorporate all that *Zen Macrobiotic Cooking* suggested, I did learn lessons that stay with me and inform the book you hold today. "I cannot urge you enough to be flexible and unafraid," Michel Abehsera wrote. In using these recipes I have gathered for you—and in supporting protection of indigenous foods, as I hope my readers will do—I urge you to be equally flexible and unafraid.

USING THIS BOOK

*I*ndigenous foods are my favorites, always have been: manoomin (wild rice), morel mushrooms, squash, smoked whitefish, salmon, potatoes, tomatoes, raspberries, chokecherries, Juneberries, real maple syrup. Corn and beans and peppers! I used to play a kind of parlor game where I would ask folks what ten foods they would take to a totally new planet. Most would list foods that originated in the Western hemisphere: corn chips or tacos, tomato sauce or salsa, chili, fried potatoes, strawberries, pumpkin pie, and so on. Plus cheese. Clearly these foods are not just my favorites, but American favorites. I enjoyed ending the game by identifying which of the selected foods existed in America before contact with Europeans. But the game was serious for me. I often imagined how, if shot into space, we could all live happily on what our ancestors ate and be grateful to them.

That game was preparation for a real-world situation I got myself into a few years ago, just after I had agreed to write this book. Following the lead of Devon Mihesuah, Choctaw author and professor who directs the American Indian Health and Diet Project, I took a one-week challenge to eat only indigenous foods my ancestors would have known. I made no special plans for the week. Since indigenous foods have always been a favorite, I figured I had enough in my pantry to carry me through. I began by eating wild rice porridge with maple and berries, sunflower seeds and walnuts for snacks, manoomin salad with berries and pumpkin seeds for lunch, and corn soup for dinner. The next day I ate nearly the same, but I added squash with maple and had salmon for dinner. My meals were filling and I felt exceedingly healthy: all that fiber and those vitamins revved me up. The week began well enough. But soon I was bored.

DON'T BE A PURIST

Because of my ignorance, my diet lacked sharp flavors: no garlic, no onions, no leeks. I had yet to be introduced to ramps (wild leeks). I missed sautéing vegetables in oil before making a meal. I had not yet discovered there had long been a traditional technique of grinding nuts and seeds to extract oils here. Oddly, I found I missed animal products—eggs and dairy. I had not thought of duck, quail, or turkey eggs. I craved cheese, though I eat very little of it in general. And I missed salt. Humans seem to need salt and seasoning, but I was not sure what salt or seasonings we used before European trade began, so I just went without. Most of all, I missed spicy-hot foods. I realized I would never make it a week without reaching beyond my region—my foodshed that straddles the Great Lakes and Mississippi watersheds. I did not take the time to research much about what I could eat, thinking I actually knew a fair amount. But there was a kind of stubbornness to my thinking: I did without the oil in an attempt to understand how foods might have tasted once, long before supermarket luxury and fusion cuisine.

Still, for all my high-mindedness, I cheated. There was no way I was going to leave off on my coffee—though I drank it black for the week, rather than with half-and-half, which is how a real Minnesotan takes her brew. I rationalized that I came by my love of coffee genetically. My Anishinaabe ancestors so loved coffee that they called it *Makade-mashkikiwaaboo,* Black Medicine Water. They respected coffee as a medicine, a drink with a powerful spirit at its center. I uphold that tradition with pride. But really, coffee was just the gateway to failure in my week of indigenous eating. Truth is, I was fudging all along. If an ingredient I used had salt or oil in it (like the pumpkin seeds in my salad), I let that slide. I've never been a purist. Perhaps because I was born of an Anishinaabe-French mother and a German-American father, I've always liked things mixed up.

LET INDIGENOUS FOODS OF THE HEMISPHERE UNITE

Although I had tried to eat only foods that could have been grown or gathered in my immediate surroundings in Minnesota, I was just not prepared to do so for an entire week. My supplies were low, and I wanted to avoid an expensive shopping trip for foods the rest of my family might not be eating. So, the salmon I ate was wild from Alaska, caught by a friend of a friend and stored in my freezer. On the third day, I used smoked salt from Oregon, justifying it as indigenous because the label called it "Yakima salt." We had grown up with a family of Anishinaabe-Yakima nearby, which lent my fudging a semblance of personal tradition. Soon I was ready to move on to indigenous foods not available in my homeland but ready to hand in most pantries. I made some chili with beans that would grow here but peppers that would not—or had not until recent times. But I ate that chili with corn tortillas, foregoing corn chips because the oil in the particular brand I had on hand was not from an indigenous plant. Animal fat was once preferred for cooking but not always available since indigenous game is generally quite lean. But by day four I was using sunflower oil, and I had branched out to the continent, making guacamole (avocados were an Aztec crop) with salsa (indigenous pre-Mexicans domesticated tomatoes), adding ground allspice berries (also from Mexico and said to taste like spiceberries, historically an Ojibwe favorite flavoring) to everything. Eventually I added select foods from South America as well, eating potatoes and pineapple. Lots of pineapple.

What I learned in a few short days was that I was simply not prepared for an entire week of eating an indigenous diet. I did not know enough about what my ancestors ate, and I had not stocked the larder with items that might make such eating possible. I'd also held myself to a standard I later learned was a bit excessive. Even with my cheating, I had aimed for 100 percent when the goal was to use *mostly* indigenous ingredients. Likewise, the idea behind the recipes in this book is to explore using *mostly* indigenous ingredients from the Upper Midwest.

REMEMBER THAT A RECIPE IS A STORY

The recipes in this book focus on but do not restrict ingredients to indigenous foods of the region, nor do they require ancient cooking methods. Let's be practical. Knowing and appreciating our indigenous foods and the people whose passions they arouse is at the heart of this book. I am not offering a consumer sport challenge to take the most "authentic" approach to what can be simple and natural, a daily practice of including foods with a long history, with stories we should know.

A recipe is a story. It suggests the characters (or understudies in the form of substitutes) and narrates how the whole comes from parts. Recipes are middles; they rarely give a full sense of the beginning—the gathering of the ingredients—or the ending—the eating. Recipes for *Original Local* center on foods that grew in the Great Lakes–Great Plains area for centuries and, through brief portraits of indigenous people, also tell the story of the gathering and the eating where they can.

LEARN ABOUT INDIGENOUS FOODS ISSUES

I thought I knew which foods were indigenous, but the two years since that November "week of indigenous eating" have taught me more about my ignorance than almost anything else. It has been delicious but at times disheartening research. Indigenous foods mirror indigenous struggles. Climate change is terribly real, and it is threatening the food ways of people in the Upper Midwest more than anywhere in the United States.

Although the topic of indigenous foods is timely, this volume is decidedly not a new diet book or a lifestyle plan or prescriptive trend. These recipes are meant to help cooks focus on ingredients that have grown in and been planted, stewarded, and eaten in the Great Lakes and Mississippi River watersheds for centuries, if not millennia. A glance through the tables of contents for each section will show that the recipes are not all that exotic. It would be ironic if they seemed so, since the foods we are working with originated in this area, and we have all probably seen if not eaten them.

THINK OF THE THREE SISTERS

To prepare for the approach used in these recipes, think of the Three Sisters: corn, beans, and squash. These staples of indigenous North American eating have fed the world, especially in terms of corn and beans, now dominant food species across the globe. These foods have been grown or carefully stewarded by the first peoples of our region, my ancestors included, for a very long time. Of course, we did not engineer genetic modifications, but we did cultivate many of these foods. We did not just pick them here and there when we stumbled across them in the wilds, as the term *hunter-gatherer* suggests. We grew in relationship to the foods and they to us. We continue to protect the Three Sisters in their early (and non-GMO) forms, and we hope a little advice will encourage you to do so, too.

FEAR NOT, VEGETARIANS, VEGANS, AND THE GLUTEN FREE

I've been taught that Anishinaabe people do not eat their clan animals. Not so hard if you are bear clan, but if you are fish clan, I guess you do not eat fish, or at least your clan's specific fish—say, sturgeon. Some tribes shun eating their spouse's clan animal, too. Women of tribes related to Anishinaabe told me to avoid certain meats (and vegetables) while I was pregnant. I've heard holy people of several nations explain that they refrain from hunting for the sake of their particular spiritual medicine. The stereotype is that the region's original inhabitants ate a lot of meat, but these rules suggest otherwise. In fact, I've been told that if I ever dream an animal makes love to me, I am not to eat that animal. And, well, I am an imaginative dreamer. My culinary choices have been limited.

There's the old joke: What do you call an Indian vegetarian? A bad hunter. That witticism used to make me mad, not because most of my life I have practiced an odd sort of quasi-vegetarianism but because it assumes we were always strictly carnivores and our love of bacon and beef is some kind of cultural tradition. Something always told me that was not so, and the lessons I've learned from elders make me think we were, as all humans are, people with diverse tastes and inclinations. That said, I cannot claim to be a pure vegetarian; I am not a pure anything. But I never eat, or cook with, beef, pork, or chicken. In fact, I rarely eat meat of any kind. I have made this choice (and it is a choice, not a religion) not in denial of my ancestry but in reverence to it and to the reciprocal relationships people once had with animals.

I've developed many of these recipes as vegetarian. Also, because there was no dairy or wheat in this area before European contact, many of the dishes in this book are not only vegetarian but dairy free, and if you are careful you can cut the gluten, too. (For a western hemisphere egg substitute, use 2 teaspoons arrowroot powder mixed well with 3 tablespoons warm water. And for gluten-free cooking, try wild rice flour, available from realwildrice.com.) But don't fret, carnivores: an entire section collects recipes centered on indigenous fish and game animals or their domesticated descendants: bison, duck, venison, rabbit, turkey, and small wild fowl.

TAKE THIS ADVICE

Think of the critters we see only in this part of the world, and you have yourself a menu: Three Sisters plus brother bison, or turkey, or fish. Following this approach of substituting an indigenous ingredient where it is easy—butternut squash for carrots, sunflower seeds for almonds, ground turkey or cooked manoomin (wild rice) for ground beef—you can easily "indigenize" your own recipes and your shopping list.

Do not be afraid of the cost of manoomin, a staple that infuses these recipes. It's a good investment and goes a long, long way. The good stuff, the real manoomin, as opposed to cultivated wild rice, can quadruple in volume and cooks in twenty minutes or less. A pound can make six to eight recipes here, as most call for a cup of cooked manoomin.

Shop the bulk herb and tea aisle to find seasonings once used in cooking. Our food is our medicine, the Ojibwe ancestors said. Nettle tea as an herbal remedy is more commonly available than nettle greens in the produce aisle, so at some level I think the knowledge of our medicines is still out there. Whether an item is available as remedy or recipe ingredient is not as important as the fact that we can find our indigenous foods around us if we just learn to look.

When possible, I urge you to buy ingredients from Native American sources to support efforts to protect indigenous foods. But check out your discount stores, too. Many foods indigenous to our region are staples of the midwestern kitchen and easily available in supermarkets and farmers markets. Food co-ops generally carry all the items used in these recipes, but many ingredients (maple, smoked fish, duck, polenta, frozen and dried wild berries) are available at discount stores such as ALDI, Trader Joe's, and even Costco.

Resources such as Native Food Network (nativefoodnetwork.com) feature news, videos, and articles on recent developments in the growing indigenous foods movement; use the "Online Ordering Market" tab to see what seasonal items are available in the Upper Midwest. In Minneapolis, the Four Sisters Farmers Market on Franklin features indigenous foods vendors weekly. Also in Minneapolis, indigenous farm Dream of Wild Health sells at the Midtown Farmers Market on Lake Street. An internet search will yield current days and addresses.

Google it. Internet resources such as localharvest.org make finding duck eggs or bison or mushrooms near where you live easier all the time, and the Upper Midwest has a bounty of options. In this book you will also find resources that focus on food businesses owned and operated by tribal members and their families. Please support American Indian–owned food businesses and projects. Updated information about these resources can be found at my site, heiderdrich.com.

INDIGENIZE YOUR PANTRY

A little list of less-often stocked items for use in these recipes

SWEETENERS AND FLAVORINGS

- *chokecherry and wild berry syrups; wild berry and wild fruit jellies and jams*
- *maple sugar (granulated); maple syrup (100 percent pure)*
- *natural salt and natural smoked salt*

HERBS AND SPICES

- *asafran, Mexican oregano (dried spices used in Mexican cooking)*
- *herbal teas (naturally flavored mint, sage, wild cherry, licorice root)*
- *juniper berries (at spice stores)*
- *nettle (dried, in bulk at natural food stores and co-ops)*
- *sumac (ground or powdered, at spice stores)*
- *whole allspice (as a substitute for indigenous spicebush berries)*
- *wild mint, wild oregano, bergamot (grow or order online)*

CANNED VEGETABLES

- *beans (black, great northern)*
- *nopales (cactus)*
- *pumpkin*

DRIED FOODS

- *beans (scarlet runner, cranberry, and other heirloom varieties)*
- *berries (cranberries and blueberries)*

- *cornmeal (all varieties, including blue corn)*
- *hominy, parched corn, dried sweet corn*
- *manoomin (hand-harvested wild rice)*
- *mushrooms (dried morels or woodland mix)*

NUTS AND SEEDS

- *black walnuts, pecans, hickory nuts, wild hazelnuts*
- *sunflower seeds, pumpkin seeds or pepitas (roasted and raw, salted and unsalted)*

FISH, MEAT, EGGS

- *duck and quail eggs*
- *game meat (farm-raised bison, venison, turkey, duck, rabbit)*
- *jerky (bison, venison, salmon)*
- *smoked whitefish and lake trout*

FRESH SEASONAL ITEMS

- *berries (Juneberries or saskatoons, gooseberries or currants)*
- *fresh seasonal wild greens (lamb's-quarters, dandelions, fiddleheads)*
- *ground cherries (substitute tomatillos)*
- *mushrooms (morel, puffball, chanterelle)*
- *ramps (also called wild leeks or wild onions)*

Spirit Plate, Bagijigan,
by Aza Erdrich

··· MANOOMIN—PSIN

WILD RICE •••

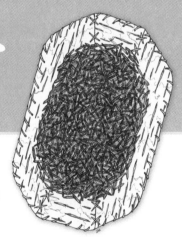

*M*anoomin, often translated as "good seed," is what Anishinaabe people call wild rice. Dakota call it *psin,* and other tribes had their own names for this important food source derived from an aquatic grass. Real manoomin differs significantly from the very dark, hard, shiny, cultivated "wild rice" grown mostly in California. Products labeled "wild rice" are not required to be hand harvested or even truly wild; however, they must be labeled "cultivated," so you should easily be able to differentiate between the two types. Packaging for real manoomin uses terms such as "hand harvested" in order to distinguish itself from cultivated or "paddy rice" and, since tribes near the Great Lakes retain treaty rights to the waters that produce manoomin, the packaging may make reference to the particular band whose members harvested it. Minnesota state laws curtail use of imagery associated with Native Americans on cultivated wild rice and on manoomin harvested by non-Natives.

The real stuff must be gathered using traditional methods—from canoes, rather than airboat, using poles and sticks called *knockers.* Ojibwe rice harvester Ron Libertus, former special services director for the Minnesota Department of Natural Resources, whose activism in the 1980s resulted in laws around manoomin, told me he wished efforts had gone further to enact larger protections for the food considered sacred by his people. Others have taken up Ron's fight, and in 2007 Congress passed a law requiring disclosure and environmental impact statements from anyone attempting to create genetically engineered wild rice, but that law is already considered inadequate protection from contamination of natural manoomin by any genetically modified plant using "wild rice" genes.

Real manoomin varies widely in color, texture, aroma, and shape depending upon where and when it was harvested. Finished manoomin displays many differences in appearance and flavor as well, from the lightness of new rice to the more substantial hand-parched rice. Hand-harvested, hand-parched manoomin can be dark and smoky or medium toned, even somewhat translucent. Other manoomin can be light green, almost milky, if picked early. Some manoomin is machine processed and may lose much of its brown-green outer coating. River manoomin, much less frequently harvested, tends to be longer and thinner than lake manoomin. Some folks like only hand-parched manoomin from a particular lake for all recipes; others prefer new rice or lightly colored rice for breakfasts and salad recipes. Differences in taste and texture of particular sources influence the preferences of cooks who are very familiar with manoomin, but these differences should not be a significant factor in these recipes unless specifically noted. You can use any hand-harvested manoomin for all these recipes, but if you are new to this ingredient, try a few different kinds of manoomin over the course of a year to see which best suits your style.

Throughout this book, I use the word *manoomin* to refer to the real, hand-harvested product grown wild in the Great Lakes region. I reserve the term *cultivated wild rice* for the cultivated variety often used in pancake mixes and other commercial products. However, none of the recipes in this book that call for manoomin were tested on cultivated wild rice, and I do not recommend substituting cultivated wild rice for manoomin.

BACON AND CREAM OF MUSHROOM SOUP

No that is not a recipe suggestion, although I am sure some of you will prepare this combination for lunch now that I've mentioned it. Dozens of favorite recipes from friends and family members in Indian Country call for cream of mushroom soup and bacon. One contributor mentioned that, due to diabetes, he uses olive oil rather than bacon grease.

Bacon and cream are not indigenous, and mushrooms swathed in whey, MSG, and salt just do not make the most healthful food, no matter how traditional Campbell's or Walmart soup has become. Many people choose lean meats because of health concerns but add weird fats and sodium when they pick up the can opener. In these recipes, I often suggest a splash of half-and-half rather than a starch-based sauce because many people already have half-and-half available for their coffee and a little goes a long way. Brown a few mushrooms with onions and finish with a splash of half-and-half, light cream, milk, or even evaporated milk, stir vigorously, and you have a quick mushroom cream sauce without added sugar, salt, or engineered ingredients.

The rage for bacon is harder to assuage. Humans must be hardwired to get their bac on. But in the spirit of learning the local and the indigenous, I try to persuade folks to leave off on the pork. Perhaps I can appeal to those who want to be ahead of the crowd rather than trending with it. The next big thing is jerky. You heard it here.

Jerky can be ground, chopped, chunked, mixed with dried berries or hot peppers, and seasoned sweet, savory, or both. Jerky works beautifully in soups, casseroles, even in breads. Beans and wiiyaas (dried meat) went together during several centuries of human eating before bacon and fatback came along as ration foods. Beans and dried meat love one another, and bacon has been interloping too long.

Jerky is a convenient, less-risky way to experiment with game meats, too. In gas stations all across Wisconsin, Minnesota, and the Dakotas, I have seen bison, elk, venison, even turkey jerky. Let's not talk about emu sticks, since emu is not indigenous. Several Native American food businesses also sell bison jerky and summer sausage. I've found salmon and bison jerky at Trader Joe's, at a price below any beef jerky at any super pump gas station. That salmon is good! And, of course, you can get excellent Great Lakes dried fish at markets along Michigan and Superior shores, too.

My point: it is all good, and bacon can step aside for awhile.

MANOOMIN BASICS

Be sure to examine your rice before you cook it to make sure there's no sand or chaff present. If your manoomin looks like it needs it, clean it before cooking. Most rice is nice and clean, but even clean manoomin might appear a bit dusty. Some people say the dust adds flavor. Some people wash it off. If your manoomin is very dusty or appears sandy, pick it over carefully before cooking and perhaps toss it in a colander a few times to allow grit to sift out. I wash mine right in the pot by spraying with cold water several times, allowing any chaff and any unhusked rice to float to the top, stirring and skimming by hand, and carefully pouring off the excess water. Out of respect for the indigenous folks who hand harvest and process manoomin, I always break the husk on any unhulled seeds and return the seed to the pot. I know from watching the harvest that ricers would never let a grain go to waste, so I try my hardest never to toss one, either.

There may be as many directions for basic stovetop or oven cooking of manoomin as there are families in which it is cooked. In fact, my own family recommends assorted techniques. My sister Angie, a doctor and therefore a scientific cook, advises: "One pound wild rice [manoomin] is roughly 2¾ cups and this yields 20 generous servings. Dry wild rice [manoomin] will puff up to at least 4 times its size when cooked. A general rule: add 3 cups water or broth for every cup dry rice."

Sister Louise says to put manoomin in "a good solid pot" and wash off the dust with cold running water in two to three rinses, then add stock up to the first knuckle of your thumb. She instructs the cook to boil manoomin, but cautions: "the time varies depending on how it was finished and where it grew. Watch it closely as it approaches done. Test for al dente. You don't want mushy rice."

My husband, John Burke, uses 1 ½ to 2 cups of water to 1 cup rinsed manoomin and a heavy pot with a good lid to cook all varieties of manoomin the same way: bring to a boil, reduce heat to low and cover, simmer for 12 to 15 minutes, then turn off heat and let sit for 12 to 15 minutes—no peeking. (Lighter rice needs less water and less time; darker rice needs more water and more time.) This approach makes a mess of the stove, with the steam spurting out "rice milk" to cook about the burner, but it works to make good rice.

I suggest that for most recipes here, 1 cup of *rinsed* manoomin in 2 cups of water, brought to a boil in a heavy, medium-size pot with a lid and allowed to simmer on low for 15 to 20 minutes, will result in nicely cooked rice that can be used in recipes where it will cook further. My recipes call for cooked manoomin because uncooked rice can soak up a lot of liquid. Cooked manoomin continues to expand as well, a factor I've taken into account in these recipes.

Some cooks boil manoomin uncovered, watching the liquid level and the swell of the rice to get just what they like. Whatever you do, you do not want to "break" manoomin and have it curl up on you, although you do want it to open up a bit and give off its wonderful aroma of toasted nut and lake and smoke.

For breakfast porridge or for use in baked goods, I cook manoomin until it nearly breaks but does not curl. For recipes in which manoomin is accepting sweet substances (maple, honey, sugar), it must be soft cooked and a little wet or it will harden. White and brown sugars seem to make manoomin harden up more quickly. Eat your treats right away (or plan to share) if you want sweet manoomin recipes at their best.

TYPES OF MANOOMIN AND CULTIVATED WILD RICE

There are several types of manoomin that you might see labeled with different terms, including long-grain wild rice, hand-parched wild rice (or hand-parched manoomin), or lake-harvested natural wild rice. Native Harvest labels their wild rice as Manoomin. These recipes call for any hand-harvested manoomin, whether it be lake or river rice or a combination of both. For recipes in which manoomin is the main ingredient, I prefer manoomin that has been hand parched, which tastes a bit richer and often smokier than other manoomin. Do not confuse hand-parched manoomin with cultivated "roasted wild rice," which is marketed by a Minnesota supermarket chain as the basis of the popular wild rice soup sold in their deli.

Tribally owned Red Lake Nation Foods in Minnesota markets several types of cultivated wild rice, including a quick-cooking variety that takes twenty-five minutes, comparable in preparation time to most hand-harvested manoomin and less expensive and easily available. In many supermarkets, Red Lake Nation's cultivated wild rice has earned a "Local Food" label or is featured in the regional product area.

Occasionally I use "broken rice"—the manoomin grains that were damaged in processing, also sometimes called "soup rice" by manoomin packagers. It tastes no different from whole manoomin; it just has a different texture. Broken manoomin is good in recipes that do not need really pretty grains or for times when you grind up or blend the rice. For such recipes, you might, in the spirit of support for tribal ventures, experiment with Red Lake Nation's cultivated wild rice product marketed as "soup bits."

MANOOMIN TROUBLESHOOTING

If the bottom of your pot of manoomin burns, simply serve the unburned portion if it tastes good. I have been known to pour boiling water over burned rice, let it steep a bit, and then strain out that water to drink as tea. It tastes a little like Japanese bancha. Even burned, manoomin smells good.

If manoomin is too wet, don't worry; just drain off the extra liquid and return to heat for one to two minutes, or put a lid on the pot and let the liquid absorb.

If chaff has been cooked into the manoomin, it is most likely on top where you can see it because it will be much lighter, tan rather than brown, and you can remove most of it by hand. If manoomin is gritty from sand or pebbles, there's nothing you can do about it once it is cooked except tell people to be careful—so clean it as well as you can before cooking. See Manoomin Basics (page 22) for cleaning instructions.

BARBARA MESABA MORRISON'S MANOOMIN

SERVES A CROWD | *For fifty years Hazel Belvo has painted Manido-giizhikens, the four-hundred-year-old spirit tree. This tree grows from a rock cliff above Lake Superior on the Grand Portage Reservation, where her son Briand Morrison, a musician, now lives. One summer when I visited her studio, I brought some hand-finished manoomin. In return, Hazel shared this recipe from the painter George Morrison's mother, Barbara Mesaba Morrison.*

2 cups manoomin, rinsed and drained
6 cups water or stock
8 slices bacon, cut into thin strips
1 large onion, chopped
1 cup slivered almonds
salt and black pepper

In a large saucepan, combine manoomin and water or stock. Bring to a boil, reduce heat to low, and cook until rice begins to swell but is still firm. Pour off excess liquid.

In a separate pan, fry bacon strips over medium heat until crisp. Add chopped onion and cook until transparent. Using a slotted spoon, remove bacon and onion pieces. Discard excess bacon grease.

In an oven-safe dish, combine bacon-onion mixture, cooked rice, and slivered almonds. Add salt and pepper to taste. Put in a 250-degree oven to keep warm until dinner. ●

activist and director, Native Harvest | Each year, my family and I join hundreds of other harvesters who return daily with hundreds of pounds of rice from the region's lakes and rivers. We call it the Wild Rice Moon, Manoominike Giizis. On White Earth, Leech Lake, Nett Lake, and other Ojibwe reservations in the Great Lakes region, it is a time when people harvest a food to feed their bellies and to sell for zhooniyaash, or cash, to meet basic expenses. But it is also a time to feed the soul.

Fifteen hundred miles away, in Woodland, California, a company called Nor-Cal has received a patent on wild rice. Conceptually, it seems almost impossible—patenting something called wild rice. The Ojibwe now find themselves at the center of an international battle over who owns lifeforms, foods, and medicines that have throughout history been the collective property of indigenous peoples. —*"Ricekeepers: A Struggle to Protect Biodiversity and a Native American Way of Life,"* Orion Magazine, *July/August 2007*

 RITA ERDRICH'S MANOOMIN

SERVES 6 | *Our mother, Rita Gourneau Erdrich, published a version of this recipe titled "Rita Erdrich's Wild Rice Casserole" in the* Bagg Bonanza Farm Heirloom Cookbook. *Like my sisters, she was sure to advise that cooks "not allow grains to break or curl." Mom also specified manoomin rather than cultivated wild rice (which will not break or curl under any circumstances), noting in the ingredient list "genuine type harvested by Native Americans."*

  1 cup manoomin, rinsed and drained
  2 cups sliced mushrooms
  ½ cup sunflower seeds
  3 tablespoons chopped shallots or green onions
  1 bay leaf
  3 cups stock
  ¼ cup water
  1–2 tablespoons butter

Preheat oven to 350 degrees. In a 2-quart casserole, combine rice with mushrooms, sunflower seeds, shallots, bay leaf, stock, and water. Dot the top with butter to taste and cover with aluminum foil. Bake 30 to 40 minutes, checking once or twice to see if more liquid is needed. When manoomin is fragrant and has swelled to nearly double in the pan, remove foil and allow sunflower seeds to toast, about 5 minutes. Remove casserole from oven, and let stand to absorb any excess liquid. Remove bay leaf before serving. •

MANOOMIN AND HOMINY

SERVES 6 GENEROUSLY | *The painter Jim Denomie was in line with me at a lunch given for us by the kind Lac du Flambeau Ojibwe folks who run the art program at Woodland Indian Art Center. What a feast! Walleye fried crisply and lightly, raspberry-blueberry-strawberry salad, bangs (fry bread), deep orange squash, and, of course, manoomin. We sat outdoors in the bright sun marveling at our plates.*

We discovered that Robin Thompson had produced a delicious dish of manoomin and white hominy. I am not sure if she cooked the rice and corn together, but the result was a perfect pairing: steamy hand-harvested manoomin with corn nuggets soft as butter. Hominy's firm and somewhat waxy texture gives superb richness to the rice dish.

> 1½ cups cooked manoomin
> 1½ cups cooked hominy or 1 (10-ounce) can hominy, drained
> 1 cup mushroom or vegetable stock
> 1 tablespoon butter, optional
> salt and black pepper

Stovetop: In a medium saucepan, combine manoomin, hominy, and stock, stirring to distribute hominy evenly. Cook over medium heat until all liquid is absorbed. Rice will swell considerably but should not break. Fluff before serving, adding butter if desired, and pass salt and pepper at the table.

Oven: Preheat oven to 350 degrees. In a shallow baking dish, combine manoomin, hominy, and stock, stirring to distribute hominy evenly. Dot top with butter. Bake 20 minutes or until liquid is absorbed but the dish is not dry. Rice will swell considerably but should not break. Fluff before serving, and pass salt and pepper at the table. •

CADILLAC MANOOMIN LOUISE'S WAY

SERVES A CROWD GENEROUSLY | *When I told my sister I was going to title her manoomin dish after our ancestor Antoine Laumet Cadillac, Louise let me know that revised history calls him "one of the worst scoundrels in New France." She suggested I call her rice "Scoundrel's Cadillac Manoomin Louise's Way." Frankly, I think Louise has redeemed our line with her saintly tendencies and her language table offering of luxurious manoomin dishes sure to "put a hustle in your bustle" whether you dance fancy or not.*

> 1 pound manoomin
> 4 cups mushroom or other stock
> pine nuts (as many as you can afford)
> sea salt and white pepper
> drizzle olive oil

Here's how Louise says to make this dish:

Put the manoomin in a good solid pot under cold running water. Wash off some of the dust: two or three rinses should do it. Add a good quality stock to the wild rice. Use the thumb measure: your thumb touching the top of the wild rice, the stock measuring up to the first knuckle of your thumb. Boil the wild rice; the time varies depending on how it was finished and where it grew. Watch it closely as it approaches done. Test for al dente. You don't want mushy rice.

Meanwhile, those expensive pine nuts. Use a cast-iron skillet to toast them first on high, stirring constantly so they sweat before they toast, then remove the pan from the heat. Don't burn them: it brings out the bitterness. As with us all.

Toss the wild rice, sea salt and white pepper to taste, and olive oil. Cover with the toasted pine nuts for effect. This dish is best served in a wooden bowl. ●

MANOOMIN PORRIDGE IN COCONUT MILK

SERVES 6 | *Commodity foods, though relics of a system that kept American Indian people dependent on the federal government, are still fondly recalled by many whose memories of their grandmas making cheese sandwiches off a huge rectangular block are a comfort that has lasted. I loved canned milk that we used on cereal— hot bowls of farina (also a commodity item)—and that we mixed with water to make drinking milk from time to time. Our usual fare was nonfat dry milk, or blue water, as we thought of it, so canned milk was creamy-dreamy to us.*

While this recipe is more wholesome and satisfying than any of the hot mush cereals we ate as kids, it reminds me of school days and the kindness of my elders making me a steaming bowl upon which I poured canned milk. I've replaced the cow's milk with coconut milk to make a nondairy treat that even my kids will eat.

    2 cups cooked manoomin
    1 (14-ounce) can unsweetened coconut milk, shaken,
        or evaporated milk, ½ cup reserved
    ½ teaspoon ground allspice or cinnamon
    ⅛ teaspoon salt
    1 teaspoon vanilla extract, or 1 vanilla bean, split,
        seeds scraped into milk
    ¼ cup maple syrup
    ¼ cup chopped dried blueberries and cranberries
    ¼ cup hazelnuts, butternuts, walnuts, or pecans, toasted

In a medium saucepan, combine cooked manoomin, coconut or evaporated milk, allspice or cinnamon, salt, and vanilla. Over medium-high heat, simmer until rice begins to puff open and porridge begins to thicken; remove from heat. Stir in maple syrup and berries. Serve into bowls and top with nuts and reserved milk.

Porridge will thicken when cooled and is excellent reheated with additional fresh or frozen fruit. It can be served as a dessert.

Over the top: Add Maple-Berry Whipped Cream (page 201), or experiment with whipped coconut cream to remain dairy free. ●

SERVES 6 | *Many indigenous grains and seeds have been enjoyed ground and formed into small cakes and dried or cooked on hot flat rocks. Early Americans made cakes on hoes and even shovels heated over a fire. Pancakes, hoecakes, journeycakes, even Hopi piki bread—all show the ingenuity of hungry humans making tasty meals with whatever was available. Crêpes may sound fancy, but they are just the thinnest of pancakes. We make them over winter break as a treat for the kids.*

1 cup cooked manoomin, divided
¾ cup water, plus more as needed
2 large eggs
¾ cup half-and-half, plus more as needed
¾ cup unbleached white flour
¼ cup whole wheat flour
½ teaspoon salt
3 tablespoons butter, melted, plus more for pan

Put ½ cup manoomin in a blender with the water and blend 20 seconds. Add eggs, half-and-half, flours, salt, melted butter, and remaining manoomin. Blend 10 seconds or so. Refrigerate mixture for 1 hour (see note, page 31).

Preheat oven to 250 degrees. Heat an 8-inch or larger shallow skillet over medium heat, and add butter to coat surface. Add ¼ cup batter to pan, swirl to spread evenly, and cook 30 seconds to 1 minute. Flip, and cook another 10 to 30 seconds. Repeat with remaining batter (unused batter will keep in the refrigerator for up to a couple of days). After every third crêpe, swirl in a little more butter. Stack crêpes on a plate and keep them warm in the oven until serving time. Add fillings as desired.

FILLINGS

• For a savory filling you could not do better than cooking morel mushrooms and ramp greens in butter. Brown mushrooms in butter with a little tarragon and then toss in some wild greens or a little baby spinach or watercress, close the lid, and let it all wilt in the pan.

- Shredded cheese is traditional crêpe filling in the United States. Eichten's Cheese and Great Midwest Cheese make a number of suitable (and affordable) cheeses with indigenous ingredients such as morel and leek; or try burning nettle from Holland's Family Cheese.
- Manoomin crepes are perfect with smoked Lake Superior fish or Superior herring caviar. Serve both with a little sour cream, goat cheese, or crème fraîche.
- For sweet crêpes use any berry, fresh or frozen, warm or chilled. Add a little Maple-Berry Whipped Cream (page 201) to take it over the top. My kids slather crepes with hazelnut-chocolate spread. Whatever sounds good is good!

Note: The batter should pour like heavy cream, and some of the manoomin should still be in identifiable pieces. However, different manoomin behaves a little differently depending on the body of water it comes from, so sometimes you'll need to add liquid. If the mixture is too thick, combine 2 tablespoons water and 2 tablespoons half-and-half, add to the batter, and blend 5 seconds to incorporate. Repeat until the texture is right.

MANOOMIN COOK-OFF: SNAG BALLS VS. HEAVEN REZ LUMPS

Some years ago, when I worked for All My Relations Arts, I hosted a manoomin cook-off in the old gallery next to Maria's Café on Franklin Avenue in Minneapolis. It was amazing how creative the offerings were and how not a grain of rice was left after the crowd finished judging. There were three salads, one soup, three appetizers, and something we did not know how to categorize called a Heaven Rez Lump, which consisted of a manoomin stuffing rolled up in dough and baked into a little pocket of, well, heaven. Jonathan Thunder made these, but producing a recipe was not easy since he just used whatever was available and never made them the same way twice. He tied for first place with Elizabeth Day, who brought Snag Balls: manoomin tempura. Her concept was brilliant and particularly midwestern: roll very cold cream cheese in cooked and cooled manoomin, dip in tempura batter, and deep-fry. Dang, that was tasty.

When I moved to Minnesota, I was intrigued to note the constancy of "wild rice salad" on the table at any potluck or celebration that involved American Indian people. We had not eaten manoomin cold before. It was a little odd to me at first, the way pasta salad is said to be odd to Italians. Soon I was appreciating the variety and seasonality of the manoomin salads I encountered. However, when my sister Louise actually put salad greens into her offering, I laughed. It was as if the salad had been taken over by manoomin, the genre revised. But Louise's salad tasted so good, I have been hooked ever since.

Here are four salads, one for each of the seasons.

NIIBIN/SUMMER CONFETTI MANOOMIN SALAD

SERVES 6 AS A MEAL OR 12 AS A SIDE

> 1½ cups cooked manoomin, cooled or room temperature
> 1 small zucchini, shredded
> 1 yellow summer squash, shredded
> 1 carrot, shredded
> ½ cup shredded red onion
> 1 tablespoon capers or milkweed capers
> ½ cup finely shredded basil
> 1 tablespoon pesto
> 2 tablespoons balsamic vinegar
> 1 cup roasted, salted sunflower seeds

In a serving bowl, toss first 7 ingredients (manoomin through basil). In a small bowl, whisk together pesto and vinegar. Add to salad, toss again, and sprinkle with sunflower seeds.

Note: To make Niibin/Summer Confetti Manoomin Salad work as a finger food, serve in roasted mushroom caps, make pastry cups by filling mini muffin tins with phyllo dough weighted down with dried beans and baked until golden (discard the beans), or just serve in tiny paper cups. The indigenous disposable plate was the maple leaf. If you use leaves, make sure they are green, blemish free, well

It may be that I was born in the birthplace of manoomin, the "food that grows on water" told of in Ojibwe prophecy. It may be that the Ojibwe came west in search of this food, as our traditions tell, and it may also be that the source of the rice was my hometown river, as early European visitors to the area were told according to Thomas Vennum, who wrote *Wild Rice and the Ojibway People.* Maps tell stories, even when the names are translated: the Red River of the North flowed just under the window of the hospital room where I was born. Tributaries of the Red, which became the border between Minnesota and North Dakota, include two rivers both called Wild Rice.

I do not know if manoomin still grows on the Wild Rice River in North Dakota, but I know it did when I was a girl. My first memory of rice is of my father harvesting the long, thin grains with a neighbor and hauling it home. Recently, when I asked my father when that was, he thought 1969 or 1970. That fits with my sense of how old I was at the time. I have a glimpse of a memory of a blue plastic kiddie pool full of manoomin ready for processing in the yard between our house and the Warrens, our neighbors from White Earth who eventually ran a large ricing operation on the reservation in Minnesota.

Ricing was not our family tradition, so not long ago I asked my dad how he came to harvest manoomin on the Wild Rice River. As we talked, my mother slipped away. I assumed she was bored with us. But soon she returned from her canning cache in the basement to produce a jar of rice from that very harvest! In a beautiful old glass jar, composed of rings to create a shape like a honey skep, there remained several cups of long, very thin rice, smoky-brown manoomin, less opaque than Minnesota lake rice. Astoundingly, it looked perfectly edible. I opened the jar and it smelled of parching kettles, wood fire, and river water all at once. Forty-four years old, and I would eat that rice today. But I don't. Mom says she keeps it in a cool spot in the cellar and that she would use it for a special occasion. I think of all the enormous moments in our large family's history: births, graduations, weddings, awards, more births, deaths, times of need, and times of rejoicing, and I wonder what occasion might be momentous enough.

My mother gave me some of the manoomin, which we will keep to help remember a long-ago adventure and in the hopes it might one day be of interest to those restoring manoomin to rivers in our region.

washed, and allowed to dry. Let your guests know to carefully lift the leaf and tilt food into their mouths, then toss the leaf in the compost bin afterward. Sounds fun, doesn't it? Kinda like doing shots, but sober and nutritious. Maple leaves don't taste good, though they won't hurt anyone who gets curious and takes a bite. Grape leaves and cornhusks also make good "paper" plates. •

DAWAAGIN/FALL MANOOMIN SALAD

SERVES 6 AS A MEAL OR 12 AS A SIDE

1½ cups cooked manoomin, cooled or room temperature
1 small sweet onion, minced (about 1 cup)
½ cup chopped roasted mushrooms, optional
1 red bell pepper, diced
1 small green apple, diced
1½–2 cups mixed salad greens
1 cup black walnuts, hickory nuts, or pecans, toasted
salt and black pepper to taste
Berry-Maple Dressing (page 215)

In a serving bowl, toss all ingredients together and serve. ●

BIBOON/WINTER MANOOMIN SALAD

SERVES 6 AS A MEAL OR 12 AS A SIDE

1½ cups cooked manoomin, cooled or room temperature
1 cup minced celery
1 cup dried cranberries
1½ cups baby spinach leaves
2 green onions, minced
2 teaspoons toasted sesame oil
1 teaspoon celery seed
1 cup black walnuts, hickory nuts, or pecans, toasted
2–3 generous grinds black pepper
malt vinegar
salt

In a serving bowl, toss first 9 ingredients (manoomin through pepper); test and splash with malt vinegar and sprinkle with salt to taste. ●

MARY ANNETTE PEMBER *Red Cliff Ojibwe*

Since so many factors affect the health of manoomin, it is difficult to pin down a single cause for this year's loss, but Peter David, wildlife biologist at Great Lakes Indian Fish and Wildlife Commission (GLIFWC), says climate change appears to be behind many of the factors. Manoomin is designed for a cold northern climate, he explains, while mild winters combined with high spring rainfall are associated with climate change. The 2011 winter was unusually mild, and heavy rains during the spring damaged the young rice plants during their formative floating-leaf stage. He suspects these conditions have also contributed to higher rates of disease for the crop. "It seems that we are having more bad years for rice." —*"Climate Change Threatens the Ojibwe's Wild Rice Harvest,"* Indian Country Today, *November 2, 2012*

ZIIGWAN/SPRING LOUISE'S MANOOMIN SALAD

SERVES 6 AS A MEAL OR 12 AS A SIDE

> 1½ cups cooked manoomin, cooled or room temperature
> 1 clove garlic, crushed
> 1 cube vegetable bouillon, crumbled
> 2 cups assorted wild or cultivated fresh spring greens (lamb's-quarters, watercress, arugula, baby spinach, dandelion greens), rinsed, toweled dry, and chopped
> 2–3 tablespoons minced fresh mint
> ½ cup chopped hazelnuts, lightly toasted
> ½ cup dried, sweetened blueberries
> 3 tablespoons balsamic vinegar
> 1 heaping teaspoon Dijon-style mustard
> 1–4 teaspoons pure maple syrup
> 6 tablespoons hazelnut oil, or substitute extra-virgin olive oil
> salt and freshly ground black pepper to taste

In a serving bowl, toss together first 7 ingredients (manoomin through blueberries). In a small bowl, add remaining ingredients and whisk to combine. Dress salad, tossing to combine.

LIMON FAMILY MANOOMIN SOUP
(ONEIDA/OJIBWE)

SERVES 6 | *Like many of us, the Limon family's active life can include attending powwows and art shows and helping out in the community.*

The Limons' recipe serves a crowd: "We make a kettle full of soup each week so that we can quickly eat something healthy and filling and then be on our way. It is very economical for us as well." I've adapted this recipe so it serves just six. Double or triple it and enjoy.

water or stock
2 cups manoomin, rinsed and drained
1 cup chopped butternut squash or carrot
1 cup chopped celery
1 onion, chopped
1 clove garlic, minced
2 cups shredded cooked turkey or chicken, light and dark
salt and black pepper

Fill a large stockpot three-quarters full with water or stock, add manoomin, and place over medium-high heat. Stir in chopped vegetables, onion, and garlic. Bring to a boil, then reduce to simmer. Stir every 15 minutes for about 2 hours. During the final 15 minutes of cooking, stir in cooked turkey or chicken and heat through. Add stock or water to reach a consistency you like. Season with salt and pepper to taste before serving.

This recipe can also be prepared in a slow cooker: combine water or stock, manoomin, and vegetables, and cook on high setting for 3 to 4 hours. When vegetables and rice are tender, add cooked turkey or chicken, season with salt and pepper to taste, and serve when heated through.

If you have leftover soup and the grains have swelled up, add water or stock to reheat.

MANOOMIN CORN BREAD STUFFING

SERVES 6 | *We double this recipe many times to serve our crowd. For me, the stuffing—cooked outside the bird to maintain crispiness—is the main event. One of my sisters does not like celery, so I made it optional in this version of the dish. My mother adds an egg, and she mixes the cranberries right in. The combination of cranberry with corn bread is so good you might be tempted to forgo the cranberry sauce at your feast table. Don't. If you have leftovers, you could make a stuffing sandwich, and you'll want that cranberry relish then.*

6 cups cubed stale corn bread or other bread
1 cup seasoned bread cubes
2 tablespoons butter, plus more as needed
1 onion, chopped
1 (10-ounce) package fresh mushrooms, sliced
1 cup chopped tender leek greens, or substitute celery
1½ cups cooked manoomin
¼ cup dried cranberries
2 cups stock, plus more as needed

Preheat oven to 325 degrees. In a large bowl, toss corn bread and seasoned bread cubes; set aside.

In a large skillet set over medium heat, melt butter and cook onion until translucent. Add mushrooms and leek greens, cooking until just tender. If pan is dry, add more butter or a bit of stock.

Pour cooked vegetables into bowl with bread and toss to mix. Add manoomin and cranberries and mix again, adding stock to moisten the contents. Place stuffing into a 9x13 or 2-quart baking dish, dotting the top with butter, if you wish, and bake until toasted on top, about 25 to 30 minutes.

Serve as a filling for roasted acorn squash, as a traditional stuffing with turkey, or as a side with any meat or fish.

MANOOMIN LASAGNA WITH ROASTED SQUASH AND GARLIC

SERVES 8 GENEROUSLY | *Creamy, smoky, silky, and mellow, the flavors of this dish are an indulgence, to be sure. In the dead of winter this hearty meal warms you through like nothing else, but with fine ingredients it can be elegant, too, and makes a crowd-pleasing main course for a dinner gathering.*

Like all lasagnas there are a lot of steps to this recipe, but attention to each layer gives this dish delectable texture, so take your time and follow the directions carefully. We prepare the roasted squash and garlic the day before to make assembling the lasagna a bit more simple. Instead of goat cheese and cottage cheese, we sometimes use an equal amount of ricotta.

1 butternut squash, cut into ¾-inch cubes (about 4–6 cups)

2 tablespoons olive oil

4 leaves fresh sage, chopped, or 1 teaspoon dried

½ teaspoon celery seed

2 teaspoons fresh rosemary, minced, or 1 teaspoon dried, crushed

1 bulb garlic, cloves separated and peeled

½ teaspoon salt

1 pound lasagna noodles

1 cup manoomin, rinsed and drained

1 tablespoon butter

1½ cups mushrooms, sliced

1 cup cottage cheese

¾ cup (approximately 5 ounces) goat cheese

1¼ cups stock, divided

¼ cup half-and-half, or use light cream or whole milk

grated fresh nutmeg

¼ cup grated Parmesan cheese

2½ cups shredded mozzarella

Preheat oven to 375 degrees. Lightly grease a 9x13-inch roasting pan. In a large bowl, toss cubed squash with oil, sage, celery seed, rosemary, and garlic cloves. Pour into roasting pan, sprinkle salt over top, cover tightly with aluminum foil, and place in oven. After 20 minutes, remove foil and increase temperature to 400 degrees. Roast until squash is tender and garlic and squash are mostly caramelized, about 30 to 40 additional minutes.

Meanwhile, prepare lasagna noodles according to package directions, reducing cooking time by 1 minute. Drain noodles and toss with a bit of oil so they don't stick together; set aside. Cook manoomin in 1½ cups water. In a skillet, melt butter over medium heat and cook mushrooms until tender. While the manoomin is still hot, toss it in a bowl with the cottage cheese and goat cheese.

When squash is tender, remove pan from oven and reduce temperature to 375 degrees. Immediately pick out garlic cloves and place in a medium bowl. Add ½ cup of the squash to the garlic, and mash together with a fork. Add 1 cup stock and half-and-half to the mashed garlic and squash, mix until smooth, and set aside. Scrape remaining squash chunks into a separate bowl and set aside.

To assemble the lasagna: Cover bottom of 9x13-inch pan with remaining ¼ cup stock. Layer 3 noodles on top of stock. Cover noodles with squash chunks, mashing lightly. Add a second layer of 3 noodles. Cover with manoomin mixture. Add a third layer of noodles. Cover with mushrooms and garlic-squash sauce. Sprinkle nutmeg and then Parmesan over the top, followed by mozzarella. Cover pan with foil, tented to keep it from sticking to the cheese if necessary. Bake for 30 minutes. Remove foil, then cook uncovered another 10 to 20 minutes, until the cheese has browned at the edges. Remove from oven, let sit 15 minutes, slice, and serve.

SERVES 6 | *A longtime friend once served my mostly vegetarian family a seriously tasty manoomin dish that, in my mind, was stuffed manicotti. Revelation! It had never occurred to me to use manoomin in place of ground beef. I devised my own version and at some point thanked my friend for the inspiration, describing the dish I had created in tribute. It sounded good, she replied, but her meal was an experiment with manoomin enchiladas.*

Oh, well. Sometimes sharing recipes is like a game of telephone and the resulting understanding hilariously altered but usually delicious.

You can substitute six ounces of any pasta sauce for the red peppers; however, you might want to taste a bit with manoomin first to see if you like the flavor combination.

> 1 (8-ounce) package manicotti noodles
> 1 tablespoon olive oil, divided, plus more for pan
> 1 cup sliced fresh mushrooms
> 4 cloves garlic, crushed
> 1 small onion, minced
> ½ teaspoon oregano
> 1 cup cooked manoomin, cooled or room temperature
> 1 (6- or 8-ounce) jar roasted red peppers with liquid
> 1 cup ricotta cheese
> ½ teaspoon salt
> ½ teaspoon cracked black pepper
> 1 cup shredded smoked mozzarella or gouda

Preheat oven to 375 degrees. Prepare manicotti according to package directions, drain, and cool. Grease an 8x8–inch baking pan with olive oil; set aside. In a skillet set over medium heat, warm ½ tablespoon olive oil and cook mushrooms until browned. In a separate pan, heat remaining ½ tablespoon olive oil and cook garlic and onion until soft, then stir in oregano. Allow all ingredients to cool until comfortable to handle.

To a large bowl, add manoomin and cooled mushrooms and garlic-onion mixture, stirring to combine. Prepare roasted red peppers by removing any very charred and black areas; if some are whole, slice to match width of manicotti tubes. Stir ricotta into manoomin mixture. Stir in salt and pepper. Transfer mixture to a large resealable plastic bag. Snip a hole in one corner of the bag to pipe the filling into the cooled manicotti shells, or just spoon it in. Place filled manicotti shells in the prepared baking dish. Place roasted red pepper segments over each manicotti shell, like a little blanket. Pour liquid from red peppers into bare areas of pan, and cover with aluminum foil. Bake for 15 minutes. Uncover, add shredded cheese, and bake another 10 to 15 minutes, until cheese bubbles and browns. ●

BOB RICE *White Earth Ojibwe*

Pow Wow Grounds Café | "Everything in life revolves around wild rice—it's how I know the seasons, the new year, everything," Bob Rice says. His passion for rice centers his world. Bob harvests manoomin the old-fashioned way, by hand, from a canoe. He also runs Pow Wow Grounds Café on Franklin Avenue in Minneapolis and caters events throughout the area. Bob says his first memories are of harvesting rice. Then he tells me his birth date, September 2. He grew up in Minneapolis but was born in Bemidji, and I realize that his mother, pregnant or not, was going to make the harvest. Her determination brought Bob into the world ready to rice.

Bob takes youth out ricing at the end of summer, and he willingly shares his wisdom with anyone who asks about the beauty and importance of manoomin. Bob has even created a singular menu that features wild rice blueberry muffins, wild rice quiche, chicken wild rice soup, a vegan Four Sisters soup, and a scrumptious wild rice and berry parfait.

Of course, people ask Bob Rice about his name, but it is not a translation from Ojibwe; it's just a coincidence. Or is it?

MANOOMIN MOUSSAKA

SERVES 6 | *I love eggplant, but I do not love béchamel sauce. One of my greatest-hit potluck dishes is a moussaka lasagna with feta topping. It occurred to me that I could make a gluten-free version if I substituted potato, and then, to double-indigenize it, I thought what the heck, let's get manoomin in there, too. This recipe is adapted from one in* Blue Corn and Chocolate *by Elisabeth Rozin that focuses on potato, but to me it isn't moussaka without the eggplant.*

You can prepare the eggplant a day in advance.

> 1 large eggplant, sliced into ¼-inch rounds
> olive oil
> 4 small potatoes, sliced into ¼-inch rounds
> 1 medium onion, chopped
> 2 cloves garlic, chopped
> 1½ teaspoons salt
> ⅛ teaspoon black pepper
> 1½ teaspoons ground cinnamon
> ¼ teaspoon ground allspice
> 2 cups plain tomato sauce
> 2 cups cooked manoomin
> 2 cups (16 ounces) small-curd cottage cheese
> 2 large eggs
> 3 tablespoons grated Parmesan cheese
> freshly grated nutmeg

Soak eggplant slices in lightly salted water for 1 hour, using a plate weighted with a can to submerge slices. Preheat oven to 400 degrees. Drain eggplant and pat dry. Lightly oil each slice of eggplant on both sides, place on a baking sheet, and bake until just soft, about 25 minutes. Allow to cool. Remove and discard any large or hard seeds. Set aside eggplant, or refrigerate for up to a day.

GREG BISKAKONE JOHNSON *Lac du Flambeau Ojibwe*

culture and language instructor | I remember when I was growing up my grandmother would sit on the couch and watch soap operas and take the hulls off of wild rice one by one. The smell of her coffee in the percolator permeated the air of her little house. There were beaver traps, fox traps, muskrat traps, and connie bear traps hanging on the bathroom walls. Every once in a while she would complain about her arthritis. People would bring her garbage bags of roasted green rice with the hulls still on. She would sit there all winter and one by one she would remove the hull and produce the world's cleanest rice. She would scold us because we didn't know how to dance on the rice like our people did a long time ago. She cleaned the rice by hand because her grandchildren didn't know how to dance on the rice. We didn't care and didn't realize how important it was until she was gone. Then, we had to learn from others.

Adjust oven temperature to 350 degrees. Grease baking dish or lasagna pan. Bring a large pot of water to a boil; add potato slices and cook for 5 minutes; drain and place slices in bottom of baking dish.

In a skillet set over medium-high heat, cook onion until browned and then stir in garlic and spices (salt through allspice); cook for 5 minutes. Add tomato sauce to onion mixture, stirring to combine, and then stir in cooked manoomin. Simmer briefly. Pour tomato sauce–manoomin mixture over potatoes. Top with eggplant.

In a medium bowl, stir together cottage cheese and eggs until smooth, then top eggplant layer with cheese mixture. Top cheese mixture with grated Parmesan and a generous grating of fresh nutmeg. Bake for 1 hour, until edges are bubbling and top begins to brown. Let rest 5 to 10 minutes before slicing and serving. •

SERVES 4 | *A traditional handheld meal in the Upper Peninsula of Michigan, the pasty came to the area with Cornish miners. While the traditional pie is meat filled, dozens of variations are in play now. Why not try one with manoomin in place of the ground meat? This pie uses mushroom stock for richness and butternut squash instead of carrots. Although there's nothing indigenous about the rutabaga and the pastry crust, the little spark of nettle gives the gravy a flavor of the woods. You can find dried nettle in the tea area of food co-ops. Here I use a pinch crumbled straight into the stock, but you could create nettle broth using a tea ball in boiling water and use the broth to replace some of the stock.*

2 tablespoons olive oil

1 medium onion, minced

1 medium red potato, peeled and diced

1 small rutabaga, peeled and diced

½ cup diced butternut squash

a few pinches dried nettle, crumbled,
    or 1 tablespoon dried parsley

1 teaspoon dried sage

1 tablespoon flour

1¼ cups mushroom or other stock

1 cup cooked manoomin

¼ cup petite peas

salt and black pepper

dough for 1 (9-inch) double unsweetened pie crust
    (from scratch or from the freezer; we don't judge)

1 large egg beaten with 1 tablespoon water

Preheat oven to 350 degrees. In a large skillet set over medium heat, warm olive oil and cook onion until soft and translucent, about 5 minutes. Add potato, rutabaga, and squash. Cook, stirring often, about 8 to 10 minutes. Do not worry if vegetables stick or brown a bit—that will only add richness to the gravy. Add dried nettle and sage, stirring to distribute. Sprinkle flour over vegetables and stir. Cook 2 minutes or until you smell the flour toasting. Add stock, stir well to break up any caramelized vegetables at the bottom of the pan, and simmer, stirring often, until sauce reduces and thickens. Stir in manoomin and peas and season with salt and pepper. Remove from heat and allow to cool.

Divide mound of pastry into 4 even portions. On a lightly floured surface, or on waxed paper, roll each ball of dough out 1/8 inch thick and approximately 6 inches wide. Use a small mixing bowl to cut rounds like a cookie cutter. Keep extra dough and scraps chilled as you make each pasty. Place a mound of filling, approximately 1 cup, on one side of dough circle. Brush bottom edge of dough with egg-water mixture. Fold top half over bottom and pinch closed. Cut a slit in the middle of the top (mounded) side of the pasty to allow steam to escape. Chill each pasty as it is assembled—much easier if you are using waxed paper under them. Repeat with remaining dough and filling, rolling dough scraps together as necessary to make 4 large pasties.

Place pasties on a baking sheet and brush tops with remaining egg mixture. Bake 30 to 45 minutes or until crust is golden brown and contents may have bubbled out a bit. Allow to cool. Contents will be quite hot for some time; originally pasties were eaten cold, so let them cool to room temperature before serving if you wish. ●

SERVES 6 | *We were lucky enough to have heirloom black turtle beans from Dream of Wild Health available for recipe testing. Dream of Wild Health organic farm in Hugo, Minnesota, teaches indigenous gardening and cooking to children, youth, and adults through programs for Native Americans in the Twin Cities area. They also sell produce at the Lake Street Farmers Market in Minneapolis and in St. Paul at the Elders Lodge.*

The black beans we used were originally a gift from Potawatomi elder Cora Baker to Dream of Wild Health founders Sally Auger (Abenaki) and John Eichhorn (Odawa). In a University of Minnesota test, these beans were found to have significantly higher antioxidant activity than commercially available black beans. This is the continued blessing from our ancestors—indigenous foods testing at higher nutrition than their hybrid counterparts. Saving those seeds may well save the world one day. We decided to do the beans tribute by making something special: the ultimate bean burger.

It seems like every bean burger recipe relies on cumin and more bread crumbs and egg than I am happy using. Husband John, who has very few dislikes but counts cumin among them, came up with this recipe. These burgers have a wonderful texture due to two chewy grains: manoomin and quinoa. Quinoa is in the Chenopodium family along with pigweed (or goosefoot), which was long domesticated throughout North America for its seeds and traditionally made into, you guessed it, little patties. We are careful to use fair trade organic quinoa that benefits indigenous folks who have suffered from the sudden popularity of their primary food. We used wild Mexican oregano from Native Seed Savers because it tastes like wild mint, but any variety of oregano will give the burgers a slightly sausage-like flavor.

These burgers are excellent even without a bun. Serve with pickles, condiments, and sweet potato fries or Sweet Potato Salad (page 120). Wild Bean Burgers taste even better the next day, so make a double batch if you can.

1½ cups cooked black beans,
        or 1 (15-ounce) can black beans, drained
¾ cup cooked manoomin
¼ cup cooked quinoa
½ cup bread crumbs
½ cup water
¼ cup minced red bell pepper
2 tablespoons minced red onion
1 large clove garlic, crushed
½ teaspoon ground allspice
½ teaspoon salt
1 teaspoon hot pepper sauce (Tabasco or Tapatio), optional
1 large egg
olive oil

In a large bowl, partially mash the black beans, leaving some whole. Add manoomin, quinoa, bread crumbs, water, red pepper, onion, garlic, allspice, salt, and hot sauce, if using, mixing ingredients together. Add egg and mix thoroughly. Form 4 to 6 patties.

In a large, preferably nonstick skillet set over medium heat, warm a bit of olive oil and cook the patties 3 to 4 minutes per side. Use a wide spatula to carefully remove patties from pan and let rest briefly before serving. ●

"Long ago, when we lived on the shores of the Great Salt Water (the Atlantic coast-line), the Seven Fires Prophecy was given to us. The First Fire reads: 'You will know the chosen ground has been reached when you come to a land where food grows on water.' We then set forth on our Great Migration that began over 500 years ago. We traveled down the St. Lawrence River, into the Great Lakes region, and thence came to Anishinaabe Aki where we found the food that grows on water.

"Nenabozho, our Great Uncle, was the first to find manoomin. Hungry, Nenabozho visited his friend Zhiishiib (Duck) for food. Zhiishiib served Nenabozho with manoomin naboob. It was the most delicious naboob Nenabozho had ever eaten. Later, Nenabozho set out to find the food that Zhiishiib had served him. After several days, Nenabozho, hungry, followed a flock of ducks to a lake. He found tall, slender plants growing from the water. 'Eat us, Nenabozho,' the plants said. 'We're good to eat.' Eating some, he realized it was the food Zhiishiib had given him. 'What do you call yourselves,' Nenabozho asked the beautiful plants. 'We are called manoomin, Nenabozho,' the manoomin aadizookaanag answered.

"As Anishinaabeg, we have a duty and responsibility to protect our manoomin. It is part of our interconnectedness to the Four Orders of Life and in accordance with the original instructions given to us by Gichi-Manidoo (the Creator). When we gather manoomin from the lakes during Manoominike-giizis (Ricing Moon), we always offer asema to the manoomin aadizookaanag to thank them for their gift and sacrifice. This is part of the responsibilities that we have been given. It connects us spiritually to the plant that Gichi-Manidoo provided us with." — Statement from Protect Our Manoomin (www.protectourmanoomin.org)

Political pressures influence our rights to hunt and gather, rights our great-grandparents and ancestors agreed to in treaties with the US government. And always there is the threat of industrial pollution, both in Canada and at home. Threats to waters that sustain our key foods loom large in the Great Lakes states and in areas of North and South Dakota in the path of proposed pipelines. Such threats have Ojibwe and other tribes protesting and joining political movements. In northern Wisconsin, tribal members are fighting fiercely to stop copper mining, which threatens both manoomin and fishing. On the Red Lake Nation in Minnesota, young women have chained themselves to doors to stop tar sands oils from being piped across tribal lands and pristine waters.

At the end of 2012 and into early 2013, Canadian First Nation and American Indian protests such as the organized round dance flash mobs of the Idle No More movement gained international attention. Leave it to North America's indigenous people to create a protest movement based in art. Singing, drumming, and dancing are an affirmation of culture and an invitation for others to join us, to dance with us. Dance is less a confrontation than a march on government offices, and it has the possibility of changing hearts as well as minds. There's an air of celebration to these protests, too, perhaps because a round dance often accompanies a feast.

These protests have been led by women because in many indigenous cultures women have the sacred duty to care for and protect the water, not just for indigenous people or humans but for all life. What is at stake for indigenous people goes beyond our treaty rights and our food: what is happening today threatens the essence of our way of being in this world—our ceremonies, tied as they are to harvests, to maple tapping, to animals and plants with which we share the world and without which we know we cannot survive.

Grace Rogers gathering wild rice near Walker, Minnesota, 1939. Minnesota Historical Society Collections.

WILD MAPLE-NUT CAKE

SERVES 8–10 | *John Burke made me love him because he told me stories of gathering and cracking black walnuts as a child. His dad would drive over the nuts with the car, and John would pick the cracked nuts clean. They collected black walnuts by the pail full in their Michigan hometown. I knew when I met him he possessed the hunter-gather soul of my mate. And if that was not enough, he liked to bake. John developed this recipe as a tribute to our shared love of German chocolate cake and black walnuts. A seemingly odd combination, I know, and in fact there's no chocolate and no coconut in this recipe, yet somehow this cake reminds us both of childhood birthdays, with a taste that is decidedly grown up.*

CAKE:

⅔ cup plain yogurt

⅓ cup water

1½ cups unbleached white flour

½ cup whole wheat flour

1 teaspoon baking powder

1 teaspoon baking soda

½ teaspoon ground cinnamon

8 tablespoons (1 stick) salted butter, softened

¾ cup sugar

2 large eggs

1 cup black walnuts, toasted and chopped

SYRUP:

¾ cup water

1 cup maple sugar

½ teaspoon ground cinnamon

¼ cup cranberry juice

¼ teaspoon ground allspice

PRALINE:

1 cup just-cooked manoomin, still warm

4 tablespoons unsalted butter, divided

¾ cup maple syrup

¼ cup half-and-half

1 teaspoon vanilla extract

½ cup roasted, salted sunflower seeds, lightly chopped

Preheat oven to 350 degrees. Grease a 9x13-inch pan. In a separate bowl, mix together yogurt and water and set aside. In another separate bowl, combine flours, baking powder, baking soda, and cinnamon, and set aside. Using a standing mixer, combine butter and sugar, mixing until fluffy. Add eggs one at a time, beating to completely incorporate each. Alternate adding flour mixture and yogurt mixture in three portions each, mixing until smooth after each addition. Stir in nuts. Pour batter into prepared pan, and bake 30 to 40 minutes, until pasta noodle or wooden pick inserted into center comes out clean.

Meanwhile, prepare the syrup: combine all ingredients in a medium saucepan, bring to a boil over medium heat, then reduce heat to medium-low and simmer for 15 minutes. When cake is finished baking, pour the syrup over the top, evenly covering the surface. The syrup will run down the sides and underneath, so be ready for a show! The cake will jump and toss in its pan like a baby about to wake from its nap. Turn off the oven and put the cake back in for 10 minutes. Remove cake from oven to cool on a rack.

While cake is cooling, make the praline. While manoomin is warm, toss with 1 tablespoon butter to coat the grains. Set aside. In a medium saucepan set over medium heat, combine maple syrup, half-and-half, and remaining 3 tablespoons butter and bring to a boil, stirring frequently. Boil 3 to 4 minutes, stirring often, until mixture is visibly thickening and beginning to smell of caramel. Remove from heat. Stir in vanilla, manoomin, and sunflower seeds. Pour praline over cake, starting in the middle and spreading with a spatula to make an even layer. Allow praline to cool and set before serving.

Note: The manoomin starts out tender but over time gets a little chewier. Our tasters enjoyed the consistency, a nice contrast to the nuts and reminiscent of coconut frosting used on German chocolate cake.

POPPED MANOOMIN WITH MAPLE SUGAR AND SPICE SPRINKLE

SERVES 4 | *Many who focus on Native American foods mention popped manoomin as a delicacy. Some describe it as an esteemed and sacred food to certain tribal groups. Many admit that success in popping the rice is harder than it seems.* Native Cooking of the Americas *gives instructions for popping manoomin, which I have adapted slightly below.*

For best results, use new rice. Manoomin harvested in September should produce popped kernels in December, but I can't promise it will work in March. So many of our foods come with their own lessons, and patience is often the first. You may just have to wait until next year.

2–3 tablespoons vegetable oil

1 cup manoomin, clean and dry

2 tablespoons butter, melted

Maple Sugar and Spice Sprinkle (page 200)

Place oil in a 12-inch, heavy-bottomed skillet over medium-high heat. Add a layer of rice and swirl over medium heat until the kernels pop. Toss with butter and Maple Sugar and Spice Sprinkle. •

RESOURCES

Bineshii Wild Rice & Goods
www.bineshiiwildrice.com
19947 Plantation Road Southeast
Cass Lake MN 56633
1-800-484-2347 x7580; 218-335-8461

Bineshii offers a full line of many types of manoomin, all hand harvested, including wood parched and slow and low-temperature wood parches for "raw eating customers," as well as the curiously named Ghost Rice: "The light color of this wild rice along with its elusive nature in the wild reflects its name 'Ghost Wild Rice.' Ghost wild rice is known for its untamed nutty flavor that only nature can establish over time." Bineshii can be appreciated for their discriminating approach to manoomin, asserting that propane parching dries the rice—they use only wood—and stating "We do not mix our batches of wild rice! All of the wild rice you receive in your order will be from the same lake or river bed, ensuring your wild rice will cook evenly every time and have the same quality taste."

Several varieties of wild rice products as well as seasonal foods and gifts are available on-line. All the manoomin is harvested by canoe from lakes or rivers on the Leech Lake Ojibwe Reservation in Minnesota. Maple syrup, blueberry syrup, strawberry, raspberry, and blueberry jam, two kinds of hominy (yellow and white), blueberry muffin mix, and fish fry mix are also offered via an extensive online catalog. Bineshii will create gift boxes with cedar and pinecones as well.

Spirit Lake Native Products (*native wild rice and pure maple syrup*)
218-644-0912

Spirit Lake Native Products is located on the western border of the Lake Superior Chippewa Fond du Lac Reservation in northern Minnesota. The Savage family has been sugaring in the region for many generations. They produce pure maple syrup each spring and also finish wild rice. Other products available seasonally.

Manoomin is also available from these Native American businesses:

Native Food Network (*"Online Ordering Market" lists resources for finding manoomin*)
nativefoodnetwork.com

Native Harvest (*manoomin products and mixes*)
www.nativeharvest.com

White Earth Wild Rice (*hand-harvested manoomin and manoomin flour in attractive packaging*)
realwildrice.com

See Resources, Organizations (page 249) for manoomin organizations that publish sources for hand-harvested manoomin.

... FISH AND

GAME •••

*W*e Erdrich children were raised by a good hunter who took us on visits to the family butcher shop full of delicious meats (my one hope for heaven is that my grandma will be there still making her smoky, pop-in-your-mouth, natural wieners) and, later, when my grandmother had a farm, I actually enjoyed butchering day, when grandma's chickens relaxed in her grasp and she said her kind good-byes. I also grew up fishing. A lot.

In high school a boyfriend with a copy of *Diet for a Small Planet* impressed me so greatly that I went off meat for most of a decade. Most days I eat vegetarian meals. Still, all these years, if someone I know has caught or killed an animal and offered me wild game, I have never refused it, and I've enjoyed it in the spirit intended. I've cleaned ducks and walked out to check snares others have set. I've gaffed fish for surf-fishing roommates, and I've fed bunnies I know I'll see browned up in a pan. I'm not the squeamish vegetarian type, but there, I've 'fessed: I am not much of a meat eater.

And yet here we arrive at a section on Fish and Game. No worries: a few meat-loving folks and much research helped me with the following recipes, which will not disappoint carnivores. At the same time, I want to question the notion that to live within an indigenous tradition is to eat vast quantities of meat. From my research, this description was far from the truth. Certainly fresh meat was not eaten on a daily basis. The meats available were lean, very different from beef, pork, and chicken as they have been bred today.

The image of the American Indian hunter running down bison on a horse with bow and arrow is a proud one. I have such an image pressed in copper foil on my TV room wall. Sometimes we forget that the horse came with Europeans and that for millennia before contact women and men (and probably children) obtained bison by running them off cliffs. Imagine that scene in copper relief! No doubt bison driving was an effort so dangerous it made such meat a luxury to be savored, at least after the initial feast. In fact, until the recent arrival of refrigeration, cultures on all continents dried and smoked meat as their main means of preservation.

If you live anywhere where you can reach a large market or food co-op, you will easily find indigenous meats much as they once were most commonly used:

smoked fish, smoked turkey, jerky of all kinds. In specialty stores or at cheese shops in Wisconsin, venison and bison summer sausage is now quite readily available.

Finding fresh or frozen rabbit and other game may depend upon the season and whether you have a good hunter in your family or friends willing to share. While markets in the Upper Midwest do carry bison and duck and wild or heritage turkey seasonally, your best bet is to use online resources (see page 249 for listings) to find indigenous food animals dressed and ready to eat, along with vegetables and fruits such as lamb's-quarters, ramps, Juneberries, juniper twigs, and dozens of other ingredients sometimes tricky to find. Sadly, there is no such thing as an Ojibwe Walmart or one aimed at the lives of any indigenous people in the region. But I am not alone in my dream of such a store. Self-described hunter-gatherer and Ojibwe teacher Greg Biskakone Johnson once joked that we needed a store that would carry not only fresh game meat and fish but spearing poles, spearing helmets, and spearheads—but it would have to stay open all night.

While I have confessed my once-vegetarian status, I also have to admit the reason it never held is that I love to eat fish. Salmon is my weakness, but my other two favorites are indigenous to the area: whitefish and walleye, or, in the Ojibwe language, *Adikameg* and *Ogaa*. I feel an odd team spirit in regard to these fish. Take my reaction to reading in a local foodie publication the words of a chef who, while touting other local foods, said that walleye was "A terrible fish": "What? That is *our* fish; watch how you talk about it," I wanted to say to him. Walleye is the fish that sustains us—had he never thought of that? What was he trying to make walleye do, anyhow? Act like red snapper? Finally I decided to pity the poor chef, who did not grow up in this region. He will never know the joys of the flaky white side of our beloved walleye.

There are some who think we nearly love our fish to death, but we protect them, too. In 2011, when Beth Dooley wrote her stupendously informative *Northern Heartland Kitchen,* she reported that "The walleye population has been growing thanks to efforts to limit the use of commercial nets in order to prevent over-fishing." Not three years later, the tribes in Minnesota and the Department of Natural Resources once again have put stricter catch limits in place in efforts to prohibit commercialization of game fish by individuals. Members are only allowed to sell their catch to a tribally operated processor such as the Red Lake Band commercial fishery, which sells and ships fish to the public.

In my dream of the Ojibwe Walmart, the produce area is stocked with every kind of squash, wild greens, ramps, edible flowers, and morels as big as my hand. The pharmacy smells like a garden, and there's an aisle of puckons (hazelnuts), hickory nuts, seeds, dried mushrooms, hominy, and an entire affiliated tribe's worth of Mandan, Arikara, and Hidatsa beans. I guess it should be called Indigenous Walmart, then, or just Indigenous Mart, a little indoor version of what a walk in the woods or along the lake or a visit to another tribe might be.

THE WAYS *Great Lakes Native Culture and Language*

Tribal commercial fishermen in Lake Superior primarily target whitefish, but also fish for lake trout, siscowet, herring, and salmon. Tribal commercial fishing is regulated through tribal codes as well as through negotiated agreements with the state of Wisconsin for the Wisconsin waters of Lake Superior. Quotas are set and adhered to. GLIFWC [Great Lakes Indian Fish and Wildlife Commission] and tribal fisheries biologists monitor the fishery through annual assessments and work with state, federal and tribal agencies on restoration and enhancement efforts and participate in the Great Lakes Fishery Commission, an international convention. Wardens from GLIFWC and the tribes enforce tribal codes on tribal commercial fishing activity and cite violations in tribal court. Many of the tribes maintain hatcheries to stock species such as walleye, perch, lake trout, and coaster brook trout. —*theways.org*

PURE WHITE AND DEADLY—
HOT SMOKED FISH SPREAD

SERVES A CROWD | *Tasty and dairy laden, this dish makes me wonder if European foods were destined to meet American foods just so we could have this union of smoked fish and cream.*

Hickory nuts are indigenous to the southern parts of this region but can be difficult to find if you do not have your own trees. Amish markets or farm stands sometimes carry the nuts in Wisconsin and Minnesota. Or substitute pecans, which are indigenous to parts of Illinois and Iowa. As for the cheese, we used Wisconsin-made morel gouda in this dish. Beyond luscious—can you imagine?

This dip is good served with woven wheat crackers. When cool, it can be sliced into wedges to freeze, and it reheats beautifully in a toaster oven.

> ¾ cup chopped hickory nuts (see head note)
> 2 tablespoons butter, melted
> ½ teaspoon salt
> 4 ounces cream cheese, softened
> 4 ounces goat cheese, or substitute ricotta
>   or cottage cheese, drained
> 2 tablespoons milk
> 1 cup flaked and deboned smoked whitefish
> ¼ cup minced green bell pepper
> ½ small onion, grated
> ½ clove garlic, crushed
> ½ cup plain yogurt, or use sour cream
> ½ cup shredded cheese, optional

Preheat oven to 350 degrees. Combine nuts, butter, and salt and spread mixture in pie plate. Bake 15 minutes. Remove from oven and set nuts aside to cool; wash pie plate. In a medium bowl, combine cream cheese, goat cheese, milk, whitefish, green pepper, onion, garlic, and yogurt; mix gently and spoon into pie plate. Cover with nut mixture and top with cheese, if using. Bake 20 minutes. Serve hot. ✐

GREEN BEAN AND SMOKED FISH SALAD

SERVES 6 AS A MAIN DISH OR 12 AS A SIDE | *Sometimes it takes time to make it fine. Chop these ingredients as finely as you can: it makes all the difference in the world. This salad is a sort of Northwoods Niçoise that seemed an obvious combination to me but that is greeted with surprise whenever I offer it. It is finished with a fairly simple dressing, but if you make Roasted Ramp and Juniper Dressing (page 232), try it on this salad and let me know how it comes out.*

Foragers and fermenting fanatics: if you pickle your own milkweed buds or other delicacies, substitute them for capers in this recipe.

> 1 pound green beans
> 2 tablespoons capers, chopped (see head note)
> 2 green onions, minced
> 2 tablespoons olive oil
> 1 tablespoon white balsamic or other clear vinegar
> 1 tablespoon juniper berries, crushed
> 1 teaspoon black peppercorns, crushed
> 2 large or 4 small boiled potatoes
> 2 hard-cooked eggs
> 1¼ cups flaked smoked whitefish
> salt

Bring a large pot of water to a boil, then cook green beans until crisp and tender but still brightly colored; drain and rinse under cool water. Chop green beans very fine (¼ inch or less) and place in bottom of salad bowl; add capers and onions.

Whisk oil, vinegar, juniper, and pepper for dressing and stir into bean mixture; let marinate 5 to 10 minutes.

Chop potatoes into medium chunks, chop eggs coarsely, and add to bean mixture, mixing gently and taking care not to break up ingredients. Add smoked whitefish and gently mix once more. Taste and add salt if needed; the fish provides quite a bit. Salad may be refrigerated, but it is best served at room temperature. 　•

NICK VANDER PUY *Man Made of Whitefish*

journalist, activist, fisherman | I am a poor fisherman, living off the products of this great inland sea. My father Sgt. William Vander Puy (USMC) came back to his hometown Sheboygan, Wisconsin after the Korean War. During the war he dreamt about coming home and fishing for perch on Lake Michigan off the North Pier. Still wearing his khakis he walked down to Stockinger's bait shop on Ontario Ave. He purchased two cane poles, some no. 6 Eagle Claw hooks, a minnow bucket and several dozen shiners for bait. He fished for perch every day for two weeks. He'd put them in a wicker creel, scale them in the kitchen, get some hot grease going in a black cast iron fry pan, bread the perch with flour and make a fish fry. When he didn't catch perch he'd stop by the fish shanties in the harbor and purchase some whitefish. He served these fish on a red and black tablecloth to his parents John and Dena Van Der Puy and his girlfriend Betty Ann Esser. I'm sure they ate some potatoes, coleslaw and some frosty brown bottles of Kingsbury beer, too. About a year later I was born. I am made of fish.

The Sheboygan River was used as a dumping ground for upstream industry. The whitefish and perch disappeared and the harbor was declared a Superfund site. Eventually, I made my way up north for better fishing. I guided fishing parties near Eagle River for thirty years. I love catching, dressing and eating fish from local water. I was one of the last shore lunch guides in northern Wisconsin.

An Anishinabe friend fluent in the language says, *adikameg* means "caribou of the sea." Just think we live in such a place! I'm astounded we can even talk about building a "responsible" mine in the Penokees [of northern Wisconsin] when no evidence exists this can be done safely without damaging the wild rice and water. I'm astounded we can talk about a mine offering "jobs" in our territory when the Chequamegon Bay is a designated Superfund site with the responsible parties squabbling over the cleanup.

About three years ago, after ceremonies at Bad River, I came to live on Madeline Island and Bayfield. And I'm finally beginning to understand the late activist Walter "Makoonse" Bresette's advice to us to love this land as deeply as the Anishinabe do and be willing to defend it with our lives. For I know in my body and soul I'm made from whitefish.

SUPERIOR FISH CHOWDER

SERVES 6–8 | *Our inland sea tilts at the rim like a bowl of eternal blue light. I could look at it forever, thinking of the abundant life in its cold waters, ciscos running to the surface, bringing with them the scent of watermelon, or so fisherman Nick Vander Puy tells me. Watermelon: isn't that a mystery? The Great Lakes are a miracle unfolding even now. I wonder if we really appreciate what we share. Vast freshwater inland seas, a wealth of a substance we truly need: water. My ancestors lived on Great Lakes islands and shores long ago, and I am always drawn to the waters of Michigan and Superior.*

I adapted this recipe from the Angry Trout Café Notebook *to remind me of a day spent looking out over Lake Superior. I had been up to Grand Marais, where I bought manoomin harvested by Grand Portage Band tribal members and which I later used in this chowder. Around that time, I read that Anishinaabeg were fond of sassafras in the old days, so I added filé powder as a seasoning and thickener all in one. If I could make this chowder with water straight from the waves that I love, I would. When I make it right, it tastes of love for and a longing to return to those rocky shores one day.*

    5 cups stock
    2 cups cubed yellow potatoes, skin on
    ½ cup minced butternut squash
    2 tablespoons butter
    1 small red onion, minced
    1 stalk celery, minced
    8 ounces lake trout, salmon, or other Superior fish,
        cut into bite-size pieces
    1 cup cooked manoomin
    ¾ cup half-and-half or light cream
    salt and white pepper
    filé powder to thicken
    fresh dill for garnish

In a large stockpot set over medium-high heat, bring stock to a boil and cook potatoes for 5 minutes. Add butternut squash and boil until just tender; reduce heat to simmer. In a skillet, melt butter over medium heat and cook onion and celery until just softening. Add mixture to stock. Add trout to stock and cook until done, about 5 minutes. Stir in manoomin and half-and-half and continue to cook for just a minute. Season with salt and white pepper to taste. Turn off heat before adding filé powder, a quarter teaspoon at a time, until stock begins to thicken. Stir gently to avoid breaking up the fish. Serve immediately with fresh dill to garnish. •

 ## FISH EGG BANNIC

SERVES A CROWD | *How delightful to find a third spelling of bannock/banik! My friend Pauline Brunette Danforth tipped me off that this recipe existed and that her mom had saved it years ago. We couldn't find it, and then when a friend was looking at old poetry publications, of all things, it came to me. Luck works this way. This recipe appeared in* Angwamas Minosewag Anishinabeg *(Time of the Indian), a compilation of poetry by American Indian students edited by James White and published by St. Paul's Community Programs in the Arts and Sciences (COMPAS) in 1976. It was accompanied by the note, "These recipes given by Mrs. Lois Benner to her daughter Dawn Benner, Nett Lake School."*

I imagine these would be delicious with Superior Fish Chowder (page 62) or with a salad for a light lunch.

    3 cups flour
    1½ teaspoons baking powder
    ½ teaspoon salt
    ½ cup water
    1 cup sucker fish eggs, or substitute any fish roe

Preheat oven to 375. Mix dry ingredients; add water and fish eggs to make batter. Make buns and bake until done. •

WALLEYE CAKES AND RED PEPPER–PINEAPPLE RELISH

SERVES 8 | *Recipes are stories, that much I have learned. I asked Austin Bartold for the story of his walleye cakes, and he gave me a cast of characters: the ingredients. I've worked the rest out for myself.*

2–3 tablespoons olive oil
1 onion, minced
grated fresh ginger
salt and black pepper
1 teaspoon chopped fresh rosemary
1 teaspoon dried thyme
2 large walleye fillets, baked until flaky and then chilled
1 stalk celery, minced
1 red apple, minced
1 green bell pepper, minced
1 large egg, beaten
1 cup panko bread crumbs, plus more as needed
½ cup mayonnaise
1 teaspoon red pepper flakes
1 teaspoon curry powder
flour
Red Pepper–Pineapple Relish (recipe follows)

In a skillet, heat 1 tablespoon of olive oil over low heat and slowly cook onion until caramelized; add ginger, salt, pepper, rosemary, and thyme. Stir to mix, then chill for at least 2 hours.

Mash fish fillets with chilled onion mixture. Stir in celery, apple, green pepper, egg, panko, mayonnaise, red pepper flakes, and curry powder. Use an ice cream scoop to create several balls of fish mixture. Hand form scoops into patties and dip in flour. In a skillet, heat 1 to 2 tablespoons of oil over medium-high heat and pan-fry patties on each side until golden, about 5 minutes.

Allow to cool slightly before serving with Red Pepper–Pineapple Relish.

RED PEPPER–PINEAPPLE RELISH (MAKES 3–4 CUPS)

1 red bell pepper

1 cup pineapple chunks

1 red apple, chopped

½ cup chopped cilantro

1 tablespoon apple cider vinegar

2 tablespoons extra-virgin olive oil

salt and black pepper to taste

In a medium bowl, combine all ingredients, mixing well. Serve with Walleye Cakes.

AUSTIN BARTOLD *Lac Courte Oreilles Ojibwe*

chef | Austin Bartold trained at Lac Courte Oreilles Ojibwe Tribal College and Le Cordon Bleu. He worked for Famous Dave's (restaurateur Dave Anderson is an LCO tribal member) and then the Minnesota favorites Napa Valley Grill and California Café and hotels in the Twin Cities area. Eventually Austin found his culinary calling in working with community, first at Open Arms, a kitchen that feeds people in need. Austin works as executive chef at Waite House Neighborhood Center in Minneapolis, where he is also an instructor in the diabetes program and in the culinary arts program for youth ages sixteen to twenty-one as well as for a course in food justice where youth learn to cook and eat. In 2013 Austin won the first Great Native American Cook-off in Minneapolis. His entry was manoomin salad, and his secret ingredient was bacon.

Austin took over as chef at Gatherings Cafe at the Minneapolis American Indian Center in 2017. Gatherings menu items range from a walleye Benedict breakfast to a wild rice wrap. The cafe offers catering, including delivered lunches. www.maicnet.org/gatherings-cafe/.

SERVES 4 | *Historian, professor, and Red Lake tribal member Brenda Child gave me the idea for this dish. Tart and bright, wild plums with a little spike of passion fruit (an indigenous southern cousin) put the sweet in the sour. Enjoy this crispy, gluten-free fish that really tastes—and smells—terrific when cooked in coconut oil.*

WILD PLUM SAUCE

¼ cup passion fruit juice, or use cranberry juice

2 cups plums, skins on, cut in half-inch pieces,
  plus more for garnish

6 cloves garlic, crushed

1 tablespoon grated fresh ginger

⅛ teaspoon cayenne

1 teaspoon tamari or soy sauce

1 shallot or ramp bulb or the white of 1 green onion, minced

1 teaspoon maple syrup

1 teaspoon cider vinegar

Combine first 7 ingredients (juice through shallot) in a small saucepan and bring to a boil over high heat, stirring a couple times. Reduce heat to low, cover, and simmer for 10 to 15 minutes. Stir in maple and vinegar, and remove from heat. Allow to cool to room temperature before serving, or make a day ahead.

PAN-FRIED FISH

1 cup buttermilk

4 fillets perch, trout, or other freshwater fish

3 tablespoons coconut oil, or use corn oil

1 cup cornmeal

¼ teaspoon salt

½ teaspoon cracked black pepper

½ teaspoon smoked paprika

Pour the buttermilk into a pie plate, add the fillets, and gently turn the fish pieces to thoroughly coat. Heat the coconut oil in a heavy-bottomed skillet over medium-high heat. While the oil and pan are heating, mix the dry ingredients together in a second pie plate. When the oil is thoroughly heated, remove fillets from buttermilk and dredge both sides in the cornmeal mix. Fry two at a time, 3 to 4 minutes per side (a little less for thin pieces, a little more for thicker pieces). As you remove the fish from the pan, place them on a paper towel–lined plate to drain briefly. Serve with Wild Plum Sauce.

Uncle Ron Manson gives Ralph Erdrich and Aaron Erdrich a lesson in filleting northerns—a somewhat tricky fish.

SECRET MUSKIE RECIPE

SERVES 4–6 | *Greg Biskakone Johnson is an educator and artist whose birch-bark baskets are inscribed with beautiful images of leaves, birds, and animals. I've enjoyed seeing Greg's artwork and beadwork and hearing about his hunting and cooking exploits, so I asked him for a recipe or two. Greg says: "The more fish you have the more people can eat. Muskie or northern caught in winter have a better flavor then post-spawn muskie. Garnish with parsley. Serve with drawn butter and lemon slices. Minopogwad!"*

Everyone has a secret recipe for fish, but in collecting for this book I learned something: the secret recipes are all the same. I think the potato is what makes this "Old Indian Secret" so special, especially if you follow the instructions carefully.

4–6 (5-ounce) boneless muskie fillets
1 large potato, quartered
2–4 wild onions, stalks only, chopped,
   or substitute 1 large onion, quartered
1 bunch parsley, minced
8 tablespoons (1 stick) butter, melted and kept warm
1 lemon, quartered, or ground sumac for serving

Bring a large pot of water to a boil. Add muskie fillets, potato, and onion. Boil for 10 to 20 minutes, until fish begins to flake. Remove fish from pot; discard potato and onion. Sprinkle parsley on fish. Serve with drawn butter and lemon quarters or a sprinkle of sumac. ●

PICKLED PERCH

MAKES 4 QUARTS | *Auntie Dolores lived for decades at the fish hatchery in North Dakota where Uncle Ron worked. Some of his stewardship included a project to reintroduce indigenous fish such as the pallid sturgeon in the Upper Midwest. The little fish were nurtured to a safe size in large, shallow tanks in darkened sheds. I remember patting the backs of some prehistoric and sleepy-looking garfish one day. I probably should not have done that. Aside from raising fish, Uncle Ron is, as they say, an avid sportsman who ventured away from the hatchery to make his catch. Auntie Dolores has come up with a lot of ways to use the fish that fill the freezer each year. Pickling is one of her favorites, and my mom's, too. Maybe because pickling also leaves more room in the deep freeze?*

       4 cups white vinegar
       4 cups cold water
       ½ tablespoon juniper berries
       1 tablespoon whole allspice
       1 tablespoon whole mustard seeds
       1 bay leaf
       ½ cup pickling salt
       2 cups sugar
       ¼ cup lemon juice
    4–6 pike or perch, cut into bite-size pieces
       2 large onions, thinly sliced

In a large bowl, combine brine ingredients (vinegar through lemon juice), stirring to mix. Place fish pieces in a gallon jar, alternating with onions. Fill to top with brine, completely covering fish. Let stand loosely covered at room temperature for 48 hours. Tighten lid and refrigerate indefinitely, or until one of your pickled fish–loving relatives visits and eats it all gone.

You can also decant pickled fish into 4 sterilized quart jars, tighten lids, and store refrigerated. Give jars of this "prairie sushi" as gifts. ●

SMALL GAME BIRDS IN WILD BERRY BLACK PEPPER SAUCE

SERVES 4 | *This dish was created by my niece, Pallas. That girl can cook! And she has been cooking since she was wee. I'll never forget how, when she was about ten years old, we stopped by my sister's house and found Pallas working a huge profes-sional mixer like she was the boss of it. About Pallas's culinary gifts, my sister has written: "When I first saw her kneading a raw egg into a little mound of flour I was filled with confusion. I could not be more surprised if I had given birth to a math prodigy." We have all grown to accept and maybe even anticipate displays of Pal-las's special talent. When I heard she would be visiting my parents, I gave her this assignment: "Dig in the freezer and find the game birds—I bet some are hiding in there." Sure enough, they were.*

Small game birds traditionally eaten by this region's indigenous people include quail, partridge (timber chicken), and grouse, some now protected from hunting. Pheasant, plentiful and very much a typical and traditional food on many reserva-tions these days, is an interloper from Asia, alas. Pallas describes small game birds as lean and distinct in flavor. She also provided me with her inner narration as she prepared a meal to complement her dish:

> *If only I could have killed the birds myself, it would have seemed more authentic. Re-ceiving the bloody packages from the hands of my grandmother will just have to do. I focused on the wild foods, which means no wrapping the bird in bacon (first thought) or pairing it with some kind of seafood—wouldn't that be bizarre? Nope, girl, stay wild. I decided to pick my favorites: blueberries, chokecherries, wild rice, mushrooms, sage, and squash. I figured these are rich enough to satiate my flavor lust without getting too heavy. Yum on.*

Pallas says to serve "with tons of sauce" and to dress the dish up with plenty of shredded fresh sage. She served it with Buttery Butternut Squash with Sage and Butter (page 152) and sautéed mushrooms on a bed of Cadillac Manoomin Louise's Way (page 28).

½ cup chokecherry syrup (preferably homemade by Grandma)

½ cup pomegranate juice

¼ cup sugar

1 cup Juneberries or wild blueberries, fresh or frozen

4 breasts of small game birds: quail, partridge, or grouse, or substitute pheasant or Cornish hen

salt and cracked black pepper

2 tablespoons butter

1 bunch fresh sage, shredded

In a large saucepan or Dutch oven, combine chokecherry syrup, pomegranate juice, and sugar. Cook on medium high, stirring occasionally to dissolve sugar, until liquid is reduced by half, about 15 to 20 minutes. Add berries and let simmer on low heat while you prepare the bird breasts.

Pat bird breasts dry and generously season both sides with salt and pepper; let sit for a couple minutes. In a heavy-bottomed skillet set over medium-high heat, melt butter. When the butter is foaming but not yet brown, add the bird breasts and cook for about 3 to 4 minutes, turning to brown both sides. Remove from heat and set aside to rest for 5 to 10 minutes.

Add bird breasts to simmering sauce. Add several generous grinds of black pepper, enough to create a layer atop pan. Allow to simmer until the breasts are fully cooked, about 10 minutes. Serve breasts with sauce and shredded fresh sage. ●

DUCK AND CORN SOUP

SERVES 6–8 | *My mentor in critter cooking has been Richard LaFortune, an activist and fundraiser who also writes a food blog and is working on a manoomin cookbook. Every time Richard made this duck dish in front of me, I did my best to follow his alchemical ballet, but he moves in mysterious ways. Finally I figured out that I needed to include his process of making duck stock, which follows the soup recipe here.*

Meat and corn soup has perhaps the longest tenure on the indigenous menu of the Great Lakes and nearby prairie states, so when you eat it, you are participating in a lengthy tradition. Duck is available both from commercial sources and from local farmers or your favorite family hunter. You will not need butter to brown the duck as the breasts render out a great deal of fat very quickly. Reserve duck fat as you would bacon grease: it is a terrific ingredient that has been credited with all sorts of curative powers by Indian grandmas for generations.

Serve soup with Gullet/Bannik (page 110) or Tea-infused Biscuits (page 241).

skinless duck pieces: breasts, wings, legs, thighs
¼ cup all-purpose flour
6 cups duck stock (recipe follows), or substitute chicken stock
1 bunch green onions, greens reserved, whites chopped
1½–2 cups chopped sunchokes, or substitute new potatoes
2 cups frozen roasted corn
2 cups cubed butternut squash
1 teaspoon juniper ash, or substitute natural smoke flavor
salt to taste
garlic chives for garnish

Dry duck breasts and score by making 3- to 4-inch cuts in the fat with a sharp knife; turn and score the breasts in the opposite direction. Cut breasts into 1-inch cubes. Pat all duck pieces dry and use hands to coat with flour. In a skillet set over medium heat cook breasts first, then when the breasts release fat, add duck pieces and continue cooking until lightly browned. Bring stock to a boil over medium-high heat, then reduce heat to simmer. Add duck to stock and cook, checking meat for tenderness after 1 hour.

Add chopped onions, sunchokes, and corn to stock, and cook over medium-high heat for 15 minutes, until you smell the corn. Reduce heat to low, and continue cooking for 30 minutes, then add squash and simmer until tender, about 10 to 15 minutes more. Stir in juniper ash and salt. Serve with onion greens and garlic chives, to garnish.

Variation: Brown duck breasts with a teaspoon of asafran (safflower threads, a Mexican cooking ingredient) or a pinch of saffron threads for a special treat. ●

DUCK STOCK (MAKES 6 CUPS)

6 cups water, plus more as needed
duck bones
1 onion, quartered
2 stalks celery, chopped
1 carrot
1 clove garlic, chopped
1 sprig fresh thyme
2 green onions, tops and trimmings
black pepper to taste

In a stockpot, bring water to a boil and add duck bones, onion, celery, and carrot. Reduce heat to simmer for several hours, adding water if needed. When meat has fallen off bones, stir in garlic, thyme, green onions, and pepper. Simmer at least 1 additional hour. Remove and discard bones and large vegetable chunks with a skimmer, or strain broth for a more clear soup. ●

DUCK EGG MEATLOAF

SERVES 6 | *Cooking buddy Richard LaFortune had a bolt of inspiration when I handed him ground turkey and duck eggs. The whites of duck eggs have higher protein levels than chicken eggs, and the yolks are more rich; do not overcook, as they will become tough. Richard suggests serving this meatloaf with peeled, boiled potatoes and sunchokes mashed together and Mushroom Sage Gravy (page 102).*

4 duck eggs, or substitute jumbo chicken eggs
2 tablespoons vegetable oil or duck fat
1 large onion, chopped
1 clove garlic, minced
1 stalk celery, minced
1 cup chopped fresh mushrooms
1 teaspoon salt
½ teaspoon freshly ground black pepper
1 bay leaf
1 teaspoon crumbled dried thyme
2 cups crumbled corn bread, or substitute bread crumbs
2–3 tablespoons water
2 pounds ground turkey
dash hot pepper sauce (Tabasco)
1 teaspoon smoked paprika

Preheat oven to 400 degrees. Place 3 eggs in a saucepan with water to cover; bring to a boil. Remove from burner, cover, and wait 7 minutes. Drain water and plunge eggs into an ice-water bath. Using a spoon or the back of a table knife, carefully crack the shells all around and allow to chill in the water. Peel eggs gently because the yolks are very softly set. Set aside.

Meanwhile, heat the oil or duck fat in a large skillet over medium heat and add onion, garlic, celery, mushrooms, salt, pepper, bay leaf, and thyme and cook, stirring, until onion is translucent, about 6 to 8 minutes. Remove to a large mixing bowl and stir in finely crumbled corn bread or bread crumbs and water. Allow to cool completely before adding ground meat, remaining uncooked duck egg, and hot pepper sauce. Mix well with your hands, but do not overmix.

Place half of the meat mixture into a well-greased 9x5–inch loaf pan, and nestle the soft-cooked eggs end to end in the center, covering with the remaining meat mixture. Sprinkle the top of the meatloaf with smoked paprika, and bake for 1 hour. ●

FLAMING BLUE GIZZARDS

SERVES 6 | *One autumn my mother, sister, and our youngest aunt all went to Paris. Imagine such a thing! Mom in Paris. Well, she enjoyed herself, there is no doubt, and partially because at one point, after an apologetic host offered "a simple country dish," the entire party was thrilled to discover that French people and Turtle Mountain folks share a love for gizzards.*

Deep-fried gizzards sell at a brisk pace at the gas station on my rez, a fact that amuses some visitors and shocks others. But why should we forget the lowly cuts of meat and the parts most often tossed away? Surely our Anishinaabe ancestors ate tongue to tail. Even our German grandfather, a butcher, made head cheese from the scrap meat. Oxtails and sweetbreads, or beef glands, were family favorites when we were growing up. When I asked my father about his favorite foods, he mentioned, in faraway tones, "de bris," the guts of a freshly killed animal. "Full of delicious pepsin," he recalled and actually touched his tongue to his lips at the memory.

The gizzard recipe the French host shared is a comfit method, meant to first preserve the gizzards, then carefully reheat them. That recipe calls for great delicacy and patience: I stock neither in my pantry. My adaption follows.

> 1 pound duck gizzards (don't try this with chicken gizzards: too tough; you are on your own with turkey)
> coarse salt
> 1 tablespoon wine vinegar or balsamic vinegar
> 2 cloves garlic
> 1 sprig fresh thyme or ½ teaspoon dried
> 1 bay leaf
> 1 teaspoon dried marjoram
> several grinds black pepper
> ½ cup duck fat or lard, plus more as needed to cover
> 1 little glass of cognac   >>

Rub fresh gizzards with coarse salt. Shake to remove any excess salt. Refrigerate for 48 hours. Rinse with warm water and drain.

In a large skillet set over very low heat, slowly cook gizzards, vinegar, garlic, and herbs in enough duck fat to cover. Do not allow the gizzards to come to a boil. They should become very tender, so a sharp knife enters easily. Drain most of the duck fat, reserving it for later use, and place gizzards in a flame-proof serving dish with a lid. Add the cognac and set on fire just as you are serving. Use lid to quench the flames if they do not go out themselves while guests *ooh* and *ahh.* ●

DUCK AND BISON CASSOULET

SERVES A CROWD | *Of course this is a French dish, but clearly it came from the land of beans and duck, North Dakota. Our version does not cook for days but is as rich and satisfying as any goose cassoulet I had in France. Oh, and a little fun fact: my spell checker does not know the word* cassoulet *and instead offers me* capsulate, *which is what the beans do with the multiple flavors that bathe them in this fancy comfort food.*

2½ cups stock, divided
7 cups cooked white beans (great northern or navy)
2 tablespoons sunflower oil
4 cups coarsely chopped onion
1½ tablespoons dried bee balm, or substitute dried thyme
1½ teaspoons dried rosemary
¾ teaspoon dried sage, crushed
1 teaspoon juniper ash, optional
8 cloves garlic, crushed or sliced
2 cups butternut squash cut into half-inch cubes, optional
1 (24-ounce) can crushed tomatoes
2 skinless duck thighs
4–5 links bison sausage, sliced into bite-size pieces
2 skin-on duck breasts

Heat 2 cups stock to a boil, then pour into a slow cooker turned to high; stir in beans and cover. To a heavy skillet set over medium-high heat, add oil, stir in onions, and cook until onions soften and begin to turn translucent. Add bee balm, rosemary, sage, and ash (if using), stirring frequently until you can smell the herbs. Add ½ cup stock and ½ cup water, stirring to scrape up any browned bits in the pan. Stir in garlic and squash cubes (if using). Pour onion mixture into slow cooker with beans. Stir in tomatoes, and turn heat to low. Cook 5 hours.

Add duck thighs, and cook 2 hours, until meat falls off bone; remove bones. In a skillet set over medium heat, brown sausage. Add ½ cup water and scrape up any browned bits in the pan. Transfer sausage and pan drippings to slow cooker. Stir.

Cook duck breasts in a skillet or oven until skin is crispy, scoring skin to let out the fat and reserving fat for later use. Serve cassoulet with duck breasts cut in four portions each and nestled on top of a serving of beans. ●

LISE ERDRICH *Ojibwe, Turtle Mountain Band*

gardener and author | Rezipe for Drunken Goose: I have two Canada goose breasts that I traded for with my homegrown corn and some dried mushrooms and green wild rice that I may bake up with sunflower seeds in turkey broth…oh this always has Campbell's soup all over it and wine but this goose going cold turkey now.

There's a cookbook I treasure, though in truth it belongs to my sister Angie. It is called *The Family Rezipe Book,* and there are dozens like it made by reservation communities in much the same way cookbooks are assembled by parishes, synagogues, and other religious groups. This book of "rezipes" was created by the Mountain Plains Region Nutrition Advisory Committee and produced by United Tribes Technical College Land Grant Programs in my home state, North Dakota. It has a sense of humor sometimes intended, as in the obligatory Coot Soup recipe, which calls for 1 coot and a brick ("Throw away the coot and eat the brick"), and sometimes unintended, as in "Broiled Vegetarian Beans," which turns out to be toast topped with canned vegetarian beans broiled with onion and bacon!

From such rezipe books, I've gleaned recipes for foods I heard of in my youth—Tu du (ground and dried chokecherries) and Rubba-Boo (rabbit and corn soup)—as well as fascinating facts of food ways ethnobotanists missed:

> We would take a lake area that is shallow, about 3 feet deep. The bait we would use would be corn or wild rice. We would make snares out of wire or plant (nettle) fibers to about 2½ to 3 inches diameter and suspend these hoops about 4 to 6 inches from the bait. The snare would be directly over the bait. The bait would be a little mound of about a teaspoon or so. Ducks are experts at spotting grains and such on lake beds. *—Donald Cain, Ojibwe, Turtle Mountain Band*

I never met Mr. Cain, but I would like to thank him for both the description above and a now vivid notion of how ingenious my ancestors were in making my favorite snack: "Throw desired amount of corn on hot flat rock. Put woven basket over corn. When popped, the favorite was to mix popped corn with maple syrup—presto cornballs."

Other rezipes tell us how to cook every critter from squirrels to fawn with the occasional rezipe for Family Pie: "ingredients include forgiveness, love and unselfishness." I love these cookbooks and referred to them regularly when working on this book. The Lovesick Lake Native Women's Association cookbook let me know how fat and tender a groundhog can be, and an anonymous mimeographed page rescued from an elder's kitchen led me to add a section on tea. There are usually several recipes that are nearly identical because the editors do not want to play favorites. And almost always there's a reference to muskrat, the only food I ever heard my mother say she disliked.

MUSKRAT TAILS

Denise Lajimodiere, Ojibwe, Turtle Mountain Band

Skin the muskrats,
nail the skins to a board
and put up high
so the dogs don't get at 'em,
boil the muskrats over a slow fire
using just enough water to cover the meat,
when almost cooked, add Red River
potatoes, prairie onions,
and wild turnips. Pour everything
in a cast iron kettle, bury the kettle
in the hot ashes. Take the muskrat tails
and stick them in the hot ashes,
after just a few minutes
peel the skin off.
This treat, delicate and white
as snow, is best eaten immediately,
serve as Indian hors d'oeuvres.

PAN-ROASTED RABBIT

SERVES 6 | *Adapted from a recipe shared by Les LaFountain. Les remembers watching his grandma Mary, whose father raised domestic rabbits, demonstrating her enjoyment of rabbit by "licking her fingers to avoid losing succulent morsels and smacking her lips."*

Serve with Sunseed-crusted Sunchokes (page 137).

> 2 tablespoons olive oil
> 1 rabbit, dressed
> 2 cups Mushroom Sage Gravy (page 102; or 1½ cups sliced
>   fresh mushrooms and 1 onion, chopped)
> water or stock
> salt and black pepper

Preheat oven to 350 degrees. In a large oven-safe skillet with a lid, heat olive oil and briefly fry rabbit legs and chopped loin (reserve other parts for soup). When meat is crisp on both sides, add gravy (or fresh mushrooms and onions) and enough water or stock to keep the meat moist. Cover the skillet and place in the oven for about 1 hour, checking rabbit occasionally, until meat is well done (internal temperature reaches 160 degrees). Remove lid to allow sauce to cook down if necessary. Season with salt and pepper to taste, and serve. •

SERVES 6 | *This recipe is adapted from one that Christina Sipla and Tom King submitted to* Tribal Cooking: Traditional Stories and Favorite Recipes, *published in 1996 by the Nutrition Project of the Great Lakes Intertribal Council, Inc. Serve roasted rabbit with juices on a bed of Red River Red Garlic- Smashed 'Taters (page 101).*

1 tablespoon oil
1 rabbit, dressed
1 large onion, chopped
½ cup sundried tomatoes, chopped, optional
1 carrot, chopped
½ cup red wine or water
1½ cups tomato juice
1 teaspoon dried wild mint, or substitute dried thyme
salt and black pepper

Preheat oven to 350 degrees. In a skillet set over medium heat, warm oil and then cook meat until lightly browned. Place meat in roasting pan with onion, tomatoes, carrot, wine, and tomato juice. Sprinkle with mint, salt, and pepper. Roast 1 hour or until meat is well-done (internal temperature reaches 160 degrees) and juices have thickened. Serve. •

LESLIE HARPER *Leech Lake Ojibwe*

Anishinaabe educator | Waaboose and Napoodin: 1 waaboose, an onion, a couple of carrots, salt, pepper, a handful of garlic. Brown the bunny parts in the stockpot with onions and carrots for a few minutes. Add nibi to an inch or two above the wiiyaas. Simmer all day long. Toss in parsley if you like that. Maybe a little more salt and pepper. At hour three or four, mix up the napoodin fixins: A couple handsful of bibinebakwezhigan, a tidge of zhiiwitaagan, some ombisijigaans, tablespoon or two of doodooshaaboo and some nibi 'til it looks all goopy. Drop goopy napoodin mix into soup and cover 'til the napoodin are cooked through, a few minutes, about eight to ten minutes, depending on how many and how big they are.

SERVES 6–8 | *When I cook with my friend Richard LaFortune, it all goes by in a flash for me: like the kids in Willy Wonka's factory, I am just in it for the ride with genius and, before I know it, it's over. Somehow, in the wild fun of inventing this dish, I missed the moment when Richard fed my sister Louise a duck tongue, but I heard about it later, at an author's event, when a child asked her what was the weirdest thing she had ever eaten.*

This extravagant party dish celebrates the best of our good foods while nodding at the history of Spanish paella. Not always a seafood concoction, paella was once made with duck, rabbit, and snails. In past times, indigenous people of the Upper Midwest ate dozens of kinds of freshwater mussels, but none are now safe to eat and most are endangered. I've substituted smoked oysters here.

To serve, place the entire pan on the table and allow guests to choose their own northwoods tidbits. Offer a side of steamed lima beans, another indigenous North American food that often appears in a seafood paella.

2 cups "broken" or "soup" manoomin

4 cups stock

2 tablespoons nettle broth (see page 44), strained

2 tablespoons olive oil

2 cloves garlic, minced

1 onion, chopped

1 teaspoon asafran (safflower threads), or substitute ⅛ teaspoon turmeric

1 tablespoon sumac

salt and black pepper

2 duck thighs, skin and fat removed and reserved

2 rabbit legs and loin, cut into bite-size pieces

2 bison sausage links (about 1 pound)

2 cups fresh mushrooms

sprinkle dried dandelion or calendula flowers, optional

1 (3- to 4-ounce) can smoked oysters

3 ounces smoked trout, optional

1 bunch watercress for garnish

LES LAFOUNTAIN *Ojibwe, Turtle Mountain Band*

educator | Les LaFountain, a faculty member in the social science department at Turtle Mountain Community College, periodically "dabbles" with raising rabbits and has a large garden. His home is located on his maternal great-grandparents' property, where his great-grandfather raised large domestic rabbits. But, Les says, despite the availability of domestic rabbits, "wild bush rabbits were snared or shot and eaten as a mainstay during more difficult times on and near the Turtle Mountain Indian Reservation." Certainly my own mother spoke often of eating rabbit when she was growing up at Turtle Mountain. In fact, our cultural love of rabbit has been a bit of a joke to folks from other tribes. As Les says, "Despite popular folklore, I never heard of any of my Chippewa relatives choking rabbits, but I have Lakota and Dakota friends who would beg to differ."

Preheat oven to 250 degrees. In a pot set over medium-high heat, cook broken manoomin in stock and nettle broth until soft and nearly dry (time will vary: watch rice closely, adding water if need be). In a skillet set over medium-high heat, warm olive oil and cook garlic and onion until onions are translucent, then add asafran, sumac, salt, and pepper. Stir mixture into cooked manoomin. Place manoomin in the bottom of a large, oven-safe dish (preferably a paella pan) and set in oven to keep warm.

Render duck fat trimmings by cooking them in a shallow pan at low heat until fat comes out. Discard skins. In a small saucepan set over medium heat, cook duck thighs in duck fat to cover for 30 minutes, taking care to keep the oil from boiling. Remove meat and drain on paper towel–lined plate. In a skillet set over medium heat, brown rabbit pieces on both sides and then cook, turning often, until well done, about 10 minutes. Remove and set aside to rest. In the same skillet, cook bison sausage about 10 minutes (if precooked, simply heat through). In a separate pan, cook mushrooms until browned; set aside.

Remove the dish of manoomin from the oven, toss, and sprinkle with dandelion or calendula flowers (if using) or additional asafran. Arrange mushrooms, duck, rabbit, bison sausage, smoked oysters, and smoked trout (if using) on the bed of rice, slightly embedding each bit into the manoomin. Garnish with watercress. •

Ralph and Rita Erdrich take aim for the heart, 1954

I ask my brother Ralph when he got his first deer. He says he has a poor memory and tells me I should ask "Big Ralph," our eighty-six-year-old father. Dad settles onto the couch and removes his glasses; he glances at my brother to signal he will tell a tale that has two sides. He remembers going out to track Ralph's first deer, which triggers Ralph's memory of coming home to get Dad to help track it. Ralph had hit it with a good shot, but still it had gotten away.

We are in a darkening room, and there's noise of many children nearby, but Dad and Ralph pause and look at each other a moment. My dad has a long, white beard; my brother a long, brown braid. They both give me gentle smiles, as if they are about to laugh at the sweetness of the memory or the foolishness of youth. Turns out it is both. Ralph explains to me how hard it is to track a deer over a plowed field if you just can't wait and go out to hunt before it snows—maybe without letting your dad know you were going hunting. Even if you have a blood trail, he tells me, it can be hard to discern when so many tracks crisscross it that you don't know which deer to follow. Ah, that is the hard part, I think to my non-hunting self. Then I remember that both my dad and my brother were bow hunters—and I am not talking compound bows. I try to imagine how unlikely it was that a young boy would get a deer using a bow. I am sure my dad had been expecting Ralph to come home empty-handed, and who knows how he even had time to help track, but he did. Dad says, "I knew the Sand Hills pretty well, and when Ralph showed me where he shot the deer, I had a good idea where that deer might end up." Sure enough, they found it.

We pause a moment. I ask Ralph how old he was when he shot that first deer. He says with pride, "Eleven years old." I am amazed. I look at Dad so he can see I am amazed. Slowly Dad says, "He was eleven then"; and he turns to Ralph, waggles a finger, and adds, "And now he is a liar." >>

We whoop it up and I ask for more stories. Dad tells me he shot his first deer "just like that" and then he had to track it quite awhile. He tells me he remembers the last deer he shot, too, but at first he does not elaborate. Then I recall the gruesome tale of how, when he saw a deer at the end of a day hunting on the Wild Rice River, Dad loosed an arrow, way up in a kind of last-minute free-throw-from-midcourt attempt. The arrow caught the deer in the eye. He hasn't hunted since.

I ask Dad if he got a deer every year. He says he *shot* a deer every year, and I begin to understand and respect the challenge of bow hunting. Dad hunted about thirty years. The son of a German immigrant butcher, he did not hunt as a kid. I ask him why he started hunting with a bow, and he says, "Well, I married an Indian—I thought maybe hunting with a bow would make it . . . better."

 SLOW COOKER VENISON STEW

SERVES 6–8 | *My brother Ralph's secret ingredient is "not vinegar" and "not tomato paste." He tells me he has only one recipe: "Cook it on high. Don't let it burn." Oddly, he makes this stew in a slow cooker on low heat over the course of hours. I ask him, what about seasoning? It's in the tomato sauce, he assures me. I am baffled. I have read a lot of venison recipes, and there's a good deal of fuss with vinegar and brine. Ralph explains that as a relic of the past, when cooks used vinegar to remove "gamey" flavors. These days, he says, we all have sweet, fat, corn-fed deer.*

2 pounds venison roast, cut into half-inch cubes

1 (24-ounce) jar tomato or spaghetti sauce, any flavor

2 potatoes, chopped

2 carrots, chopped

1 onion, chopped

Put all of the ingredients in a slow cooker set on low, and cook all day, until meat is tender. Add water if need be. ●

SERVES 4 | *Greg Biskakone Johnson shared this recipe. He lives with the seasons on the Lac du Flambeau Reservation in Wisconsin and is an artist, teacher, and avid hunter. He recommends serving this stew with boiled potatoes.*

3½ tablespoons butter, divided

2 pounds boneless deer shoulder meat, cut into chunks

¼ medium cabbage, sliced into thin wedges

¼ small rutabaga, sliced

1 large carrot, cut into chunks

5 leeks, chopped

salt and black pepper

2 teaspoons grated fresh ginger

⅓ cup all-purpose flour

maple sugar

maple syrup

Melt 1 tablespoon butter in the bottom of a stockpot set over medium heat. Add the meat and then the vegetables. Sprinkle with salt, 1 teaspoon pepper, and ginger. Pour water over to cover. Bring to a boil and skim scum that rises to the surface. Lower heat and simmer, shaking the pot now and then so the meat won't stick, until the meat is tender, 60 to 75 minutes. Remove from heat and scoop out meat and vegetables, arranging them on a serving platter and keeping them warm; reserve cooking liquid, adding water as needed to make ¾ cup.

In a skillet set over medium heat, melt the remaining 2½ tablespoons butter and stir in the flour. Gradually add reserved cooking liquid, stirring well. Season with salt, pepper, maple sugar, and a touch of maple syrup. Serve meat and vegetables with sauce. ●

BLACK AND BLUE BISON STEW

SERVES 8–10 | *I need no excuse to make savory berry dishes: the combination of tart, deeply colored berries with other intense flavors seems natural to me. Cooked in a cast-iron Dutch oven, this rich stew turns as black as the night once was on the North Dakota prairie. Of all the foods I created for this cookbook, this dish has been the most favored. Enjoy it and imagine a time beyond the glow of energy development when (who knows?) the bison return to help restore the prairies.*

2 teaspoons sunflower oil

5 green onions, chopped

2 teaspoons juniper berries, crushed

2 pounds bison roast, cut into bite-size pieces

¼ cup all-purpose flour (or gluten-free substitute)

1 cup chopped sunchokes (4–6 knobs)

1½ cups frozen wild blueberries or Juneberries,
   or substitute regular blueberries

1 tablespoon dried wild mint, or substitute dried mint

2½ cups hot water

salt

1 recipe Tea-infused Biscuit dough (page 241)

melted butter, optional

Preheat oven to 350 degrees. In a Dutch oven or other large oven-safe pot with a lid, warm oil over medium heat and cook onions and juniper until onions begin to soften. Coat bison with flour, then add to the pot and brown meat on both sides. When meat is browned, add sunchokes and cook 5 minutes. Add berries, mint, and water. Cook 30 minutes or until stew becomes bubbly and thick. Season with salt to taste. Top stew with biscuit dough, brush dough with butter, and place pot, covered or uncovered, in hot oven for 10 to 15 minutes, until biscuits are fluffy, golden, and cooked through, testing doneness with a wooden pick. •

LOUISE ERDRICH *Ojibwe, Turtle Mountain Band*

author | Woodchuck Stew: This summer, for health reasons, I began to eat red meat—bought solely at a meat shop like the old world Erdrich's. In a burst of creative cookery inspired by P.—who, on her most recent visit, got me to dump a 24 dollar bottle of wine into her beef stew—I began mixing ground chuck with chopped tiger lily buds. I added crushed nasturtium flowers for their pep- pery tang, garlic scapes, chive blossoms, marigold, geranium, rose petals, and the leaves and yellow blooms of a weed my father taught us to eat—we called it sauerkraut plant because of its pleasantly sour taste. My popular resulting burger caramel- izes tastily at high heat, maybe because of the sugar content of the petals. I call it the Ferdinand Burger, for the flower sniffing children's book bull.

FERDINAND THE BISON BURGER GETS LOOSE

SERVES 6 | *Minnesotans, Twin Citians in particular, like to claim as local the inven- tion of the Juicy Lucy—a burger stuffed with cheese, onion, and other items usually reserved for toppings. I don't eat beef, but the concept is not a mystery to me. Years ago, I recall making hamburgers for my older brothers that had the cheese inside. Very popular, if a bit messy.*

For our more indigenous burger, I asked a Mandan tribal elder to help me ex- ecute my idea. He put rosemary and feta cheese in the meat to make a less messy burger. That was not exactly what I meant, but the Bison Juicy Lucy seems like a winning concept, so I went with it. The Mandan have been living in my home state of North Dakota since long before it was a state, for thousands of years, in fact. Mandan, or Nueta, as they call themselves, lived amid the bison herds and were re- nowned farmers and gardeners. They were the key traders on the river. If they could have traded for cheese, I am sure they would have. I know from historical accounts that Mandan cooked with flowers. In this recipe, I feel a fullness of the circle that began with my sister Louise's Ferdinand Burger and ends with sliding this bad bull into a Pumpkin Bang (page 96).

If you choose to use daylilies, make sure you positively identify any lily you eat as hemerocallis. Google it.

2 tablespoons chopped chives or garlic chives

2–4 dried lily buds or golden needles (available in Asian groceries) or petals of wild daylilies (see head note), chopped

1 pound ground turkey

1 pound ground bison

salt and black pepper

1 (1-ounce) package edible flowers, or 1 cup fresh edible flowers, washed (nasturtiums, pansies, violets, garlic and chive blossoms, dandelion, borage, zucchini or squash blossoms without pollen, sunflower petals, rose petals— be sure none are chemically treated), or ½ cup dried flowers, crumbled (calendula, lavender buds, clover, chrysanthemum, safflower threads, etc., from the bulk tea aisle or from a tea mix such as hibiscus tea), divided

1 (10-ounce) package feta cheese

coconut or other oil for frying

In a large bowl, mix chopped chives and lily buds with turkey and bison and salt and pepper; set aside. The flowers and greens will help the lean burger cook without burning. Reserve half the flowers for garnish. Pull petals from the rest of the flowers or tear to make small flower petals and pieces. In a small bowl, combine feta and the flower pieces.

Divide burger mixture into 4 to 8 balls (about ½- or ¼-pound patties). Make a well in each ball of meat and place a tablespoon of the feta mixture in it. Reshape into patties. Fry in a hot pan that has been seasoned with a bit of oil. Add oil as needed—this meat is very lean. Serve with remaining cheese mixture and reserved fresh flowers to garnish. ●

Eichten's Cheese & Specialty Foods Online Store

eichtenscheese.com
16440 Lake Boulevard
Center City, MN 55012
651-257-4752

Eichten's specializes in 100 percent grass-fed bison/buffalo meat. As they advertise, "Bison is a lean red meat source that is safe, flavorful, and healthy for you and your family . . . excellent texture and flavor plus the benefits of low fat, fewer calories, and lower cholesterol. Bison is also high in iron, vitamins, minerals, and protein. Eichten's herd is fed on naturally grown, pesticide-free native grasses. The herd is raised without growth hormones. All bison is USDA inspected and available to order online."

Red Lake Nation Fishery

www.redlakewalleye.com
19050 Highway 1 East
Redby, MN 56670
877-834-2954; 218-679-3513

Owned and operated by the Red Lake Band of Ojibwe, the nation's only hook and line commercial fishery has been providing freshwater walleye since 1919. The fishery's website focuses on efforts to sustain fish in Minnesota's largest lake: "Our wild fish products share more than an amazing taste of where we come from. They illustrate to the buyer our Native American culture by teaching our ways of balance and harmony in our sustainable practices." All fish are wild caught by tribal fishermen and filleted by hand. Red Lake Nation Fishery sells fresh and frozen walleye, perch, crappie, northern, and whitefish and smoked whitefish.

Native American Natural Foods
www.tankabar.com
287 Water Tower Road
Kyle, SD 57752
1-800-416-7212; 605-455-2187

Tanka Bars and Tanka products include traditional wasna and pemmican made of high-protein, prairie-fed buffalo and tart-sweet cranberries. Dried bison meat products come in bars, bites, sticks, and summer sausage and as Bison Dogs—an indigenous answer to the all-American hotdog. Native American Natural Foods is owned by Oglala Lakotas on the Pine Ridge Reservation, in South Dakota. Its products are sustainably grown by Native American producers and "minimally processed with care and respect, to help you feed mind, body and spirit." Grass-fed bison contains omega-3 fatty acids and is low in saturated fat. Gift baskets available. Order online or find distributors at tankabar.com.

Louis (Ludwig) Erdrich butchered this record-size bear brought in by a hunter who accidentally sat down on the animal in the snow, 1950

··· GATHERING ···

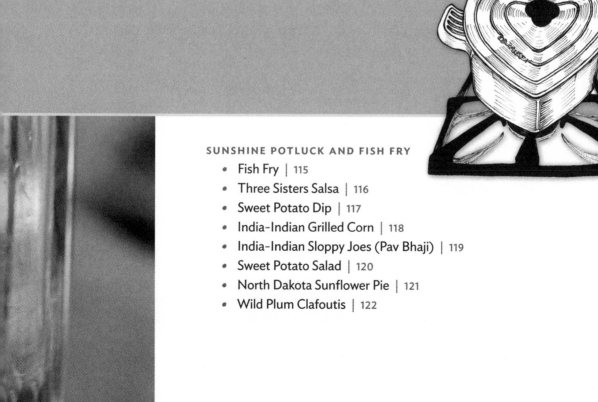

When we gather as a family, we cook. Our annual big family get-together is a tremendous feast and a feat of indigenous cooking: Mom makes at least one turkey with manoomin–corn bread stuffing and, to skip ahead to dessert, Juneberry pie, and cherry pie from our parents' own tree, as well as "Secret Ingredient Pumpkin Pie"; sister Lise presents an enormous enameled roaster of her renowned "Porkypine Bullets and Bangs," made not of porcupine but of a ground bison mix; she also roasts butternut squash with sage and often brings a vat of her Three Sisters Salsa as well; brother Ralph offers pan-fried fresh venison—if he or his sons are lucky that morning—if not, we often get a slow-cooked venison stew, or Ralph thrills us with a fish fry, usually of Red Lake walleye; sister Louise brings a huge pan of her fragrant manoomin with pine nuts or creates eclectic wild rice salads that are gobbled up first thing; my husband, John Burke, hauls out ten pounds of roast garlic "smashed" potatoes and an entire Crock-Pot of mushroom sage gravy, a vegetarian treat; sister Angie makes delectable cranberry chutney; brother Louis has a wonderful way with mushrooms and green beans, or perhaps those offerings come from sister-in-law Peggy? My sisters-in-law are all good cooks, too, but it is a rare occasion when all of my family can make these events. My brother Mark and his wife, Mary, live in California, and if only half of my twenty-some nieces and nephews arrive we have a huge crowd that extends as well to beloved elders and tribal sisters, aunts, and cousins. And not everyone's dish of choice is strictly indigenous, either: brother Louis makes his own sauerkraut, wine, and beer; sister Angie's "Rez Water Pickles" are fought over, and though she cans nearly a hundred jars a year, there's never enough.

Remarkably, our family feasts include vegetarians, people who stay dairy free or gluten free, and others with requirements of a diabetic diet—all satisfied by our offerings. Perhaps that's why our dishes have grown so varied—many needs, and equally diverse opportunities (the luck of hunters, a good squash crop) mean much to share.

And we have always gathered our food as well. What is called *foraging* to us was just getting food. To many Native people living in the Upper Midwest, gathering remains an important part of eating right, protected by treaty rights. While I do not give detailed foraging suggestions here, some recipes contain foods that we "wild harvest" or that are now readily available at markets. Not every food featured in this section's recipes would be classified as indigenous to the Great Lakes, Mississippi region, or Great Plains area, but still these are traditional foods eaten and enjoyed by people whose cultures are indigenous to the area and whose tastes and trade are as dynamic as they have ever been. As ethnobotanist Huron Smith wrote in the early part of the twentieth century, "The Ojibwe are fond of visiting and, in the summer time, some are always away on visits to other tribes in Wisconsin, Iowa, Minnesota, the Dakotas, Kansas or Oklahoma." Many of these recipes result from culinary visiting we practice today.

Our big family visits and the feasts involved require the expertise of our sister, Dr. Angie Erdrich, who is an organized person. Angie e-mails a list each year to help us remember what to bring to our family feast. Last year the list snowballed to over one hundred items and contained requests for an enormous variety of goods, from the usual (green bean hot dish) to the specific (Munchkin board game) to the mysterious ("nesting disposables"), and grew more eccentric as we e-mailed it back and forth. Eventually someone listed "caveats" right next to "caper berries," and it went downhill from there. Still, everything you need to know about our family feast is revealed in the first and last items on a list that starts with "bangs" and ends with "gizzards."

Three Sisters Potluck, including Sunny Corn Muffins (page 172), Tanka Bite Bread (page 173), squash with Garlic-roasted Cranberries (page 218), and Black and Blue Bison Stew (page 87)

A NOTE ABOUT FRY BREAD

Fry bread was treaty ration food made of the flour and lard many indigenous people waited for—and starved for—when promised provisions did not arrive from governments that demanded we stop hunting and start eating the colonial diet. Yet, even with that conflicting history, we love fry bread. It's a complex world.

A poem fragment on fry bread technique by Denise Lajimodiere:

> You know the grease is just right when you drop a round
> piece of dough in and it sinks to the bottom then pops
> right back up. Turn your bread the second it pops back up.
> You can eat this one right away
> to make sure it's cooked all the way through.
> Watch carefully for dough to turn a golden brown,
> turn it over and fry on other side. Use a long fork
> to take out of the pan and put on a cookie sheet
> with paper towels to absorb the grease.
> Be careful, these will float to the ceiling!

Fry bread and the Indian taco have become the most recognizable food traditions of American Indian people today. When I first started this book, I vowed not to include fry bread, but I had forgotten about bangs, the Turtle Mountain version of fry bread. Our mother would make bangs for us on special occasions, and memories of those doughy treats warm my heart to a golden-fried glow. Thus, fry bread made it into the book in the form of a special kind of bangs.

 ## PUMPKIN BANGS

MAKES 12 PIECES (2 PER PERSON IS INDULGENT, BUT LET'S SEE YOU RESIST) | *While visiting with a Wisconsin Oneida student, I heard about the pumpkin fry bread her mother makes out of her powwow food truck. It occurred to me that I could develop a slightly decolonized bang recipe to be used for tribal gatherings, big doings, or other special occasions only. Now ask the next Native American you meet how often such occasions occur. We can't help our propensity for gathering, but we should develop some kind of fry bread dance to burn off the calories.*

This recipe is inspired by Marlene Divina's submission to the spring 2008 issue of Repast. *I've seen a few others like it, but I wanted something with more pumpkin and less sugar. The allspice is important—making it taste less like dessert or a donut than the usual cinnamon—but you can cut it altogether if you are making fry bread tacos or some savory dish. Or, heck: put some cayenne in there for a little zip.*

3 cups unbleached white flour,
  plus more for dusting
½ cup whole wheat flour
1 teaspoon sea salt or coarse salt
2½ teaspoons baking powder
¼ teaspoon ground allspice
1 cup pumpkin puree
¼ cup honey
¾ cup warm water
½ tablespoon sunflower oil
  coconut or sunflower oil for frying

In a large bowl, combine the flours, salt, baking powder, and allspice, mixing well. In a separate bowl, combine the pumpkin, honey, water, and oil, mixing well. Make a well in the center of the flour mixture and add the pumpkin mixture. Work the wet ingredients into the dry ingredients and form the dough into a smooth ball. Spread a thin layer of oil over the dough and cover with plastic wrap. Let rest for 10 minutes before rolling and shaping.

Lightly dust a work surface and your hands with flour. Separate the dough into 12 pieces and form into balls. Sprinkle flour over the balls and roll out to ¼-inch-thick rounds—"bangs." The dough may be slightly sticky; sprinkle with flour as necessary.

Pour oil into a heavy skillet to a depth of 1 inch and place the pan over medium-high heat. Once the oil reaches between 360 and 375 degrees, place the bangs in the pan, one or two at a time, and fry, turning once, for about 3 minutes on each side, until the dough puffs and turns golden brown.

Using tongs, remove the bangs from the pan and place on paper towels (or brown paper bags) to drain. Serve warm. ●

Why not just call it Thanksgiving Dinner? Well, there's much wrong with our collective myth of the first Thanksgiving, starting with its official declaration, long after the actual events, as a day to thank God for the massacre of indigenous peoples in the American colonies. But it is also my favorite holiday. In protest, I have long referred to it as Indigenous Foods Day or Turkey Day or T-Day. Now, I am sure that will seem way too politically correct for some, but you can probably see my point. The traditional Thanksgiving meal is based on foods (turkey, pumpkin, cranberries, corn) that indigenous people living on the Atlantic long knew, and they generously introduced these new foods to the entire world. Why not celebrate that history and be thankful?

HARVEST FEAST MENU
- *Heritage Turkey (page 99)*
- *Manoomin Corn Bread Stuffing (page 37)*
- *Dawaagin/Fall Manoomin Salad (page 34)*
- *Slow Cooker Venison Stew (page 85)*
- *Decolonized Green Bean Casserole (page 100)*
- *Garlic-roasted Cranberries (page 218)*
- *Red River Red Garlic-Smashed 'Taters (page 101)*
- *Mushroom Sage Gravy (page 102)*
- *Rez Water Pickles (page 102)*
- *Cranberry Meringue Pie (page 219)*
- *Secret Ingredient Pumpkin Pie (page 106)*
- *Oswego Tea (page 243)*

HERITAGE TURKEY

In the book Renewing America's Food Traditions, *Gary Paul Nabhan introduces us to the turkey varieties that were nearly extinct until recently. These are not wild turkeys, but they look much more like the rainbow paper cutouts we all remember coloring in grade school. And they can walk and breed, unlike the commercial birds that most of us eat.*

The last time I ate turkey, some years ago, it was a wild one that had been smoked into a tender slice of what ham dreams of on its best day. It is no easy feat to hunt a wild turkey, though they seem to be everywhere urban and rural in the Upper Midwest these days. We have a jaywalking flock in our neighborhood less than a mile from downtown Minneapolis. You don't want one of them coming at your windshield, I can tell you! So eat them, please. Or at least get a heritage turkey.

Heritage turkey should be pre-ordered and can be pricy, but demand is bringing the price down every year. The online service Local Harvest (localharvest.org) can help you find heritage turkey for sale nearby and gives recipes (including one suggesting you baste the bird with rosemary and maple, yum!) and important advice:

> *Heritage turkeys are also much leaner and smaller than sedentary commercial birds. This means that fast cooking at high temperatures is a better method than slow roasting—another big plus since you won't have to set your alarm to get the bird in the oven to be done in time for an early dinner. Heritage turkeys should be cooked at 425–450 degrees F until the internal temperature reaches 140–150 degrees F. Butter or oil can be added under the breast skin to add flavor and moisture during roasting.*

Just as the term Indian *was mistakenly applied to the people of an entire hemisphere, the turkey, it is said, was named for the middle eastern country. Turkey was once* Mizise *in Anishinaabemowin. No doubt the bird has hundreds of names in other indigenous languages, some of which must have meant* really, really tasty.

DECOLONIZED GREEN BEAN CASSEROLE

SERVES 6 GENEROUSLY | *People are passionate about the holiday green bean casserole, and since it features an indigenous ingredient, the green bean, it has earned its place at the feast. The dish used to leave me cold, so I set to work on my own version. If you have indigenous mushrooms like morels or chanterelles, by all means use them. And why not go one better and take out the dairy and gluten entirely? I know: whoa. Fear not, there are now gluten-free Funyons available if you require the trash factor on this once-a-year treat.*

> 1 pound green beans, fresh or frozen
> 4 tablespoons high-quality sunflower oil or olive oil
> 1 large leek, chopped, or 2 ramps, stalks and bulbs only, chopped
> 10 ounces fresh mushrooms, sliced
> ½ teaspoon garlic powder
> about ½ cup potato flakes
> 1½ cups stock
> salt and black pepper
> gluten-free Funyons for garnish, optional

Preheat oven to 350 degrees. Bring water to a boil in a large saucepan, and cook beans until they turn bright green. Drain and set aside. In a skillet set over high heat, warm 2 tablespoons oil and cook leeks until they soften and begin to brown; remove from pan and set aside. Add remaining 2 tablespoons oil and mushrooms to the skillet, and cook, stirring, until mushrooms begin to give off juices; add garlic powder and stir. Continue cooking for 1 to 2 minutes. When mushrooms are soft and have given off a lot of juice, slowly sprinkle in potato flakes a bit at a time, stirring constantly and also adding stock a bit at a time, until a thick sauce forms. You may need to add more potato flakes. Season with salt and pepper.

Place green beans in a shallow oven-safe dish, and add a splash of stock so beans do not stick to bottom of dish. Pour mushroom mixture on top of green beans. Spoon leeks over the top.

Bake 30 minutes or until leeks are crisp and beans cooked to taste. If the casserole seems to be drying as it cooks, add a splash of stock at the edges of the pan, taking care not to water down the mushroom sauce. Remove from oven and garnish with those freaky onion things you love, if you really must. ●

RED RIVER RED GARLIC-SMASHED 'TATERS

SERVES 6 | *For generations, Ojibwe people (and probably Dakota, too) living near the Red River Valley hired on to harvest potatoes each season. Our grandparents and great-grandparents picked so many potatoes, you'd think they would never have wanted to see another in their lives, and yet potatoes were a beloved vegetable on their tables. My grandmother Mary Gourneau made delicious "badada salad" with eggs and mayo—you know the one. My father demands kartfel salat, the German version served warm with oil and vinegar. At holidays, Uncle John serves up ten pounds of Yukon Gold and ten pounds of Red River Red from Hughes, an organic farm in North Dakota that supplies most of the Upper Midwest. For these smashed 'taters, you'll want to use organic potatoes if you're leaving the skins on, which is what makes them so, so good.*

6–12 cloves unpeeled garlic
1½ tablespoons olive oil
6 medium Red River Red potatoes, skins on
1 teaspoon salt, plus more to taste
4 tablespoons (½ stick) butter, softened
¼ cup half-and-half, at room temperature
black pepper

Preheat oven to 375 degrees. In a small oven-safe dish or ramekin, place unpeeled garlic in oil. Cover with aluminum foil and roast for 45 minutes, checking after 30 minutes to make sure the skins are not burning; add oil if necessary. Remove dish from oven, let garlic cool, and remove and discard skins; reserve garlic and oil.

Place potatoes in a 3- to 4-quart stockpot, cover with water, add salt, and bring to a boil over high heat. Cover, reduce heat to medium low, and simmer 20 to 30 minutes, until potatoes are fork tender. Remove from heat, drain, and add butter, half-and-half, and garlic and oil. Smash to desired consistency with potato masher. Season with salt and pepper to taste. ●

MUSHROOM SAGE GRAVY

MAKES 6 CUPS | *Uncle John's smashed 'taters (page 101) deserve a rich gravy that lets the mushroom flavor shine. This one tastes traditional and is brown and rib-sticking but also vegetarian, gluten free, and dairy free. I probably should not have told you that. Make it and you will never open a can of Campbell's cream of mushroom again.*

This gravy also works well on Duck Egg Meatloaf (page 74) and rabbit dishes and as a side with any of the Esteemed Manoomin Ways (pages 25–28).

> 1 tablespoon olive oil
> 2 medium yellow onions, minced
> ¼ teaspoon dried rosemary, crushed, or 1 sprig fresh
> 12 ounces mushrooms, fresh or rehydrated
> ½ teaspoon dried thyme
> ¾ teaspoon dried sage, or 2 leaves fresh
> 3 cups stock

In a saucepan set over medium heat, warm oil and cook onions until lightly browned, then stir in rosemary, and cook 1 minute. Add mushrooms, and cook, stirring, until they begin to release liquid and onions are well browned. Add thyme and sage, stir, and let cook a minute. Add stock, stir, and let simmer 10 minutes, then reduce heat to low. Transfer half of gravy to a blender, and puree until completely smooth. Stir pureed gravy back into pan. If not thick enough, scoop out more mushrooms and onions and puree them as well. Make sure to leave some mushrooms whole. •

REZ WATER PICKLES

MAKES 8–10 QUARTS | *The type of cucumber makes a big difference in the quality of the pickle. Angie Erdrich goes to great lengths to get the right one. She claims that "Cross Country cukes" from a particular Hutterite colony are best, and so she makes a pilgrimage each year. Other advice from Angie: "Thicker skin is better. Thinner skin gets too mushy. Signs that you might have Rez water even though you are not on a Rez are that you have calcium and iron deposits around your sink fixtures. In the pickle making process, the garlic will turn blue-green. Water tastes like iron? That's good for pickles!"*

Warning: our mother, Rita Gourneau Erdrich, studied home economics in college, and she says that pickles should be packed tightly, straight up and down, pointy side down. Fill in as tightly as you can get them. She will notice if you don't.

10–15 pounds pickling cukes

13 cups tap water (softened water will ruin things; go rural water or go home)

6 cups white vinegar

1 cup pickling salt

3 cloves garlic, sliced

1 tablespoon sugar

dried red chili peppers

8–10 sterilized quart jars with lids and rings

1 bunch dill

Pick cukes and put them directly into an ice-water bath for 1 to 2 hours prior to pickling.

In a large saucepan, combine (unsoftened) tap water, vinegar, salt, garlic, sugar, and peppers. Bring to a boil and let bubble for at least 15 minutes. Start another pot or two of water to boil to seal the jars.

Fill wide-mouthed quart jars with pickles, packing very, very tightly, the Rita way (see head note). Add dill on top. Pour brine over cukes to the top of jar, just below the lid threads. Put on seal and ring and screw down as tightly as you can.

Put jars into hot-water bath for 5 minutes, or, if you have enough space for two baths of boiling water, the pickles turn out better if you just put them into the bath and immediately turn off the burner. Let jars sit in the water until cooled, typically the next morning. This technique makes the pickles very crisp. If using a single bath, after 5 minutes, remove jars to cool on the counter, and repeat with remaining jars.

The lids should be flat and not make a *pop* when you tap them the next day. If the jar pops, just put it in the refrigerator and eat the cukes as refrigerator pickles. They will keep a long time. Properly sealed jars will be ready in 6 weeks. •

If you can get your cukes from a religious colony,
then that's double-holy on you!
Rez Water makes for better pickles.
Protect our sacred waters. Rez Water is life.

REZ WATER = BETTER PICKLES

Dr. Angie Erdrich, Ojibwe, Turtle Mountain Band | Rez water makes better pickles. Yes, that's right: Rez water. Now I don't mean to minimize legitimate water struggles that threaten the water table across Indian country, the existence of Superfund sites on reservations, and sulfite emissions that endanger manoomin/wild rice. All these are true struggles. I'm just saying that Rez waters make for better pickles.

If you are traveling to the Turtle Mountain Reservation and want a quiet place to stay, there is a lovely bed and breakfast, the Queen of Peace, aptly named as it is housed in a former convent. The beds are very narrow, which makes me wonder if there is a special mattress just for nuns. Sometimes the Virgin Mary appears in the toast markings because my sister gifted them with a BVM toast embosser. The holy pickle water moniker fits the real dill. You see, one summer, I was traveling with my sisters (who thought I was just visiting relatives), returning to North Dakota intent on canning pickles. So convinced was I of the superiority of Belcourt, ND, water (and, later, Sisseton, SD, water) that I was on a pilgrimage. And I forced my sister, Heid, to join me.

We returned from a powwow, put the kids to bed. It was nearly midnight, and we had 86 empty quart jars and 90 pounds of "Cross Country" cucumbers (imagine a bathtub full) from the very earnest Hutterite ladies who grew and washed all these hand-picked, teeny, tiny pickling cucumbers. In order to get the quantity of pickles desired, I needed the help of a colony and, perhaps, a psychiatrist because at first Heid's mind boggled, as a non-manic person's mind should have. She tried to understand the quantity of cucumbers and my insistence that we finish all while they were crisp in the ice bath, while fathoming my brash request to use the stove in a bed and breakfast. In retrospect, as an armchair shrink, perhaps Heid assessed the whole situation as a psychiatric condition and was merely following her codependent tendencies.

Actually, she was good in a pickle. She took no breaks, made no whiny excuses. We commenced to packing those pickles, and before long we were efficient factory workers. Our skin kissed by the briny steam, we became two salty bitches who, bemoaning our lot, began to curse the oldest sister, who was asleep upstairs upon her very narrow mattress. The nerve! Our sister Louise, for whom the word *no* does not exist, was upstairs fast asleep. She's all "yes" the rest of the year when she wants to eat a pickle! We started jamming produce in those wide-mouthed jars, cursing at first the tiny cukes, but soon laying foulest curses upon Louise and even our friend Denise, who was just along for the powwow. Totally unreasonable of them, deciding not to pickle at midnight!

Around 2 AM, I made some vile threats to keep Heid going—she seemed to think we were reaching an end. But I have a saying: "if it is worth doing, it is worth overdoing." She has a saying: "We canned all we can can." Around 3:30 AM, we ran out of jars, congratulated ourselves, and cleaned up in the lingering piquant steam we knew would offend the hostel guests when they came to break their fast and pray at dawn. Finally my sister took a break and left the kitchen—but came running when she heard a terrible noise. I will never forget it: a distinct *crack-boom-sizzle*. I spun around in time to see shards of glass flying and chemical smoke emitting from the stovetop. Heid arrived seconds later to witness the eyes like saucers, the pallor, the gaping mouth, and me, in disbelief, wandering about aimlessly, uttering F-n-A!

At first we thought our curses in the holy place had caused the tragic explosion, but we soon figured out that glass-top stoves are not meant for heavy canning equipment. We wrote late-night, mortified apologetic notes. In shame, we dared not show our faces until breakfast, when we claimed our quarts and opened our checkbooks to donate to the stove fund. The convent staff was kind and accepted pickles in numbers. In penance we offered up a pickle sacrifice even to the pickle slackers, our sister and dear friend, for whom, a few hours earlier, we had harbored nothing but ill will.

Never has a batch of pickles matched the Rez Water Pickles of that summer, but I have already made plans to go back and repeat the process this year, so we will see.

SECRET INGREDIENT PUMPKIN PIE

SERVES 8 | *My mother has an almost identical recipe she calls Favorite Pumpkin Pie, but when I made it, the result was not nearly as good as hers. When I asked why her pie was so good and mine not, even though I followed her recipe, she off-handedly told me she always uses butternut squash, which she says makes perfect pumpkin pie. Little detail left out there, Mom. But I guess that's the nature of the secret ingredient.*

1 (9-inch) unbaked pie shell
2 cups cooked and pureed butternut squash
3 large eggs, slightly beaten
1 cup packed light brown sugar
1 teaspoon ground cinnamon
¼ teaspoon ground cloves
¼ teaspoon nutmeg
¼ teaspoon ground ginger
1 cup evaporated milk

Preheat to 450 degrees. Grease pie plate with butter; line with pastry shell. Use a standing or hand mixer to blend squash, eggs, sugar, spices, and milk. Pour mixture into pie shell. Bake 10 minutes, then reduce heat to 350 degrees and continue baking for an additional 40 to 50 minutes. The pie is done when a knife inserted at the center comes out clean.

For pumpkin pie without crust: add two heaping tablespoons of Bisquick to the filling and blend. Pour into greased pie plate and bake as directed. ●

NEW YEAR'S WELCOME FEAST

When the new year starts is a matter of perspective. Friends who harvest manoomin have told me they think of ricing season, late summer, as the start of a new year. Growing up, we heard stories of how, on the first day of January, families on our home reservation would visit house to house sharing potato and meatball soup, dancing to fiddle music, and greeting one another with the phrase "Bon Anee"—which folks say less French-like, more like *Bonny Nee!* Funny how some people's customs are another's cure: when I told a friend from another tribe about our New Year's soup, she said, "We call that hangover stew."

These days the start of a new calendar year brings a sobriety powwow in many communities, and families may celebrate quietly at home, which is a good thing, since the names on this menu sound loud enough already.

NEW YEAR'S WELCOME MENU
- *Porkypine Bullets (page 108)*
- *Gullet or Bannik (page 110)*
- *Biboon/Winter Manoomin Salad (page 34)*
- *Cowboy Kicker Beans and Wiiyaas (page 112)*
- *Sour Cream and Craisin Pie (page 113)*
- *Maple Custard in Nut Crust (page 204)*
- *Bon Annee Tea (page 243)*

PORKYPINE BULLETS

SERVES A CROWD | *Lise Erdrich works at Circle of Nations School in our hometown, Wahpeton, where she helps American Indian kids learn about healthy living and growing their own food. My sister Lise would rather be known as a gardener than a writer, although she is author of several books. Lise is also known to cook for a crowd. For decades she kept an open-house policy for a big bunch of boys who could really tuck in. No matter how big a roaster of bullets she made, it all got eaten up.* Bullets *supposedly comes from the French word* boulettes, *or, as Lise says, "a Native phonological of the French word but the use predates standard American pronunciation." Folks on the Turtle Mountain Reservation, where our mother grew up and where Lise lived for several years, eat bullets as a celebratory New Year's Day food. We keep that tradition wherever we are today.*

Lise says, "I don't follow recipes, just use anything in whatever proportions suit the occasion," but she typed it all up when I asked her for her secret recipe for Porkypine Bullets.

She says: "When cooking the bullets, add more water or broth gradually as needed. Don't just drown everything, even though that's another version I love from childhood. There would be big pieces of onion swimming around with the potatoes and bullets. The resulting consistency is thinner than the prescribed method, which makes its own gravy. Some people like the bullets on top of potatoes cooked separately and maybe mashed."

TRADITIONAL BULLETS

1 pound lean ground beef or bison, or mix in ground pork or turkey
1 large onion, minced
pinch salt
1 teaspoon black pepper
¼ cup flour
water or beef broth
4 Red River Red potatoes, peeled and quartered

In a medium bowl, mix together meat, onion, and salt and pepper. Place flour in a small bowl. To a large stockpot with a lid, add 2 to 3 inches of water or beef broth and bring to a boil. Form golf ball–size meatballs, roll them in flour mixture until coated, and drop them in the boiling broth one by one. Reduce heat as soon as the flour mixture sticks and makes a coating; turn balls gently to make sure the flour adheres, but don't boil it plumb off. Add the potatoes, cover, and cook gently about 30 minutes.

PORKYPINE BULLETS

For this recipe, the manoomin must be native-harvested, genuine wild rice. The commercially produced paddy rice won't work.

1 pound lean ground beef or bison, or mix in ground pork or turkey
1 large onion, minced, or ½ cup dried chopped onion
1 packet beefy onion dry soup mix, or 1 cup old-fashioned oatmeal
1 large egg
½ cup uncooked manoomin
¼ cup flour
water or beef broth
4 Red River Red potatoes, peeled and quartered

In a medium bowl, mix together meat, onion, soup mix or oatmeal, egg, and uncooked manoomin. Place flour in a small bowl. To a large stockpot with a lid, add 2 to 3 inches of water or beef broth and bring to a boil. Form golf ball–size meatballs, roll them in flour until coated, and drop them in the boiling broth one by one. Reduce heat as soon as the flour mixture sticks and makes a coating; turn balls gently to make sure the flour adheres, but don't boil it plumb off. Add the potatoes, cover, and cook gently about 30 minutes.

VARIATION: ROOSTER GLAZE BALLS

Make Traditional or Porkypine Bullets but leave out the potatoes. Mix together 2 cups cranberry sauce and as much Rooster Sauce (Sriracha) as you like. Or use Heinz chili sauce, as in the old traditional party meatballs recipe. Use as little water or broth as possible, and as it cooks down, add cranberry mixture. Serve with Gullet or Bannik (page 110) or with Pumpkin Bangs (page 96).

VARIATION: MANCAKE

Make Porkypine Bullet meat mixture, omitting flour, potatoes, and broth. Place half of mixture in Bundt pan. Add a layer of approximately 1 cup sauerkraut; top with remaining meat mixture. Bake at 350 for about 45 minutes. Allow to cool slightly; turn out of pan onto serving platter. "Frost" with ketchup, mustard, or Sriracha Rooster Sauce. ●

GULLET OR BANNIK

SERVES 6–8 | *Auntie Gladys is known for her flaky, delicious gullet (la galette), also called bannik or bannock bread. The only change I made to her recipe was an attempt to bring the indigenous into this treaty-ration food by using a sunflower-based fat. This bread, which is really a giant biscuit, looks good baked in a cast-iron skillet and cut into wedges, so give that a try. And don't forget to poke it all over with a fork. I'm not sure why the ladies always did that, but I do know it allows butter to run into the holes when you get your mitts on your hot portion.*

Gullet is served with jam and tea as often as it is served with bullets or other soups. Try gullet with Gooseberry-Raspberry Jam (page 211), and you will taste one of the sweetest memories of my childhood, straight from the Turtle Mountain Reservation, circa 1975.

4 cups all-purpose flour

4 teaspoons baking powder

1 teaspoon salt

8 tablespoons (½ cup) Earth Balance sunflower "butter" sticks,
  or substitute shortening

2 cups milk

butter for serving

Preheat oven to 350 degrees. Grease a cast-iron skillet or cookie sheet with oil. In a large bowl, sift together dry ingredients. Melt the Earth Balance "butter" or shortening. Make a well in dry ingredients and pour in milk and melted butter. Mix until dough just holds together. Turn dough onto a floured surface and knead until you can form it into a slight mound.

Move dough into prepared skillet or form in a round on prepared cookie sheet; do not overflow the edges of the pan. Use a fork to poke all over, scoring the dough in a pattern of your choosing. Bake in center of the oven 1 hour. Remove and brush with butter; cut into slices and serve, or place in the middle of the table and let everyone pull off pieces as they eat. ●

RICHARD WRIGHT *Leech Lake Ojibwe*

elder | Bannik: this is an early version of fry bread, cooked over a campfire. No grease: just plain dough and fire. I still cook it as I learned from my parents when we went camping and harvested wild rice. We would stay for up to two weeks at a campsite and rice out the lake. We built tar paper shacks to live in. Not a bad cost for a house—five dollars for a roll of tar paper, and the rest of the building blocks were willow forming a room big enough to hold two beds and five children with two parents and a grampa. Then we moved to the fish camps for another two weeks, but all this time we lived on bannik. Plus wild rice and fish feeds.

COWBOY KICKER BEANS AND WIIYAAS

SERVES 6 | *Sometime in the 1970s, some Don Draper advertising genius urged every-one to make "cowboy beans" by adding barbecue sauce to canned beans to serve at cookouts. Well, that was also the era of Billy Jack, the Indian-Hippie B-movie hero who took off his socks to kick racist behinds. These tribute beans use sauce from Ojibwe restaurateur "Famous Dave" Anderson and dried meat/wiiyaas. They could be made vegetarian, like Billy Jack's weeping, washed-out-blonde pacifist girlfriend.*

To paraphrase Billy Jack, "You're gonna take these beans and whop them right next to some gullet and there's not a dang thing you're gonna be able to do about it." These beans are for you, Billy Jack. So good, you'll go berserk!

1 tablespoon olive oil

1 red onion, chopped

2 cups cooked or canned black beans, drained

1.75 ounces bison jerky, cut into bite-size pieces (optional for pacifists—kick wiiyaas!)

1 cup stock

½ cup hot or mild Famous Dave's BBQ Sauce (Devil's Spit for hotheads)

¼ cup maple syrup or honey

½ cup sundried tomatoes, cut into bite-size pieces

In a medium saucepan set over low heat, warm olive oil and fry red onion until very soft, 5 to 10 minutes. Stir in beans, jerky, and stock, increase heat to medium, and let mixture bubble for 1 minute. Stir in barbecue sauce and maple, turn heat to low, and simmer for 10 minutes. Stir in sundried tomatoes and simmer 30 minutes, adding stock if mixture seems dry. This dish is done when jerky is softened (which can vary with the type of jerky) and sauce is thick. Serve hot or cold. •

SOUR CREAM AND CRAISIN PIE

SERVES 8 | *A version of this pie is a staple in commodity foods program cookbooks, no doubt because every participant got an enormous white box with the blue out-line of a bunch of grapes: what to do with all these raisins? Well, if we put cream and sugar in there, it might taste like summer in the dead of winter.*

Sour cream and raisin pie seems like indigenous cooking to me: just recall a time when fruit was gathered and dried when plentiful and reconstituted with whatever ingredients were on hand months later, and fast-forward to a time when we can get sour cream at a gas station. Everything you need to make this new family tradition is there on the Super Pumper shelves. We invented it for our own holiday, Pie Friday, which is the day after Indigenous Foods Day (Thanksgiving). John Burke switched up the raisins with dried cranberries, indigenous to the Upper Midwest in both highbush and low/bog forms. In this recipe, you'll want to use the sweetened ones.

> 1 cup craisins
> 1 cup hot water
> 1 cup sugar
> 1 tablespoon flour
> ¼ teaspoon salt
> 1 large egg, beaten
> 1 teaspoon vanilla extract
> 1 cup sour cream
> 1 (9-inch) unbaked pie shell

Preheat oven to 400 degrees. In a small saucepan, cover the craisins with the hot water, and bring to a boil; set aside for 10 minutes while they plump, and then drain off the water. In a large mixing bowl, toss together the craisins, sugar, flour, and salt. Stir in the egg, vanilla, and sour cream. Pour mixture into pie shell. Bake 15 minutes; reduce heat to 350 degrees, and bake an additional 45 minutes. The top will brown lightly. ●

At least once a summer, we all try to be home around the same time. If there's occasion to meet elsewhere, like a wedding or anniversary, or a graduation, or someone is running a marathon, or getting an award, or a baby is born, or a relative is visiting from far away, or a memorial is being observed, or a big rummage sale is on, or an art exhibit is opening, or just about any excuse, we will eat together in the park or a backyard. Potluck must include Wahpeton pasta (a noodle salad made of the usual suspects plus fresh dill), and Mom's coleslaw of napa cabbage and ramen noodles, another family favorite. As our family has grown, new traditions have entered, some from faraway lands that bring indigenous foods home all dressed up fancy from their travel abroad.

SUNSHINE POTLUCK AND FISH FRY MENU

- *Fish Fry (page 115)*
- *Three Sisters Salsa (page 116)*
- *Sweet Potato Dip (page 117)*
- *India-Indian Grilled Corn (page 118)*
- *India-Indian Sloppy Joes (Pav Bhaji) (page 119)*
- *Sweet Potato Salad (page 120)*
- *Ziigwan/Spring Louise's Manoomin Salad (page 35)*
- *North Dakota Sunflower Pie (page 121)*
- *Wild Plum Clafoutis (page 122)*
- *Crimson and Clover Iced Tea (page 244)*

SERVES A CROWD | *My brother Ralph has always been the one to whomp up the fish fry—just as I remember my mom's brothers doing when we visited Turtle Mountain in the summer. They take the action outside, deep-frying with various setups from camp stoves to wood-fired grills. Ralph doesn't care too much about the fish batter: just use a mix. Fresh fish or good fresh-frozen are the best ingredient, he says. Ralph looks forward to experimenting with grilled buffalo fish when son Aaron spears in South Dakota. When I asked Ralph what he thought of recent catch restrictions imposed by the Red Lake Nation and Minnesota DNR, he was thoughtful. When the walleye are not being fished so much, he says, the black crappies prosper and then walleye recover. He should know: he lived on that lake for ten years while working for Indian Health Services. "Red Lake has some excellent black crappies," Ralph says, looking hungry.*

Red Lake Nation Fishery (redlakewalleye.com) offers visitors to its website "Original Fried Walleye," adapted slightly here, a recipe for a crowd. And it is not a fish fry unless it serves a crowd.

   1 dozen eggs
   2 sleeves saltine crackers,
      crushed
   oil
  24 Red Lake walleye fillets

Whisk several eggs in bottom of flat dish. Place crushed saltines in another flat dish. In a Dutch oven or other large pot, heat oil to 350–60 degrees. Roll fillets in egg and then in saltines. Fry in hot oil for about 3 to 4 minutes on each side or until golden brown. Enjoy! •

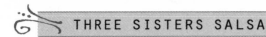

THREE SISTERS SALSA

SERVES A CROWD | *Sugar and cream–type corn on the cob is the way to go if you use fresh in this recipe. When using canned, I like "corn and peppa"–style mixes or white and yellow corn mixed. When my sister Lise makes this recipe, she must quadruple it because she usually serves it in a vat. And we eat it all with tortilla chips or as a side salad. It really is that good.*

> 3 ears very fresh sweet corn, kernels cut from cob,
>   or 1 (15-ounce) can corn, drained (see head note)
> 1 medium zucchini, minced
> 1 (15-ounce) can black beans, rinsed and drained
> 1 (16-ounce) jar salsa (red or green, fresh or canned,
>   as hot as you like)
> chopped fresh cilantro, parsley, chives, and/or green onion tops
>   for garnish

In a large bowl, combine corn, zucchini, and black beans, mixing well. Add salsa to level of "soupiness" and spice that you like. Mix again. Garnish with fresh herbs as you like. ●

SWEET POTATO DIP

MAKES 3–4 CUPS | *While sweet potatoes did not grow in most of the area surrounding the Great Lakes in the very distant past, they were common fare by the time the USDA got around to listing them. Still, I think of them as southern cousins, so charming and smooth. I love it when they visit, and they are always gone too soon.*

2 large sweet potatoes, baked and peeled
½ cup extra-virgin olive oil
2 cloves garlic, crushed
1 teaspoon red sumac
½ teaspoon white pepper
¼ teaspoon smoked paprika
⅛ teaspoon ground allspice
½ teaspoon sea salt
3 dashes chipotle hot sauce (Tabasco or Bufalo)
1 tablespoon chopped parsley
black pepper
¼ cup toasted pumpkin seeds, optional

In food processor, puree sweet potatoes. Add oil, garlic, sumac, white pepper, paprika, allspice, sea salt, hot sauce, and parsley, and puree again until thoroughly combined. Serve garnished with further sprinkles of paprika and sumac and some cracked black pepper to taste. Add toasted pumpkin seeds (if using) around the edges and serve. ●

INDIA-INDIAN GRILLED CORN

SERVES 6–8 | *The first time I saw Indians from India making sweet corn at a picnic was the night before my sister did the nicest thing and married Dr. Sandeep Patel. We threw a party with fish fry for the meat eaters and corn roast for all. I marveled at the ingenious Indian American way to prepare sweet corn. Instead of entirely shucking the corn, leave the husks on but pull them to the bottom of the stalk and leave them hanging off the grill. When the corn is charred—and you want it a little charred—the husks work as a handle and napkin in one. Season the corn with a delicious spice mix applied with a lemon. No fussy corn holders, no rolling the corn on a buttery, slippery plate: just rub a spiced lemon on the cob, and your corn is seasoned to perfection.*

Why did we never think of such a clever approach to eating corn? It seems unfair. Then again, we use the name of their entire continent (mistakenly, true), and they gave us Sandeep, so the least we could do is give Indian Americans props for terrific grilled corn. A tried-and-true version follows, but methinks sumac and cracked juniper would be good on corn, too.

8 ears sweet corn

2 tablespoons ground red chili (called Merchu at Indian stores)

2 tablespoons black pepper

1 tablespoon salt

8 tablespoons (1 stick) butter, softened, optional

2 lemons, quartered

Prepare a charcoal grill. While the grill is heating, pull back outer leaves and silk from corn but do not remove them all: keep the tightest, inner layers of leaves pulled back but still attached. Submerge the corn in cold, salted water for 20 to 30 minutes, or until coals are ready. Place ears of corn on the hot grill and cook 5 to 10 minutes, turning several times. Mix chili, pepper, and salt in a bowl. As a concession to American preference, coat cobs with butter (if using). Rub lemon wedges in seasoning and then rub lemon up and down cobs. ●

INDIA-INDIAN SLOPPY JOES (PAV BHAJI)

SERVES A CROWD | *Another recipe heavy on corn, green beans, and lima beans, in-gredients long used by indigenous peoples in the area, comes to us through my sister Angie and her mother-in-law, whom we refer to as Mama Patel. She taught Angie this recipe, and Angie has tried to teach me, but I like it when Angie makes this dish.*

Angie says, "This treat is like a Sloppy Joe—the kind of thing that one might buy from a road stand in India. It can be made in massive quantities in less than one hour and even made the day before and seasoned overnight.

"Pav Bhaji Masala—ready-made mix—comes in a little box that can be found in Indian grocery stores or ordered online. The main ingredients are ground cloves, cinnamon and cayenne pepper. Some brands are more potent than others so adjust to your spice comfort level. Recipes for the spice mix are also available online, if you want to make your own."

    1 pound frozen corn, thawed
    1 pound frozen green beans, thawed
    1 pound frozen lima beans, thawed
    1 pound frozen peas and carrots, thawed
    ¾ cup canola oil, divided
    ½ teaspoon black mustard seeds
    6 cloves garlic, pressed
    1 tablespoon grated fresh ginger
    2 large jalapeños, seeded and minced
    2 medium onions, diced
    2 teaspoons turmeric
    4 teaspoons salt
    ¼ cup water
    8 plum tomatoes, diced
 6–10 tablespoons Pav Bhaji Masala (see head note)
    2 dozen hamburger buns with or without sesame seeds
      butter, softened
    1 bunch green onions, chopped
    1 bunch cilantro, chopped
    6 lemons, quartered   >>

Use a food processor to chop thawed frozen vegetables into small but still recognizable pieces; some puree is okay. In a Dutch oven or soup pot set over medium-high heat, warm ½ cup canola oil. Add black mustard seeds and heat until they pop; immediately reduce heat to medium. Add garlic, ginger, jalapeños, and onions, and cook, stirring, until soft. Add turmeric and salt and stir. Add veggies and water and cook, covered, for 30 minutes, until soft, stirring often and adding remaining ¼ cup oil as needed. Stir in diced tomatoes and Pav Bhaji Masala. Simmer, covered, for an additional 30 minutes, stirring often.

Meanwhile, prepare the buns: spread on a little butter and then fry or grill on both sides, flattening with a spatula. To serve in classic fashion: garnish each serving with green onions and cilantro and a squeeze from a lemon wedge. Use the buns like chapattis (India-Indian bread): tear off little pieces and pick up the pav bhaji. This dish is fairly spicy: adjust to taste. Freezes just fine or tastes great as leftovers. ●

 SWEET POTATO SALAD

SERVES 6 | *While this method calls for roasting the potatoes, in the summer, rather than turn on the oven, I boil them until tender but firm. I've also taken thickly sliced sweet potatoes and peppers and lightly grilled them outdoors the day before and then chopped them to use in this salad. Sweet potatoes just get better the next day, so save yourself a step and do them ahead, I say. Don't let them get mushy, but if they do, use them to make Sweet Potato Dip (page 117) instead.*

> 2 large sweet potatoes, skins on, cut into bite-size pieces
> olive oil
> 1 bell pepper, chopped medium
> ½ cup minced cilantro, plus a few leaves for garnish
> ¼ cup minced red onion
> 1 tablespoon balsamic vinegar
> 2 tablespoons walnut oil or other light vegetable oil
> 2 green onions, minced
> 1 cup whole roasted salted peanuts for garnish

Preheat oven to 375 degrees. Toss sweet potatoes with just enough olive oil to coat, place in shallow baking dish, and bake 25 to 30 minutes or until tender but firm (see head note). Allow potatoes to cool. In a large salad bowl, gently mix sweet potatoes, bell pepper, cilantro, and red onion. In a small bowl, combine vinegar and oil, stirring well. Drizzle into salad bowl and gently stir to combine. Garnish with green onions and peanuts. ●

NORTH DAKOTA SUNFLOWER PIE

SERVES 8 | *Whenever we go home to North Dakota, we patronize the local thrift shop, Mother Hubbard's Cupboard. Don't go there: there's nothing fantabulous, we swear! We would not be holding out on you about vintage clothes and household items. All you will find there are cookbooks, like* Favorite Recipes from Great Midwest Cooks, *from which we adapted this scrumptious pie.*

        3 large eggs, beaten
      ¾ cup packed brown sugar
      ¾ cup maple syrup
        3 tablespoons Earth Balance sunflower "butter" sticks
            or salted butter, melted
        1 teaspoon vanilla extract
      ¼ teaspoon salt
        1 cup roasted, unsalted sunflower seeds,
            or use ¾ cup unsalted and ¼ cup salted
        1 (9-inch) unbaked pie shell

Preheat oven to 350 degrees. In a large bowl, beat together eggs, brown sugar, maple syrup, shortening, vanilla, and salt. Spread sunflower seeds evenly in the bottom of the unbaked pie shell. Pour in the egg mixture. Bake for 50 to 60 minutes or until almost set (the center will jiggle a bit). Cool on a wire rack. Serve to friends who can't eat pecan pie and make them smile. ●

WILD PLUMS

The frosty pink skin is sour, to be sure, but tender, and the yellow interior glows with sweetness easily coaxed by cooking. We walked to shelterbelts and parked alongside drainage ditches, went out in force and picked enormous buckets of wild plums from small trees so loaded that the memory of their smashed sunset of spilled fruit marked itself forever on my child's mind. Wild plums! As psychedelic a display as my older siblings' tie-dyed T-shirts! I ate so many once that now just a little taste has the tang of a stomachache to me. I go easy on the raw plums but would happily cook down a pound to make a sweet and sour sauce for duck or fish and have enough left over for a breakfast of Wild Plum Clafoutis.

 ## WILD PLUM CLAFOUTIS

SERVES 6 | *My love loves me and I know, because he makes me clafoutis. The most tender and simple way to treat fresh fruit is all Frenched up in name but down home in fact. There is nothing more lovely to put to your lips, except perhaps a kiss.*

1 pound wild plums, or substitute cultivated plums
1 tablespoon Chambord plus 1 tablespoon water, optional
4 large eggs
1 cup coconut milk, or substitute half-and-half or light cream
1 tablespoon maple syrup
1 teaspoon vanilla extract, or use seeds scraped from 1 vanilla bean
4 tablespoons (½ stick) unsalted butter, melted,
  or substitute sunflower "butter" sticks
1 cup unbleached white flour
½ cup packed brown sugar or maple sugar
⅛ teaspoon salt

Preheat oven to 350 degrees. Grease a round 2- or 3-quart baking dish. Halve and pit the plums. Slice off the ends of the halves (they're almost all skin), then halve lengthwise to make thick slices. Toss the plums in a bowl with the Chambord and water (if using), and set aside. In a large mixing bowl, beat eggs with coconut milk, then add maple, vanilla, and butter, mixing well. In a separate bowl, mix together the flour, sugar, and salt. Beat the dry ingredients into the wet to make a smooth batter. Pour one-third of the batter into the baking dish. Set in a layer of half the plums. Cover the plums with half the remaining batter. Layer in the remaining plums. Pour in the remaining batter. Bake 50 to 60 minutes, until the top is puffed and golden and the center is set; test by poking in a wooden pick or a spaghetti noodle, which should come out clean (except for bits of plum!). ●

RESOURCES

If you can't make it to one of our family gatherings and you are in the Twin Cities, try Gatherings Cafe at the Minneapolis American Indian Center: www.maicnet.org/gatherings-cafe.

Another possibility is the Sioux Chef (sioux-chef.com), which is in partnership with Minneapolis Parks and Recreation at the Water Works. Founder Sean Sherman (Lakota) and his co-owner Dana Thompson (Dakota) have gathered a team of Anishinaabe, Mdewakanton Dakota, Navajo, Northern Cheyenne, Oglala Lakota, and Wahpeton-Sisseton Dakota chefs, ethnobotanists, food preservationists, adventurers, foragers, caterers, event planners, artists, musicians, food truckers, and food lovers. The Sioux Chef's mission: "We are committed to revitalizing Native American Cuisine and in the process we are re-identifying North American Cuisine and reclaiming an important culinary culture long buried and often inaccessible."

Sharing the canning obsession with the next generation

... VEGETABLES AND

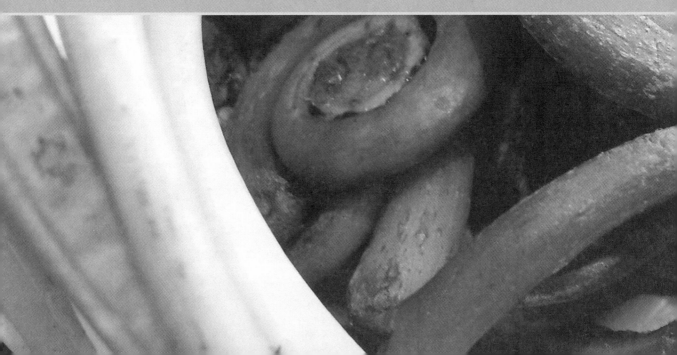

BEANS •••

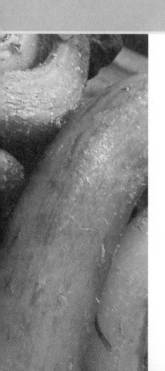

*W*e all know that once all foods were local foods. But pretty quickly humans, and before them animals, began to move food around the globe. Before most indigenous people in the Upper Midwest had ever met a European, foods from Europe, Asia, and Africa were growing and being eaten in the area. French explorers noted Native American cultivation of melons in the Mississippi River region, although watermelon originated in Africa. Cucumbers, related to melons, were being grown in North Dakota at the time of European contact as well. Numerous green plants that we now consider weeds, including dandelions and plantains, became important foodstuffs to tribal people but are in fact relative newcomers to Turtle Island. From the coastal regions of what is now the United States, squash and other plants made their way to the Great Lakes and prairie states long before European contact. In ancient times, other plants migrated from Mexico, Central America, and island nations, most notably corn, which was grown by all the cultural groups indigenous to the Upper Midwest.

The USDA lists 244 vegetables and plant foods as native to all or part of the Great Lakes watershed. Foods indigenous to the prairie areas of the Upper Midwest, such as prickly pear cactus, prairie turnip, ground cherries, and dozens of other fruits no doubt would take that number to three hundred or more. Because of intensive agricultural programs that favor hybrid produce, many of these foods are difficult to find, and some varieties, such as the cushaw squash, are becoming rare enough to be placed in the Slow Food USA Ark of Taste for endangered foods.

But many indigenous foods are not at all rare. Here's a list of thirty-one you would most likely find in stores and markets: maple, pecans, chestnuts, hazelnuts, black walnuts, crookneck squash, butternut squash, acorn squash, pattypan squash, summer squash (yellow and green zucchini), pumpkin, sunflower seeds, Jerusalem artichokes/sunchokes, mint, green beans, yellow (wax) beans, kidney beans, navy beans, pinto beans, black beans, great northern beans, persimmons, plums, cherries, strawberries, blackberries, raspberries, blueberries, cranberries, grapes, and manoomin (wild rice).

Farmers markets, food co-ops, and specialty stores often carry some of the harder-to-find foods used in indigenous cooking, including wild leeks/ramps, fid-

Studies by the University of Minnesota on the traditional foods grown in the tribal gardens found the following:

• Hominy corn is high in carbohydrates and protein. One serving of hominy yields 47% of the DRV for fiber and 33% of the B vitamin Thiamine and has half the calories of market corn.

• Arikara squash has 13% of the DRV for fiber, 64% of the DRV for vitamin A, and half the calories and double the calcium and magnesium of the market equivalent.

• Similarly, Potawatomi lima beans are low in fat, and high in carbohydrates and protein. B vitamins are found in abundance, including thiamine, pantothenic acid, niacin and B6. Po-

tawatomi lima beans also provide 24 grams of fiber per serving, and 21 times the anti-oxidants found in market beans.

In an article published in the *Journal of Medicinal Food* (10:2 [2007]) Kwon, et al. of the University of Massachusetts report that in vitro studies show that upon digestion, corn, beans, and squash perform 'enzyme inhibitory activities' that may prove conducive to blood sugar and blood pressure management, without the side effects of commonly prescribed drugs.

Restoring these traditional foods will have an impact on reducing diet-related illness in our communities. —*nativeharvest.com*

---

dlehead ferns, dandelion greens, scarlet runner beans, hickory nuts, butternuts, Juneberries (saskatoons), gooseberries/currants, crab apples, papaws, mulberries, wild grapes, and other wild foods.

Maple, berries, and wild ginger have long been the main seasoning of many foods, along with wild mints that range in flavor from the oregano- or marjoram-like savoriness of bergamot to licorice-like hyssop. Tarragon is native to North Dakota, and sassafras and sarsaparilla grew throughout the region. Seasonings available in the spice aisle or through specialty stores and online sources include sumac, sassafras, juniper, bee balm/bergamot, and wintergreen leaves.

Of course, most of the varieties of these foods now grown for market will not be exactly like those eaten for centuries in the region. A good example is the strawberry, once a small berry loaded with tremendous sweetness that can still be found wild. Many foods once indigenous to the area have been crossed with European varieties and the original food obscured. Recently an 850-year-old squash seed was germinated and grown by Native Harvest in Minnesota. The fruits matured into large, vividly orange–fleshed, oblong squash never before seen by anyone alive. One person described the taste of the squash, dubbed Gete-okosomin (Ancient Squash), as "intense" and unlike the squash we grow today. The seeds were found in a clay pot in an archeological dig in Minnesota near the Wisconsin border. Other food recoveries are underway across the region. A particular focus is corn, which deserves, and in this book has been given, its own section.

Seek heirloom indigenous varieties of beans, squash, and other plant foods at farmers markets and food co-ops, and investigate Local Harvest (localharvest.org), an online service that matches buyers with sellers of local foods. Explore online to find products containing hawthorn, shag bark hickory, birch syrup, and other items made from trees, all of which seem to be gaining in popularity. Finally, in the spirit of the Three Sisters, consider ordering seeds and renewing our food traditions by growing your own. In the past I've planted nodding onion, meadow garlic, and wild ginger. This year I am focusing on mints—wild mint, wild bergamot, mountain mint, oswego tea—and a number of other indigenous plants that would be hard to find otherwise.

Another option is to wild harvest indigenous foods. Often, as in the case with berries, cherries, and other tree fruit, an abundant harvest is nearby. But consult a good guidebook (such as *Abundantly Wild* by Teresa Marrone) and a good wild foods cookbook (such as Brett Laidlaw's *Trout Caviar*) before you forage or prepare foraged foods. That said, wild harvesting is not as tricky as you might think, and most people would recognize at least a few of these familiar wild foods: wild plums, cherries, currants, gooseberries, and blackberries; acorns, butternuts, and black walnuts; cattails, violets, and milkweed.

Several foods from non-indigenous plants that have long been important to indigenous cooking in the Upper Midwest are fairly easy to find as well. Some of these plants spread throughout the Americas so quickly, at a time so distant, their use became common in the cooking of tribal groups, as in the case of cucumbers and melons. Others are watercress (or upland cress), daylily flowers (known as lily buds in Chinese cooking), and sweet potatoes.

Finally, substitutes for indigenous ingredients that are easy to find, sometimes locally sourced, include baby spinach and arugula (for all greens); asparagus (for fiddlehead ferns); leeks or green onions combined with garlic chives (for ramps); fresh or bottled nopales from Mexican groceries (instead of local prickly

pear cactus); and roasted pepitas, also available at Mexican groceries (rather than raw pumpkin seeds). Good substitutes for wild seasonings are fresh ginger, fresh peppermint, and zatar (a middle eastern seasoning made of sumac).

Honoring the spirit of our ancestors and the foods that made them strong so we could be here today is more important than strict adherence to indigenous ingredients alone. After all, tribal people of the Great Lakes and Great Plains never turned down good food, no matter where it was from—of that I am sure.

FIDDLEHEADS AND QUAIL EGGS IN RAMP NESTS ON POLENTA

SERVES 6 | *Like a miniature woodland diorama, this appetizer or brunch treat is fussy and meant for special occasions. Having fiddleheads, ramps, and quail eggs is a special occasion, by the way. Quail eggs, as well as duck eggs, are available at Asian groceries and farmers markets.*

> 1 bunch ramps, thoroughly rinsed, roots trimmed
> 1 cup olive oil
> coarse or sea salt
> 5 juniper berries, crushed
> 1 (18-ounce) package precooked polenta, or prepare from scratch, ¼ cup per person
> black pepper
> 10 quail eggs
> 2 tablespoons butter, divided
> 1 cup fresh morel or other small mushrooms, optional (but will put this dish over the top)
> 1–2 cups fiddlehead ferns (20–40 fern heads), or substitute 6 asparagus spears

Preheat oven to 425 degrees. Prepare ramps: chop off greens, taking care to slice the green away from the rib that extends a fair distance into the leaf. Split ramps. Chop greens in bite-size pieces; set aside. In a 9x13–inch shallow baking dish, arrange the split ramps with bulb ends all facing in one direction. Pour in oil and coat ramps, using your hands to get curving stems. Season with salt and add juniper berries, submerging in the oil. Roast ramps, uncovered, until soft and caramelized, about 10 to 15 minutes, checking regularly to make sure they do not burn. If they are browning too quickly, lightly cover the browning area with aluminum foil. Continue to roast until ramps are all soft and some even slightly crispy. Remove from oven, and allow to cool.

While ramps are roasting, slice prepackaged polenta to ¼-inch rounds and place on a baking sheet. If preparing polenta, follow package directions and form into small cakes, 1 per person. Lightly oil polenta, and season with salt and pepper. Bake until crisped, about 10 minutes. Remove juniper berries from ramps, drain oil, reserving for Roasted Ramp and Juniper Dressing (page 232).

Carefully open quail eggs into a bowl. Shells are surprisingly tough on these delicate little eggs, so rather than cracking the eggs, use a serrated knife to cut off the tip and then pour each egg out of its shell. In a small skillet set over medium-high heat, melt 1 tablespoon butter until sizzling. Slide all of the quail eggs into the hot butter and fry briefly, until the whites set up. Slide the entire mass of eggs onto a plate and cut into individual portions, in any shape that works, using a sharp knife.

In a skillet set over medium-high heat, melt remaining tablespoon butter and cook mushrooms (if using) until soft, then add chopped ramp greens. Stir until greens wilt slightly. Remove from heat and set aside.

On top of each polenta cake, place 2 fiddleheads so they look like a 6 to the left and a 9 to the right. Between the fiddleheads, put a tablespoon of the ramp green or mushroom and ramp green mixture. Place 1 or 2 fried quail eggs on top, in the center. Make a nest by winding roasted ramp stems on a fork and sliding them off in the center of the polenta. If using asparagus, cut the spears into long strings or simply chop into bite-size pieces and create a tiny forest around the nests, making sure each nest resides in a forest of both tips and stems. Serve warm with a few extra fiddleheads or additional greens or mushroom mixture garnishing the plate. ●

FIDDLEHEAD AND PICKLED RAMP COMPOSED SALAD

SERVES 4 | *Our friends the Young-Walsers brought fiddleheads from their farm on just the day we were set to try the ramps we had pickled. It was also soon after Easter, so we had plenty of boiled eggs. These ingredients were likely available to indigenous people in early spring for millennia. In fact, I imagine ferns and eggs were one of the first meals, since ferns are some of the oldest plants on the planet. Indigenous people dug root vegetables as a staple of their diets, too. Not just sunchokes, but the roots of lake-growing arrowheads and cattails, as well as tiny wild sweet potatoes and other wild tubers. Potatoes are indigenous cousins, most likely introduced here with European movement but developed in thousands of varieties by Andean indigenous people of South America. Groups in the Upper Midwest quickly developed their own varieties of potato as well: the Menominee grew a blue potato that, in the 1920s, ethnobotanist Huron Smith declared had never before been seen.*

The idea of a composed salad reminds me of a still life that one can eat. Admire it first, then enjoy!

> 1–2 cups fiddlehead ferns (20–40 fern heads), thoroughly rinsed, brown bits removed, ends trimmed
> 2 cups boiled tiny new potatoes
> salt
> 4 hard-cooked eggs, peeled and quartered
> 4–6 Ramp Refrigerator Pickles (page 233)
> 6 tablespoons Roasted Ramp and Juniper Dressing (page 232) or other vinaigrette

In a large pot of boiling water, cook fiddleheads 10 minutes, and test for tenderness. (Some people drain the water, bring new water to a boil, and cook the fiddleheads for 5 more minutes in order to completely rid the ferns of any husk-like debris that might taste bitter.) Ferns should be crisp but fully cooked. Drain ferns and rinse in cold water to retain fresh green color. On a large platter, place fiddleheads and new potatoes. Sprinkle with salt. Add egg pieces to platter. Cut Ramp Refrigerator Pickles in pieces about the size of the new potatoes and arrange on platter. Drizzle with Roasted Ramp and Juniper Dressing. ●

visual artist | First greens in the spring are ferns and dandelions, then asparagus, then milkweed. Skunk cabbage is early, also, but my family did not eat it . . . When I was a young man living off the forest . . . I remember eating fiddleheads with fresh-caught trout. We just ate them plain, or they can be thrown into salads for texture. Sometimes we had them steamed with butter. They turned bright green—all wild greens turn bright green.

Wallace was an old Indian man, hired help, an important part of my youth, like a bridge, a way to get from here to there as he taught me ways of Menominee men.

Wallace was an expert at finding partridge nests along the logging roads, the old foot trails, the granite spaces between the streams and the forests. In late spring the nests are filled with eggs, and we would eat them. He and I, hidden away from Grandma and seated with our backs leaning against some friendly pine tree, would eat them raw. After puncturing the top of the eggshells with his thumbnail, he made a straight circular line, peeling off the top fifth of the shell, holding them upright to keep them from spilling. Then we poured the viscous egg into our mouths, swallowing the delicate-tasting egg in one gulp.

Sometimes Wallace would take the partridge eggs home and Grandma would boil them. But mostly Grandma fried them—Grandma fried almost everything. Grandpa always said that one of the few good things that white people brought to us was a frying pan.

Fiddleheads are the tips of ostrich ferns picked before they open

FIDDLEHEADS AND SALMON IN BLACK BEAN SAUCE

SERVES 4 | *Chinese black bean paste does not contain indigenous beans, but its garlic-salty, fermented richness brings out the sweetness in fiddlehead ferns. Find black bean paste in the Chinese food section of larger groceries or at Asian markets or co-ops. It is not expensive, and a little goes a long way, so you will be able to make several dishes from one small jar. And then you will be hooked.*

Somewhere I read that a slow and low approach to salmon is the way to get odd-sized fillets to cook evenly. Well, our method shows a bit of impatience—after 30 minutes in a 275-degree oven, we crank it to 300 for just 5 minutes to get the fillets nice and hot for serving. So far it has worked beautifully. Give it a try.

Serve the salmon with Spring Mâche Up (page 238) and Sunseed-crusted Sunchokes (page 137).

> 4 (5-ounce) salmon fillets
> 6 tablespoons black bean paste, divided
> 1 cup fiddlehead ferns (approximately 20 fern heads), thoroughly rinsed, brown bits removed
> 1 tablespoon olive oil
> 1 onion, chopped
> ¼ cup stock

Preheat oven to 275 degrees. Place fish fillets in a lightly oiled shallow baking dish. Spread 1 tablespoon black bean paste on each serving. Place pan in middle of oven and bake 30 minutes, testing periodically for doneness.

Meanwhile, in a small saucepan, bring 2 cups water to a boil. In a large bowl, prepare an ice-water bath. Drop fiddleheads in boiling water and cook 5 minutes, skimming away any chaff that comes to the surface. When fiddleheads turn bright green, drain and plunge in ice-water bath.

In a small saucepan set over medium heat, warm oil and cook onion until softened and translucent. Stir in remaining 2 tablespoons black bean paste. Add stock and stir again. Add fiddleheads, and simmer over low heat 5 minutes. Do not cook so long that fiddleheads lose their color.

When the fish has been in the oven 30 minutes, if not flaking when tested for doneness, increase heat to 300 degrees and bake another 5 minutes. Let rest 2 to 3 minutes outside the oven, where fish will continue to cook. Cover each serving with fiddleheads and black bean sauce. ●

CARSON VILES *Confederated Tribes of Siletz Indians*

Many indigenous peoples are recognizing the threats posed to first foods by climate change and are confronting these challenges in a variety of ways. The potential loss of first foods has spurred many native communities to revitalize their already struggling relationship with first foods. Conversely, native communities with a strong, ongoing relationship with the first foods are taking this challenge as an opportunity to assert the importance of first foods for their communities and the health of the land. First foods continue to nourish indigenous peoples, as they have always done. Even as they are jeopardized by climate change, first foods are inspiring cultural, physical, and ecological health in native communities. —*"Tribal Climate Change Profile: First Foods and Climate Change"*

SERVES 6 | *The first time I cooked with Richard LaFortune, it was a little embarrassing, a little like falling in love. People stared, watching us ooh and ahh over our ingredients and ideas. We were wild in my sister's kitchen that night: we made a huge mess—broke an antique periwinkle blue-glazed pot I am still seeking to replace—and we were successful in every dish. Whew, I still have that winded, satisfied feeling thinking of it now!*

Richard is a sexy cook. He uses tools I've never touched. In making this super-simple salad he used a vegetable mandoline, which scared me a little but also looked practical, so I hope to get one someday. You can use a knife or a food processor to get very thin slices that you instantly plunge in cold lemon water. The lemon juice and peppery watercress season the sunchoke. That's it. And that is all you need.

I have also served this dish using sunflower sprouts and pea greens. If you try that version, chop the stems to make them less awkward to swallow. And, if using spinach, you might first want to dress the salad with a very small amount of olive oil and white or regular pepper before mixing with sunchokes.

> 3 cups cold water
> 1 tablespoon lemon juice
> 3–4 medium sunchokes
> 1 bunch (2 cups) watercress or upland cress,
>   or substitute arugula or baby spinach (see head note)

In a large bowl, mix water with lemon juice. Using a mandoline, knife, or food processor, slice sunchokes very, very thinly and immediately plunge into lemon water, making sure all surfaces of the sunchokes are bathed in the water to prevent darkening. Chop or tear watercress or arugula into bite-size pieces. Chop stems. Drain sunchokes, and toss with chopped greens.

SUNSEED-CRUSTED SUNCHOKES

SERVES 4–6 | *Roasted sunchokes were a common food for the first people of the Great Lakes–Great Plains. They are good plain, poked with a fork, rubbed in oil and salt, and baked in an oven-safe dish, where they will whine and hiss pitifully as they dissolve into sweetness. Here I've dressed them up with a warm blanket of complementary flavors that sends them to a sleep from which they wake up transformed. A caution, however, for those who are not used to working with these warty little roots: I leave the peels on. Usually I just use a paring knife to nick off any areas that look too old or dirty, but an industrious cook could peel them entirely. Just be aware that, naked and vulnerable, they might cook more quickly than expected in this recipe.*

These sunchokes go very well with salmon, game meat, eggs, or polenta.

> 1 tablespoon olive oil
> 1 cup roasted, unsalted sunflower seeds, divided
> 1 cup roasted red peppers, drained
> 2 cloves garlic
> 4–6 sunchokes (about 2 cups), large chokes cut in halves
>   or thirds (see head note)
> salt and cracked black pepper

Preheat oven to 400 degrees. Coat the bottom of an 8-inch glass or ceramic pie plate or small, shallow oven-safe dish with olive oil. Using a food processer or blender, process ½ cup sunflower seeds until crumblike. Add peppers and garlic and process briefly—the result should be chunky but loose with some moisture.

Arrange sunchokes in pie plate close together, lumpy side down and cut side up. Cover cut side of each sunchoke with pepper-sunseed mixture, pressing gently so each choke has a tasty little jacket. Press any remaining mixture around the edges of the chokes. Sprinkle with salt, and grind pepper very generously over the top. Press the remaining ½ cup sunflower seeds into the top of the chokes, distributing equally to create a crust.

Cover with aluminum foil and bake 20 minutes, then remove foil and bake 15 to 20 additional minutes (see head note), until sunseeds puff up and toast and coating forms a soft crust. Test to be sure a fork goes through chokes easily. Let rest a few minutes before serving as a side dish or starter. •

Every cookbook of Native American foods from North or South Dakota contains a recipe for wild turnips or prairie turnips. The Dakota word for this important food source is *tipsna* and in Lakota it is *timpsula*. Although I was gifted with use of a beautiful braid of tipsna, I have chosen not to include a recipe here because the food source is now just too rare. In South Dakota, the Native American food company that makes Wooden Knife Fry Bread Mix has omitted wild turnip from its list of ingredients, saying, "Timpsala is no longer an ingredient in our frybread mix. Due to habitat loss changing environment. It is our decision to not add to the stress on the plants."

Slow Food USA has created an Ark of Taste to feature critically endangered foods in order to draw attention to threats to food diversity and to encourage, when possible, growth in markets for such foods as well as in sales of seeds for the home gardener. Foods listed there include hand-harvested wild rice (manoomin) and beans and squashes developed long ago by indigenous farmers around the Great Lakes and in North Dakota.

Other foods, such as cream peas and several types of papaw, are listed as endangered by US Fish and Wildlife, along with dozens of aquatic animals and plants too threatened to dishonor with a recipe here. And some foods, such as tipsna and ceremonial corn, are so culturally important, and their habitat so deeply within tribal lands or treaty areas, the tribes must steward them as they see fit. In an era when genes can be patented and enormous profits made from altering traditional foods such as corn, it falls to cultures to remain in control of their food resources.

In fact, we all need the means to our own food production or we owe our souls to the company store. This notion is the essence of the food sovereignty and food security movements. Food sovereignty is a central concern of the White Earth Land Recovery Project (welrp.org) in Minnesota, which encourages the adoption of tribal food policies. A draft policy posted on its website begins

> Anishinaabe people and other peoples across North America have traditionally produced all the foods we needed for our peoples. Our Miijim involves an ongoing relationship with the Creator and all of our relatives, whether they have wings, fins, roots or paws. The historical practices of harvesting wild rice, trapping, snaring, netting and gardening have provided for our people since time immemorial and will continue to do so in to the future. These practices have been explicitly and implicitly reaffirmed through treaty rights and ongoing harvesting within our reservation and within the treaty boundaries of the 1855 and 1837 treaties, and through our ceremonial practices. We intend to insure the continuation of these traditions as a sovereign nation. More recently, our people have faced diminished access to traditional foods and medicines as a result of colonization economic, ecological and jurisdictional practices.

The statement goes on to cite a rise in diabetes and obesity among children as evidence of an urgent need to return to indigenous food ways and to establish a clear policy declaring that "our health, and indeed the future of our nation is tied to secure access and relationship with our traditional Anishinaabe foods."

SERVES 8 | *One difficult thing about building recipes around indigenous ingredients was the lack of easily available green vegetables. Sure, people harvested greens that grew wild, but so few are available at market today. "What did you do for greens?" I asked Dr. Martin Reinhardt, who ate only foods indigenous to the Great Lakes watershed for an entire year. "We got creative with green beans," he said.*

There comes a summer day when everything harvested from the garden or fresh at the market is vividly green. That is the day to make these beans. Serve alone or with Tanka Bite Bread (page 173) or other corn bread. Good with any meat.

> 4 cups chopped green beans, trimmed
>
> 2 tablespoons sunflower oil, plus more if needed
>
> 4 green onions, chopped
>
> 2 medium zucchini, chopped
>
> 1 teaspoon salt
>
> ½ teaspoon Mexican oregano, or substitute regular oregano
>
> ½ teaspoon dried wild mint, or substitute any mint
>
> ½ cup stock
>
> Pumpkin Seed–Watercress Pesto (page 155) or
>
>   basil pesto for garnish, optional

If using fresh green beans, blanch first: bring 6 cups of water to a boil in a large pan. Add green beans. Stir and cook until you can smell the beans, approximately 2 minutes. Drain and set aside.

In a saucepan set over medium heat, warm oil, then add onions. Cook, stirring frequently, until onions begin to soften and turn brown. Add zucchini and cook, stirring frequently, until zucchini turns bright green. Add green beans and cook another 2 minutes, stirring and adding oil if necessary. Add salt and herbs, and cook, stirring, until the herbs' scent is strong. Add stock to pan, and continue to cook, stirring, until the liquid is reduced by half. Add a dollop of pesto (if using), stir, and serve. ●

MAPLE BAKED CRANBERRY BEANS

SERVES 6 | *The cranberry in this recipe comes from two sources, the first being cranberry beans. True Red Cranberry Bean, an heirloom variety, is included in the Slow Food Ark of Taste, created to encourage biodiversity and the resurgence of foods that are being recovered from saved seeds. Cranberries come into this recipe in the form of a contemporary pemmican, as my ancestors called it, or wasna, as the Lakota people who make Tanka Bars (tankabar.com) refer to the meat and fruit traditional food that inspired this power bar. Serve with Sunny Corn Muffins (page 172) or as a side to roasted meats.*

4 cups cranberry beans
1 large onion, sliced in rounds
2 stalks celery, chopped
1 tablespoon dry mustard
1 teaspoon smoked paprika
½ teaspoon ground ginger
 black pepper
½ cup maple syrup, or more to taste
½ cup chopped Tanka Bites, optional

Soak dry beans in water to cover overnight or for 12 hours. Drain and rinse, then place beans in a heavy pot and add water until within an inch or two of the top. Cook over medium heat for 1 to 2 hours, until tender. (Or place beans in a slow cooker set on low for 4 hours, until tender.) Do not salt cooking water. Reserve 2 cups of cooking liquid, then drain. Do not rinse.

Preheat oven to 300 degrees. Layer onions on the bottom of a medium oven-safe dish; set aside. Place beans and reserved cooking liquid in a large bowl. Add celery, mustard, paprika, ginger, and pepper to beans, mixing thoroughly. Stir in maple and chopped Tanka Bites (if using). Pour beans on top of onions; do not let onions float. Cover tightly with aluminum foil and bake 3 hours. Remove foil and bake 1 to 2 more hours, checking occasionally and adding a small amount of water or stock around the edges if the beans seem too dry. Beans will get very dark, and a caramelized crust may form at the top, but this is a good, tasty thing. •

director, Dream of Wild Health | We grow seeds for food—we want to feed people. We invite people to enjoy the food. It is not about the health only. It is about the beauty of the food.

If you eat indigenous foods, you are re-indigenizing your body. The work we do, at a deeper level, is cultural recovery. Usually language comes first, or history, but your relationship with food, that is the first importance.

ALL SISTERS CHILI

SERVES A CROWD | *The Three Sisters (corn, beans, and squash) invite the two additional sisters (manoomin and sunflower) for dinner in this deep and rib-sticking vegetarian chili. It would not be a family reunion without that cousin from the south, New Mexico chili, so pick some up before making this dish. It would be okay with chili powder, but more like a potluck than a family reunion.*

This chili is dense and full, definitely a meal in itself. A garnish of cheese or dairy would be overkill. All it needs is a topper of crumbled tortilla chips and perhaps a dollop of guacamole.

> 3 tablespoons sunflower or olive oil, divided
> 2 cups chopped onion
> 1–2 tablespoons New Mexico chili, to taste (see head note)
> ¼ cup coarsely ground parched corn, or substitute toasted cornmeal
> ¼ cup pumpkin seeds
> ¼ cup sunflower seeds
> 1½ teaspoons cocoa powder
> 1 cup pumpkin puree
> up to 3 cups stock, divided
> 1 (14-ounce) can fire-roasted tomatoes and liquid
> 1 (15-ounce) can black beans and liquid
> 1 cup cooked manoomin   >>

In a large skillet set over medium heat, warm 1 tablespoon oil and add onions, cooking and stirring until lightly browned; set aside. In a large saucepan or Dutch oven set over medium heat, briefly toast chili in a dry pot, stirring constantly, until the chili warms through and you can smell it strongly. (The chili might give off a quick burst of scent, so be careful not to breathe in over the pot.) Quickly add the parched corn, pumpkin seeds, sunseeds, and remaining 1 to 2 tablespoons oil, stirring briefly to mix all ingredients. Stir in cocoa, and continue to toast dry ingredients, stirring constantly, for about 5 minutes. Add more oil if need be. Reduce heat to low. Continue to stir. Do not let this base burn, but get it darn close. Soon you should have a dense, fragrant paste.

Slowly add pumpkin to the paste, a tablespoon or so at a time, stirring constantly, and slowly adding 1 cup stock, until pumpkin incorporates the seasonings and the mixture becomes very silky and creamy. Add onions and fire-roasted tomatoes and their liquid. Stir until all the seasonings are incorporated. Repeat with black beans and their liquid and manoomin. Simmer until the ground corn is soft and the chili is very thick. If you prefer a soupier chili, add up to 2 cups more stock.

 ## CACTUS AND BLACK BEAN TACOS

SERVES 6–8 | *Dream of Wild Health is an indigenous farm in Hugo, Minnesota, that operates farm stands and serves Native American youth through programs that bring them to their roots, literally. In summer 2012, Dream of Wild Health staff operated a food booth at the Indigenous Music and Movies in the Park series in Minneapolis. On the hottest day in August, we arrived too late for most of the food they were serving—except for the cactus and black beans, which worked beautifully in corn tortillas, so we improvised cactus tacos.*

Prickly pear cactus is indigenous to the region and was eaten by all the tribes as an important source of winter greens and vitamins. Nopales, sold canned or jarred in many groceries, are simply prickly pear cactus that grows a little bigger in the southwest. You can often find prickly pears de-spined and ready to cook; I have even seen them at Target. The cactus is sweet and savory and soft, like nothing else—except maybe a piquant cucumber with the mouthfeel of avocado. Cactus goes beautifully with avocado, by the way. The black beans are smoky, and with the crunch of the cabbage a satisfying vegetarian taco is born. Or rather reborn, as I discovered: cactus tacos are common fare in Mexico.

Prickly pear can be grilled and would work beautifully for this recipe.

2–4 pads prickly pear cactus, cut in strips,
　　 or substitute 1 (15-ounce) can nopales or nopalitos
1 tablespoon olive oil
2 green onions, chopped
1 tablespoon Mexican oregano, or substitute regular oregano
1 teaspoon ground cumin
salt
1½ cups cooked black beans, or 1 (15-ounce) can black beans,
　　 rinsed and drained
8–12 corn tortillas
2–3 cups shredded napa cabbage, or use red cabbage
2 limes, quartered
cilantro for garnish, optional
hot sauce, green salsa, avocado, or guacamole for garnish

Peel off and discard the outer layer of the cactus; chop flesh small (or open and drain nopales); set aside. In a skillet set over medium heat, warm oil and cook green onions 5 minutes. Add chopped cactus and cook, stirring, 5 additional minutes (less for canned nopales), until cactus is soft. Add oregano, cumin, and a sprinkling of salt, and cook, stirring, 1 minute. Add black beans to cactus mixture, and cook until heated through, about 5 minutes.

　　Serve in corn tortillas with shredded cabbage, a squeeze of lime, and cilantro (if using). Garnish with hot sauce, green salsa, avocado slices, or guacamole as desired. ●

GREAT NORTHERN VEGETARIAN CASSOULET

SERVES 8–10 GENEROUSLY | *Great northern beans are descended from an ancient bean grown by indigenous people in North Dakota. Scott Shoemaker, who works with indigenous plants at the Science Museum of Minnesota, told me that Son of Star, a Hidatsa farmer, gave the bean to Oscar Will, whose father owned a seed company.*

In this vegetarian version of the classic French comfort food often considered the culinary height of the white bean, we have used mock duck (made of wheat gluten) and Field Roast brand vegetarian sausage, which holds up well to slow-cooking and comes in many varieties, including one appropriately flavored with wild rice.

2½ cups stock, divided

7 cups cooked great northern beans,
  or use white kidney beans or navy beans

3 tablespoons sunflower oil, divided

4 cups coarsely chopped onions

4 carrots, coarsely chopped on diagonal,
  or 1 cup butternut squash, cut into half-inch cubes

1½ tablespoons dried thyme

1½ teaspoons dried rosemary, crushed,
  or 1 teaspoon juniper berries, crushed

¾ teaspoon dried sage, crushed

1 teaspoon juniper ash, optional

1 cup water, divided

8 cloves garlic, crushed or sliced

4–5 links firm meatless sausage, cut into bite-size pieces,
  or 1 (20-ounce) can mock duck, cut into bite-size pieces

1 (28-ounce) can tomatoes, drained and chopped,
  or 1 (28-ounce) can crushed tomatoes

Heat stock to a boil, then pour 2 cups into slow cooker turned to high; stir in beans and cover. In a heavy skillet set over medium-high heat, warm 2 tablespoons oil, stir in onions, and cook until softened and beginning to turn translucent. Stir in carrots (if using) and continue cooking until all onions are translucent and some are browning. Add thyme, rosemary or juniper, sage, and ash (if using), and continue cooking, stirring frequently, until you can smell the herbs. Add remaining ½ cup stock and ½ cup water, stirring to scrape bottom of pan, and then stir in garlic. Pour onion mixture into slow cooker with beans; replace lid.

In the same skillet, over medium heat, warm remaining tablespoon oil and brown sausage pieces (if using). Add ½ cup water, stirring to scrape bottom of pan, and then add sausage and liquid to slow cooker. Stir in tomatoes, mock duck (if using), and squash cubes (if using), replace lid, and turn heat to medium low. Cook 6 to 8 hours. ●

THE ARK OF TASTE *Slow Food Foundation for Biodiversity*

The Ark of Taste travels the world collecting small-scale quality productions that belong to the cultures, history and traditions of the entire planet: an extraordinary heritage of fruits, vegetables, animal breeds, cheeses, breads, sweets and cured meats . . .

The Ark was created to point out the existence of these products, draw attention to the risk of their extinction within a few generations, invite everyone to take action to help protect them. In some cases this might be by buying and consuming them, in some by telling their story and supporting their producers, and in others, such as the case of endangered wild species, this might mean eating less or none of them in order to preserve them and favor their reproduction. —*slowfoodfoundation.com*

BUFFALO BIRD WOMAN'S FOUR SISTERS DISH

SERVES A CROWD | *It seems sensible that what we ate before contact with Europeans was dominated by what we farmed or gathered as much if not more than what we could hunt. Corn, beans, and squash with culinary ashes provided a balanced protein and essential vitamins. Dry crops and nuts were easy to store and provided abundant protein; they sustained people when hunting was hard, which was likely often. As we were growing up, my mother and our dear adopted grandmother, Esther Horne, told of a Mandan-Hidatsa woman whose gardening stories were made into a book. In that book, Buffalo Bird Woman, who lived from 1839 to 1932, describes a dish that contains the Three Sisters—parched corn, dried winter squash, and beans—plus sunflower, the fourth sister of the prairie:*

Four-vegetables-mixed was eaten freshly cooked; and the mixed corn-and-sunflower meal was made fresh for it each time. A little alkali salt might be added for seasoning, but even this was not usual. No other seasoning was used. Meat was not boiled with the mess, as the sunflower seed gave sufficient oil to furnish fat.

This "mess," as Buffalo Bird Woman called it, goes a long way if you continue adding stock or water and keep it simmering until the beans break down. One night we served four adults, then added five cups of stock to the leftovers and served four kids who had seconds and thirds.

Each year I splurge on a few teas made with indigenous herbs from Juniper Ridge. For this recipe I once used two bags of wild mint and white sage tea for seasoning. If you can get Juniper Ridge teas, treat yourself!

2 cups dried scarlet runner beans,
  or substitute cannellini beans
4 cups stock
1 tablespoon dried mint
1 teaspoon dried sage (see head note)
1 cup parched corn, or substitute toasted cornmeal
1 cup raw, unsalted sunflower seeds
1½ cups cubed squash, or use dehydrated squash
  salt

To prepare heirloom runner beans, soak overnight in a large bowl with water to cover. Drain beans, rinse, and place in a slow cooker with enough fresh water to cover by 3 to 4 inches. Cook 6 to 8 hours on low. When beans have softened and absorbed much of the liquid, add stock and seasonings and simmer 15 minutes. (Remove tea bags if using.)

Using a food processor, make a coarse meal of parched corn and sunflower seeds. Add to "mess" and let simmer. Cook on medium until corn softens and beans are tender, about 1 hour. Add squash and cook until tender, about 15 minutes. Season with salt to taste. ●

BUFFALO BIRD WOMAN *Mandan-Hidatsa*

In the bottom of this soft-skin bag the warrior commonly carried one of these sunflower-seed balls, wrapped in a piece of buffalo-heart skin. When worn with fatigue or overcome with sleep and weariness, the warrior took out his sunflower-seed ball, and nibbled at it to refresh himself. It was amazing what effect nibbling at the sunflower-seed ball had. If the warrior was weary, he began to feel fresh again; if sleepy, he grew wakeful.

teacher, writer, actor | Lois Red Elk has been a teacher since childhood because she was the family's firstborn. A published poet and accomplished actor who now lives in Montana, Lois teaches a college course titled "Traditional Plants: Food, Teas, Medicine and Trees."

> My father was Hunkpapa and Yankton. My mother's father was a medicine healer from the Spirit Lake Reservation, North Dakota. The place where my mother grew up is primarily woods. She helped her father and older sister locate a hundred different medicinal plants. They also survived on traditional foods, such as wild turnips, wild onions, wild potatoes, and had community gardens full of Mandan and Sioux blue corn, Hidatsa squash and beans . . . Our diet also included snake, gopher, crane, porcupine, along with whitetail deer. My sisters and I know how to hunt, butcher, and preserve every kind of food you can imagine.
>
> One of my favorite recipes is squash chips. They can be eaten like banana chips as a snack. Dried squash is included in a stew of wild turnips, dried corn, and dried deer meat.

Lois Red Elk's recipe for dried squash uses traditional methods: "take one large Hidatsa squash, peel, pare, and slice into 3-inch slices, about ⅛ inch thick. Dry in full hot sun for 3 days, turning occasionally. Store in a cotton sack until you need them."

SUMMER SQUASH AND MANOOMIN TERRINE

SERVES 6 | *The green summer squash was a welcome food and often eaten raw, according to ethnobotanists. This recipe calls for two whole zucchini, perfect for when they are abundant in the garden and we wonder how to use them all.*

Some tips: Cool the loaf and then refrigerate it to eat it cold. It is better the next day. Serve with a salad as a light lunch or as an appetizer for a full meal, or serve warm as a brunch item.

olive oil

1 onion, chopped

2 medium zucchini or other summer squash, cubed

2 cloves garlic, chopped

2 large eggs, beaten

½ cup shredded mozzarella or Swiss cheese

2 tablespoons grated Parmesan cheese

1 cup cooked manoomin

½ cup chopped fresh parsley, or 1 tablespoon dried nettles, sifted

1 teaspoon chopped fresh wild mint or wild mountain mint, or ½ teaspoon fresh thyme

½ teaspoon salt

¼ teaspoon black pepper

Rita Gourneau Erdrich with some of her garden produce, circa 2009

Preheat oven to 375 degrees. Grease a loaf pan or casserole with olive oil. In a large skillet set over medium heat, warm additional olive oil and cook onion until soft, about 5 minutes. Reduce heat to low, add zucchini and garlic, and cook, stirring, for 10 minutes. Remove from heat and allow to cool.

In a large bowl, combine eggs, cheeses, manoomin, parsley, and mint. Add cooled cooked vegetables, salt, and pepper, stirring well to combine. Transfer mixture to loaf pan and bake until firm, 35 to 45 minutes. Cool and invert on a plate. ●

SQUASH NOODLE BOWLS

SERVES 6 | *Don't you love how squash and pumpkins make their own bowls? Some say that the original pumpkin pie had no crust other than the natural shell of its own skin. Desserts and stuffing have long been cupped in the original golden bowl of the acorn squash, but now the time of the noodle is at hand.*

CURRY NOODLE BOWL

      3 acorn squash, halved, seeds scooped out
     14 ounces rice noodles (pad Thai noodles)
    ¾ cup yellow or red coconut curry sauce,
          or combine coconut milk and dry Thai curry mix
      3 tablespoons chopped cilantro, plus more for garnish
      3 tablespoons chopped mint
      1 tablespoon chopped basil
      3 tablespoons sweet chili sauce
      2 tablespoons rice wine vinegar
      3 tablespoons fish sauce
    ¾ cup chopped cucumber
      3 tablespoons chopped green onions, plus more for garnish
    1½ cups peanuts, crushed, plus more for garnish

Preheat oven to 375 degrees. Place squash open side down in a roasting pan with an inch of water and place in the oven. While squash is roasting, soak noodles in warm water for 1 hour. When squash flesh is soft all the way through, remove pan from oven, discard the water, and return squash to pan open side up. Thoroughly coat squash with curry sauce. Return pan to oven for 10 to 15 minutes, allowing squash to absorb some of the sauce and become slightly more dry. Do not let skins burn.

In a large bowl, mix herbs, chili sauce, vinegar, fish sauce, cucumber, and green onions. Stir in peanuts. Drain noodles, then pour in enough boiling water to cover and let sit 1 minute. Drain again, test to be sure noodles have softened (if not, re-peat with more boiling water), then pour into bowl with sauce. Serve each portion in roasted squash bowl, garnished with cilantro, green onions, and peanuts.

PESTO NOODLE BOWL

3 acorn squash, halved, seeds scooped out

½ cup pesto

½ cup white wine

14 ounces angel hair pasta, or any long, thin pasta

¼ cup light cream

2 tablespoons grated Parmesan cheese, plus more for serving

2 tablespoons chopped basil

salt and black pepper

grated nutmeg, optional

Preheat oven to 375 degrees. Place squash open side down in a roasting pan with an inch of water and place in the oven. When squash flesh is soft all the way through, after about an hour, remove pan from oven, discard the water, and return squash to pan open side up. Thoroughly coat squash with pesto and white wine. Return pan to oven for 10 to 15 minutes, allowing squash to absorb some of the sauce and become slightly more dry. Do not let skins burn.

Meanwhile, prepare pasta according to package directions; drain. In a large bowl, toss pasta with cream and cheese. Add basil. Season with salt and pepper to taste. Toss once more. Serve each portion in roasted squash bowl topped with a bit more cheese and grated nutmeg.

DR. MARTIN REINHARDT *Ojibwe, Sault Sainte Marie Band*

Decolonizing Diet Project | How much do we know about the animals and plants, our relationship to them? We need to reawaken the spiritual and emotional relations between humans and foods in the Great Lakes.

BUTTERY BUTTERNUT SQUASH WITH SAGE AND BUTTER

SERVES 4–6 | *My niece Pallas sent this recipe for making what amounts to caramelized squash. She also sent me her charming notes, which I preserve here as instructions. To begin with, Pallas cautions, "The hardest part is cubing the gourd. The younger the squash, the harder it will be but the better this will turn out. So, try and find a buddy to help you cube it so you don't get super-bored."*

1 butternut squash
4 tablespoons (½ stick) butter
salt and black pepper
¼ cup chopped fresh sage
patience

Peel the squash and cut it into cubes. Make the pieces as even as possible, around 1½ inches per side. No need to be insane about it, but the closer in size they are to each other, the more successful this dish becomes.

Melt the butter in a cast-iron skillet over medium heat. You want it to brown, so wait until it's bubbling and then start stirring slowly with a wooden spoon. When you can clearly see it's turned toasty brown in color, take it off the heat for a few minutes to let it cool. Return the pan to the heat and dump in the squash. Toss to coat and then let the bottom layer hang out for 5 or 6 minutes until it forms a crust. Turn the whole lot over and let the next layer toast. Try and get every side: the little burned bits are epic. This will take 30 to 40 minutes to fully cook: don't turn them too often, but don't forget about them either.

Season with salt and pepper to taste. Just before serving, stir in all the sage and let it wilt on the table. For Pete's sake, that's a tasty squash. ●

BUTTERNUT CHOWDER

SERVES A CROWD | *Sometime after I began serving this recipe, I was amused to find a similar dish called Ojibwe Butternut Squash and Corn Chowder in* American Food *by Evan Jones. Perhaps genetic memory was at work on some level, but certainly not when it comes to the potatoes and dairy I've added. Use any fish that flakes well: wild Alaska salmon looks beautiful in this dish, making a nice contrast of warm orange, pink, and yellow against the white of the dairy, but Great Lakes salmon would be more in keeping. You can also substitute smoked fish as a garnish at the table. Serve as a meal with bread and a salad.*

4 tablespoons (½ stick) butter
2 large leeks, chopped, half of greens reserved
1 clove garlic, chopped
2 cups chopped potatoes, preferably Yukon Golds
2 cups stock
1 bay leaf
2 cups chopped butternut squash, fresh or frozen
1 cup corn
1 tablespoon chopped fresh sage, or 1 teaspoon dried
¼ cup chopped red onion
½ teaspoon white pepper
½ pound fish (see head note)
¾ cup half-and-half
 salt to taste
 smoked paprika for garnish

In a large stockpot set over medium-high heat, melt butter and cook leeks, reserving greens, for 2 to 3 minutes. Add garlic and stir. Stir in potatoes, stock, and bay leaf. Simmer 5 minutes. Add squash, corn, sage, red onion, and white pepper and allow to simmer. When squash is tender, add fish to top of pot. Cook until fish begins to flake. Add half-and-half and salt, and stir gently, taking care not to break up the fish too much. Serve into bowls and garnish with leek greens and smoked paprika. ●

PUMPKIN SEED FLOUR BREAD

SERVES 6 | *Dr. Martin Reinhardt—Marty—principal investigator of the Decoloniz-ing Diet Project at Northern Michigan University, found the DDP diet, as they call it, not too tasking. We talked just after he ended his year of indigenous eating.*

One thing I was wondering about when I first heard of the DDP diet was baking. How do you bake without eggs and wheat flour? This bread recipe is adapted from the Decolonizing Diet Project to use seed meal and duck eggs. When hulled, un-roasted pumpkin seeds are ground into flour, the resulting bread takes on a strong green hue. You can substitute roasted sunflower seeds for half the pumpkin seeds to get a less green bread. Either way, it is truly tasty.

> sunflower oil
> 2 cups raw pumpkin seeds (see head note)
> ½ cup cornmeal
> 1 cup corn
> 3 duck eggs
> 1 tablespoon maple sugar, or less, to taste
> 1 teaspoon sea salt
> 1¼ cups water

Preheat oven to 325 degrees. Grease a 9-inch pie or shallow cake pan with sun-flower oil. Using a food processor, grind pumpkin seeds until the consistency of cornmeal. Add all ingredients to a large mixing bowl and mix well. Pour ingredi-ents into prepared pan and bake, uncovered, until top begins to brown, about 15 minutes. Test with a butter knife or wooden pick: if it comes out fairly dry, the bread is done. •

WATERCRESS SOUP

Watercress is a wild green that grows plentiful beside many streams. The first Native Americans ate it either fresh or in a stew or soup . . . A chunk of bear, venison, or buffalo with its layer of fat would be cooked with it in a pitch-lined basket until the rich broth resulted. —American Indian Recipes, *Katherine J. Gurnoe and Christian Skjervold, Minneapolis Public Schools*

PUMPKIN SEED–WATERCRESS PESTO

MAKES 1–2 CUPS | *While watercress is likely not indigenous to the region, it is plentiful and has been for so long that, in some areas, it was a sought-after food. My dad picked watercress, and I remember him bringing it to us at a campground in Iowa where we had set up tents. These days you have to be sure the water is clean where you are harvesting, or go to the grocery store, where fresh cress is becoming more common due to health claims.*

Serve this pesto on top of roasted sunchokes, as a topping for fish, or as a garnish for soups. Also good in pasta, especially if you can find the butternut linguine that is made locally in the Upper Midwest.

> 1 cup hulled pumpkin seeds or pepitas
> 2 tablespoons fancy organic sunflower oil, divided,
>   or substitute extra-virgin olive oil
> 1 bunch watercress, or substitute arugula or baby spinach
> 2 ramp bulbs and stems, chopped, or substitute green onions
> ½ teaspoon salt

In a food processor or blender, pulse pumpkin seeds and 1 tablespoon oil until a meal forms. Add watercress, ramps, ½ tablespoon oil, and salt. Pulse until a nice paste forms. Store in a glass container with ½ tablespoon oil covering to preserve freshness. ●

PUMPKIN COCONUT CURRY

SERVES 4 | *Coconut and pineapple are allowed in the Week of Indigenous Eating promoted by Devon Mihesuah, indigenous foods activist and author of several books on indigenous foods and diet. These foods from far away meet northern cousins in a delicious stew inspired by the writer N. M. Kelby's Thai pumpkin curry. For even more local flavor, garnish with dried cranberries or toss steamed jasmine rice with dried cranberries and herbs and serve curry on it.*

1 tablespoon coconut oil, or use peanut or vegetable oil

5 green onions, greens removed, cut on diagonal in ¾-inch pieces

1 cup sliced mushrooms

1 tablespoon sweet curry

1 teaspoon hot curry, optional; increase sweet curry accordingly

2 cups stock, divided

½ cup pumpkin puree

1 cup chopped butternut squash,
    or substitute any orange-fleshed squash

1 cup boiled yellow potatoes, chopped into bite-size pieces

½ cup green bell pepper, chopped into ½-inch pieces

1 cup bite-size pineapple pieces

1 cup coconut milk

white and/or brown rice (see head note)

2 tablespoons chopped mint for garnish

2 tablespoons chopped cilantro for garnish

½ cup crushed or minced peanuts for garnish

In large stockpot or Dutch oven set over medium-high heat, melt coconut oil. Add green onions and cook for 1 to 2 minutes, stirring frequently. Add mushrooms and cook for 1 to 2 minutes, stirring a couple times. Add curry and stir briefly to toast the spices. When you smell the curry, stir in ¼ cup stock, and stir mixture, scraping any browned bits from the bottom of the pan. Slowly add pumpkin a bit at a time, stirring until it incorporates and becomes very smooth, adding ½ cup stock a bit at a time as well. Return mixture to simmering and stir in remaining 1¼ cups stock, squash, and potatoes. Reduce heat and simmer for 10 minutes, until squash and potatoes are tender but still hold their shapes. Stir in the green peppers and pineapple, and simmer 3 to 5 minutes, until the peppers turn bright green. Stir in the coconut milk, and reduce heat to low. Simmer 5 minutes, or until potato and squash pieces are cooked and pineapple is heated through. Serve over a mixture of white and brown rice sprinkled with mint, cilantro, and peanuts. ●

PUMPKIN BUNDT

SERVES 8–10 | *Kids who have birthdays around Halloween will appreciate a double recipe of this cake, stacked to resemble a pumpkin and frosted however appeals.*

> 2 cups canned or fresh pumpkin puree
> 1 cup water, divided
> ⅓ cup maple syrup
> ¼ teaspoon almond extract
> ½ teaspoon ground allspice
> ¼ teaspoon ground cloves
> 2 cups whole wheat flour
> 1½ cups unbleached white flour
> 2 teaspoons baking soda
> 2 teaspoons baking powder
> 1½ teaspoons salt
> 12 tablespoons (1½ sticks) unsalted butter, softened
> 1 cup packed brown sugar
> 1⅓ cups granulated sugar
> 4 large eggs
> ¼ cup half-and-half
> ½ cup chocolate chips, optional
> ½ cup chopped nuts, optional   >>

Preheat oven to 350 degrees. Grease and flour a 12-cup (10-inch) Bundt pan. In a large bowl, mix together pumpkin, ¼ cup water, syrup, almond extract, and spices. Set aside. In a separate large bowl, mix together the flours, baking soda, baking powder, and salt. Set aside.

In a standing mixer fitted with the paddle attachment, on medium-low speed beat the butter and sugars until fluffy. Beat in the eggs one at a time, thoroughly incorporating each before adding the next. Increase the speed to medium and beat in the pumpkin mixture, continuing to mix for a minute. Beat in the remaining ¾ cup water and the half-and-half; mix for a minute. Reduce mixer speed to low and add the flour mixture in 3 batches, scraping down the bowl in between. The batter will be very wet. Add chocolate chips and nuts (if using), and mix for another minute. Pour batter into the prepared Bundt pan, filling two-thirds to three-quarters full (if you have extra batter, pour into cupcake cups or a greased, floured cupcake pan; bake for 20 minutes). Bake cake about 1 hour, or until spaghetti noodle or wooden pick poked in the center comes out clean. ●

Rita Gourneau Erdrich, circa 1942, holding a squash Grandpa Pat grew for his truck garden

"I started paying into Social Security at thirteen years of age." This is how my brother Ralph, who holds the family title of Cast-iron Chef, begins a story. He tells me about his first job washing dishes and learning the ways of the fry cook. Soon enough he was working a summer job at Hornbacher's grocery store in Fargo, living with our older brother Mark, who was at North Dakota State University. Ralph had a job behind the deli counter, where, at the time, "you could buy anything from the best cuts to the worst," and "we would cook it up for the customers any way they asked and give it to them with hash and sides." So that's where he learned to hash, I think to myself. Ralph tells me there was a guy who came every day, selected the largest porterhouse steak he could, and asked that it be cooked exactly as he instructed. Ralph was supposed to "sizzle it on one side a few, turn it over and sizzle it on the other side." Ralph said, "I knew it was nearly cold in the middle, but the guy came every day," and so he gave the customer what he wanted.

Ralph was just fifteen at the time, so our mom went up to Fargo to visit him often. One time she surprised him by showing up after his shift. She let him know she had come in for a steak while he was working. "Oh, you should have told me," he said, probably wishing he could have done an extra-good job for Mom. "Was it good?" Our mom is a gentle but direct woman. She let him know that no, it was not good. Ralph was a little puzzled: "What did you order?" And of course Mom said, "The porterhouse."

Mom had picked out a nice, thick porterhouse. Ralph had made it just as he was usually instructed by his regular customer. Forty years later my brother still sounds dismayed when he ends the story with "Mom! Why didn't you send it back?"

Sending food back is not the usual way of the Erdrich women, who were all waitstaff at one point or another. Only a month ago, I watched one of my sisters pick at her cold eggs and refuse to return her plate because she did not want to trouble the waitress. Ralph, who went on to fry cook throughout his youth, even in Yellowstone Park, remembers that Mom presented the barely seared steak to our brother Mark, who apparently ate it with gusto. Or perhaps he, too, simply would not send it back.

The foods in this subsection remind me of my brothers. The first cooking I recall doing was tending the hash browns while my brothers cracked eggs. Not long after, I was promoted to cooking the eggs, too. At that point I guess I was just making breakfast for two of my older brothers, but that was fine by me. Louis and Ralph both work in health care with American Indian communities, one as a nurse and one as an engineer. They are fine fellows in every way; they make a good name for nice guys. Both have gardens I've admired over the years, not the least because they each face challenges—Louis outwits the critters of the north woods with well-engineered fences, and Ralph battles the drying prairie wind and wins most years. Plus Ralph knows where the wild asparagus grows, and he is tickproof, as far as I can tell.

Since the days when my brothers parked me in front of the stove over a pan of shredded potatoes, my idea of hash has grown to include just about every vegetable, chopped small and fried hard, scrambled up with onions. My siblings, it turns out, are hash purists of sorts: potatoes, peppers, and onions mean hash; everything else is derided as "stir fry."

Ralph is known to "hash it up" for a dozen kids and adults on a weekend morning, whether over an open fire or a five-burner stove.

It is hard to believe that melons and cucumbers migrated to the upper midwestern tribes from Africa, but that seems to be the case. In the mid-1600s, but most likely earlier, watermelons were being grown in North Dakota. But of all the foods that came late to indigenous people around the Great Lakes and into the prairies, I am sure the potato was the favorite. Growing up, we ate a lot of potatoes. On the steps to the basement sat a hundred-pound burlap sack to which we were often sent to fetch potatoes. Mom says we went through a lot of those hundred-pound sacks. Mom's maternal grandparents and great aunts and uncles were potato farmers and harvesters in the Red River Valley, where some Ojibwe and Métis families settled after allotment. Big burlap sacks of potatoes figured prominently in her stories of childhood, recounted with a sense of pride for her female ancestors who could carry the enormous sacks.

Remember Johnny Appleseed, the partly mythical man who spread apples across the country? Well, our father was a kind of Ralph E. Asparagus Seed. When he went hunting, he would sometimes spread asparagus seed so he could return for harvest a few years later. His technique worked. So well, in fact, that recently, as I was looking at a foraging guide, I saw a map marking where wild asparagus could be found. There was one little area apart from the others—just where Dad used to hunt. Perhaps a coincidence, but maybe not. No, I am not going to tell you which guide it was: my brother Ralph still forages there. Enough said.

This menu based on foods that came late to indigenous cooking honors our potato-picking ancestors and our asparagus seed–spreading father as well as my brothers, who first made me want to cook.

- *Three Brothers Hash (page 161)*
- *Asparagus with Black Walnuts, Cranberries, and Feta Cheese (page 162)*
- *Red Pepper Jam on Creamy Cheese Toast (page 163)*
- *Honey Buzz Melon Salad (page 164)*

SERVES 6 GENEROUSLY | *This hash requires three different potatoes because it is a tribute to my three brothers, Mark, Louis, and Ralph. Add a poached egg, some smoked salmon, decadent Red Pepper Jam and creamy toast points (page 163), and some roasted asparagus, and this is brunch. Wait, it is not brunch without melon, so make some Honey Buzz Melon Salad (page 164), too.*

My brother Ralph, as I have noted, is good at hash. He does not have much advice for actually cooking the hash, except to say, "Some veggies are good for hash; some for stir fry." We disagree on which veggies those are, but we agree on the ones that are good in both: onions and peppers, perhaps a little bit of celery. He has one step in his work at the pan: "Cook it on high; don't let it burn." But do let everything caramelize a bit.

> 2 Red River Red potatoes
> 2 Yukon Gold potatoes
> 2 white or purple potatoes
> 1 red onion
> other vegetables—peppers, celery, chives—in small quantities
> oil or butter
> patience

Preheat oven to 250 degrees. Chop or shred all vegetables, and let drain in a colander briefly, 5 to 10 minutes. To a heavy skillet set over high heat, add oil or butter, about 2 tablespoons to start. Cook vegetables in batches, lifting and turning when they threaten to burn. Using an oven-safe dish, place each batch of cooked hash in the oven to keep warm. Repeat with remaining ingredients, adding more oil or butter as needed. •

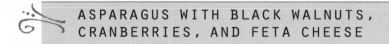

ASPARAGUS WITH BLACK WALNUTS, CRANBERRIES, AND FETA CHEESE

SERVES 4–6 | *Reactions to the concept of this recipe were varied, but the results yielded unanimous enthusiasm. You can make this dish while the hash sits and gets crispy. It might help with the impatience that ruins most hash.*

  1 pound asparagus, rinsed and trimmed
½ cup dried cranberries
  2 cloves garlic, sliced
  2 tablespoons olive oil
 dash salt
½ cup chopped black walnuts, or substitute pecans
½ cup feta cheese, or substitute another dry, crumbly cheese

Preheat oven to 375 degrees. In a shallow baking dish, lightly coat asparagus, cranberries, and garlic in oil and sprinkle with salt. To work salt into oiled vegetables, use your hands—go ahead: all the best cooks do! Keep the spears facing one way. Roast for 20 minutes.

About 10 minutes after the asparagus begins roasting, place nuts in a small oven-safe dish and set in the oven. As soon as you begin to smell the nuts, take them out and set aside.

The asparagus is done when it is tender throughout but not browned. If spear tips threaten to burn, place a bit of aluminum foil loosely over them. Remove asparagus from the oven and sprinkle with nuts and cheese. Serve hot. ●

RED PEPPER JAM

MAKES 4–6 (4-OUNCE) JARS | *Originally, there were no peppers up north, so that's one thing our southern cousins had on us. When we did start growing peppers, folks did what midwesterners do with excess produce: we sweetened them and canned them. This jam recipe was shared by Megan Treinen, who enthusiastically taste tested many recipes as I worked on this book. Although of Dutch origin, Megan has a good hand with fry bread and was key in developing the Pumpkin Bangs recipe (page 96). Yes, you could put this jam on bangs, if you want to go way over the top.*

> 12–15 red bell peppers
> 2 tablespoons salt
> 2 cups sugar
> 2 cups white vinegar
> 2 cups water
> 1 tablespoon red pepper flakes, optional
> 4–6 sterilized (4-ounce) jars with lids and rings

Seed peppers and slice the long way, very thinly. Place in a large colander and sprinkle salt over top, tossing to mix. Let drain for 2 hours. In a large saucepan set over medium-high heat, combine sugar, vinegar, water, and red pepper flakes (if using), stirring to mix. Cook until sugar dissolves, about 5 minutes. Add peppers and stir. Reduce heat to low and simmer 3 hours, or until peppers are very thick.

Boil water in a tall (1- to 4-gallon) pot. Pour pepper mixture into sterilized 4-ounce jelly jars, seal with sterilized rings and lids, and process them in a boiling water bath for 30 minutes working in batches to avoid crowding your pot of boiling water.

Use canning tongs to remove jars from boiling water. Set jars on countertop to cool overnight. The lids should be flat and not make a *pop* when you tap them the next day. If the jar pops, just put it in the refrigerator to enjoy first.

To serve at brunch: Use Mandaamin-Manoomin Bread (page 179) or other rustic bread that toasts crisply. Butter hot, toasted bread with goat cheese or cream cheese and spread on a generous amount of red pepper jam. Cut into points and serve. ●

HONEY BUZZ MELON SALAD

SERVES 6 | *This recipe reminds me of a Hairy Buffalo, which is what you call it when you spike watermelons with whisky by drilling a little hole and slowly dripping the booze into the melon. Hairy Buffaloes were popular when I was a youth in North Dakota. The result was a tangy, melting buzz of a melon slice. I've tried for the nonalcoholic version here using honey.*

Contrary to popular belief, honeybees are indigenous to the hemisphere, but they stayed south with the Maya (who kept them for honey) and other peoples of Central and South America. Sometime before the 1700s, European bees, in feral swarms, flew north, and everyone began taking honey. Thus, honey became a part of the indigenous diet and cooking long ago. There's controversy as to whether an extinct honeybee once pollinated North America. What we do know is that bumblebees, moths, bats, and other insects pollinated food plants for millennia. The latecomer honeybee arrived with colonists to the east and the Spanish to the south. Now all pollinators are suffering declines, with the likely cause being farm chemicals and other environmental stressors, according to recent news.

Buzz killer, huh? Well, this recipe should cheer you up and make you want to help a hive.

> 2 cups watermelon, cut into bite-size pieces
> 1 cup cucumber, peeled and chopped small
> ½ cup chopped fresh mint
> 1 cup Honey Buzz Salad Splash (page 217)

In a large serving bowl, add all ingredients, tossing to combine.

Over the top: If you must, splash salad with champagne or ice-cold vodka. Whisky would be too much for brunch. •

Dream of Wild Health (Twin Cities farmers markets)

www.dreamofwildhealth.org
16085 Jeffrey Avenue
Hugo, MN 55038-9334
651-439-3840

Dream of Wild Health (DWH) is a ten-acre organic farm in Hugo, Minnesota. Begun in 1998, DWH stewards a collection of more than three hundred rare heirloom seeds donated by tribes and families from around the country. In addition to growing out a select number of heirloom seeds each year, DWH raises organic vegetables for sale at weekly farmers markets in Minneapolis and St. Paul and provides educational programs for Native youth and families.

Oneida Market

exploreoneida.com/attractions/oneida-market/
501 Packerland Drive
Green Bay, WI 54303
920-496-5127

Featuring Oneida-produced and -harvested foods and all-natural specialty products: Oneida Cannery jams (including low sugar), white corn, corn bread, and other in-season products such as fresh and vacuum-packed strawberries, asparagus, and locally harvested maple syrup, along with Oneida Nation Farms bison meat, grass-fed beef, and Oneida Tsyunhehkwa farm eggs.

You can call to order foods produced by the Oneida Nation or stop by the market. Oneida foods are also sold at Indian Summerfest in Milwaukee each September.

Seed Savers Exchange

www.seedsavers.org
3094 North Winn Road
Decorah, IA 52101
563-382-5990

More than a seed catalog, Seed Savers Exchange actively preserves important foods, including many indigenous foods. Hidatsa Red and Shield Figure and Runner (cannellini) beans can be purchased dry by the pound for cooking. About Hidatsa Red, Seed Savers says, "Originally grown by the Hidatsa tribe in the Missouri River Valley of North Dakota. Introduced in Oscar Will's Pioneer Indian Collection of seeds (1915)." About Arikara Sunflower, Seed Savers notes, "Collected by Melvin Gilmore from the Arikara tribe at the Fort Berthold Reservation. First offered by Oscar H. Will in 1930." Seed Savers also stocks crookneck squash seeds, lemon mint, and other varieties of wild and Native-developed seeds.

... MANDAAMIN

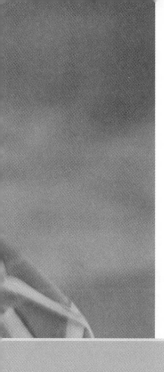

CORN •••

One of the wonderful things about talking with indigenous people about corn is hearing people refer to the corn as "our relative." From an Anishinaabe perspective, this makes sense. Corn is a gift from the creator, given through a half human–half spirit who pulled it from his own body, or so it goes in the story I have heard. Other indigenous cultures tell of corn falling from the sky world in the pockets of the first woman. Indigenous cultures from Mexico and Central America, where corn was first domesticated thousands of years ago, speak of the interrelatedness of corn and humans.

In fact, corn as we know it cannot exist without humans, and humanity would not have grown as it has without corn. Many scholars tie population growth and related development to the success of corn on every continent. Corn is the dominant global agricultural product today. But today's corn, much of which is genetically modified to suit the needs of industrial agriculture, actually threatens the ancient corn varieties that long sustained entire cultures. According to *Iowa Source Magazine,*

> The Meskwaki people plant Tama Flint in their gardens. But in recent years, farmers have also been growing yellow dent corn on 2,000 acres of the tribe's land. Pollen from the yellow corn, which is likely GMO [a genetically modified organism], is now contaminating the traditional corn. Several years ago Jerry Young Bear started seeing yellow kernels in Tama Flint corn and became concerned that the genetic purity of the heritage corn may be threatened.

Those who grow ancient corn have resorted to planting it under crop fabric and laboriously hand pollinating it. In response to such threats, indigenous people all over the western hemisphere are standing up to protect their rights to original and sacred corn; not only does the corn belong to the people, the people belong to the corn.

In the past few years the Indigenous Corn Restoration Project, which is run through the White Earth Land Recovery Project and North Dakota State University, has helped to begin reinstatement of traditional corn varieties in reservation communities in Minnesota, Wisconsin, North Dakota, and elsewhere. The project concerns itself with our stories as well, recognizing the intellectual and agricultural wealth carried in deeply metaphoric knowledge ways. Stories and songs have been shared from Mandan, Hidatsa, Arikara, Odawa, Dakota, and other tribes. Through such efforts and the hard work of tribal people, corn varieties called Bear Island Flint, Manitoba Flint, Dakota Black popcorn, and Pink Lady now return as visiting relatives who are welcomed, protected, and hopefully home to stay.

When we eat, and perhaps plant, heritage varieties of corn we are protecting indigenous cultures in the most basic, and tasty, way. Parched corn, hominy, popcorn, corn flour, blue corn, and other corn products are available from Native American growers, and they honestly taste much better than other corn. Tiny red hull-less popcorn so tender your teeth will thank you, parched corn nutty and sweet, blue corn that goes vivid purple when stirred with sumac, dry corn that grinds into perfect meal, corn mush with an Italian accent (polenta), masa harina, corn smut, and sweet corn on the cob—all of these indigenous corn foods are included in the recipes in this section. Enjoy them with relatives or friends because corn makes us all related.

DR. WALTER GOLDSTEIN *Mandaamin Institute*

Analysis of 24 different varieties of native flour corn in 2011 showed that they averaged 14.2% protein and 64% starch. In contrast, modern hybrids have been bred for yield, and our impression is that they lack taste and nutrition. Analysis of 4 modern hybrids grown in southeastern Wisconsin in 2010 showed they had about half as much protein and more starch (7.5% protein and 73% starch). The easiest way for a corn plant to produce yield is to produce starch. Perhaps even more significant are differences in essential amino acids that are crucial for building new proteins in the human or animal body. The native corns averaged 0.39% lysine and 0.33% methionine in their grain while the modern hybrids averaged only 0.28% lysine and 0.18% methionine. —*www. mandaamin.org*

GRANDMA GOURNEAU'S CORN PANCAKES

SERVES 6 GENEROUSLY | *Auntie Dolores sent me this recipe, which she said my grandmother Mary LaFavor Gourneau used to make. Grandma was a commodities trader. She always kept a store of government surplus foods so no one went hungry around her. Or, as Auntie Dolores says, "The cornmeal was a commodity staple and Mama never let anything go to waste."*

This recipe includes nonfat dry milk, which was also a surplus commodity, but these days not everyone has it in the pantry. You can leave it out and just add a bit more cornmeal if your batter seems too wet.

Chokecherry syrup is available from several of the Native American food sellers included in the Resources section at the back of this book. Another variation is to add fresh or frozen Juneberries to the batter or serve with chokecherry syrup. I won't tell you where we pick our Juneberries, but sometimes you can find frozen saskatoons from Canada at larger grocery stores near the border. Blueberries (especially frozen wild blueberries) are a great substitute.

Auntie Dee says you won't need lunch!

- 2 cups water
- 2 tablespoons butter, plus more for frying and serving
- 2 cups cornmeal
- 1½ teaspoons baking powder
- 2 tablespoons sugar
- 1 teaspoon salt
- ½ cup nonfat dry milk, optional (see head note)
- 1 large egg
- chokecherry syrup, warmed, optional (see head note)

In a small saucepan, warm water and butter until butter has melted; set aside to cool. In a large bowl, mix dry ingredients, add water-butter mixture, stir well, and then mix in the egg. Preheat a cast-iron pan and melt a little butter. Drop batter by spoonfuls onto the pan, cook until bubbles form and the cake is nicely browned, then flip and cook the other side. Serve with butter and hot chokecherry syrup. •

tribal historic preservation officer | Folks around here used to make something called *pegna* as it's said in Potawatomi and *nabaginaa* in Ojibwe. This is basically a type of corn bread made from corn-meal. In the old days you would use a botagen or bootaagan to mash the corn into a paste; you could also add ground acorns made by the same process using the botagen, and you would then get your cornmeal. Nowadays you just throw corn bread mix in the oven 'til it looks brown, throw some honey or maple syrup on it, and you've got it made in the shade.

Corn grinding dance, Veteran's Memorial Park, Ann Arbor, Michigan, 1967. Courtesy American Philosophical Society

SUNNY CORN MUFFINS

MAKES 12 MUFFINS | *Truth be told, I've never harvested cattail pollen. But some of you can probably look up from this book, glance out your windows, and see cattails. I imagine you in early summer, late June, avoiding sinking in the mud while gently tapping tops of cattails into a long, skinny plastic bag to knock off the pollen. Wait. Now I imagine you accompanied by your sweetheart of many years, your dearly beloved, and it takes you quite awhile to find enough cattails, which you discover are better cut and taken home to shake. In fact, you avoid the mud, get in a canoe, and have a long, lovely day cutting cattail spikes on the lake. When you get home, you sift the flour to get out the bugs and fluff. Then you make these muffins, look lovingly into each other's eyes, and sing "You Are My Sunshine, My Only Sunshine," or some other old, sweet tune.*

> 1 cup all-purpose flour
> ¾ cup cornmeal
> 2 tablespoons maple sugar, or substitute granulated sugar
> 1 teaspoon baking powder
> 1 teaspoon salt
> 2 tablespoons cattail pollen, optional (see head note)
> 1 egg (try a duck egg)
> 1 cup milk
> ⅓ cup butter, melted
> ⅓ cup sunflower seeds

Preheat oven to 400 degrees. Line a muffin tin with paper liners or grease well. In a large bowl, mix dry ingredients; in a second bowl, mix egg, milk, and butter. Add wet ingredients to dry all at once, stirring to moisten. Pour batter into prepared muffin tin. Top with sunflower seeds. Bake 12 to 15 minutes, until lightly browned.

VARIATION: TANKA BITE BREAD

Decolonize your corn bread with bison bits! Try chopping up some spicy sweet Tanka Bites (order directly from tankabar.com) instead of going for the hog. Make Sunny Corn Muffins, leaving out the cattail pollen. Pour batter into a greased 9-inch pie plate or baking dish and sprinkle with Tanka Bites instead of sunflower seeds. Bake 20 minutes, until golden. Allow to cool briefly, then slice into wedges and serve. ●

Lise Erdrich, Ojibwe, Turtle Mountain Band | The earth was built on the back of a Turtle after the Flood, as everybody knows. Sky Woman fell to earth just as all the birds and animals had finished the job. When she landed, she gave birth to a daughter. This daughter became a young woman, and one day she was pregnant. "Who did that?" Sky Woman asked. "It was the West Wind," her daughter replied. She gave birth to twin boys and died. These boys ran off in order to cause various stories all over the earth.

For the moment, you may call them G. Howdy and G. I. Joe. Sky Woman told them, "You will have four sisters to mind you when I'm gone." Sky Woman buried her daughter and sang a sacred song over the dirt. Corn, then Squash and Bean grew out of the ground right there. Sky Woman sent these spirits of the garden to find People. They were inside of seeds, carried on the wind and by the birds and animals. Old Magic Woman found them.

Old Magic Woman was always digging around. She would look at things and think of what to call them. She decided to invent Native American Agriculture. She made a clearing among the cottonwood trees down by the river, she worked the soil with her digging stick. The buck deer came out of the trees and raked the ground with their horns. Later, the deer came back to rake weeds. They came back one more time to eat, and they shed their horns. Old Magic Woman tied the horns onto a stick to make her own garden rake. The people followed what Old Magic Woman did, and they prospered.

Old Magic Woman went out to gather firewood. When she came back she said, "I saw the gooseberry leaves open up today, so it is time to plant the seeds that Raven brought to us." She made a hill of dirt and buried the seeds, and gave them plenty of water.

Along came the oldest sister, Corn. At first she was like a small shoot of grass. The girls and the women and birds sang to Corn to make it grow tall and straight and strong. "They sing my praises," thought Corn. "The sky is the limit, so I shall not quit." Even when Corn had grown quite high and sturdy, the girls and women kept watch over her and chased away all the birds and animals and boys who might be hungry. "When the geese come back it is time to plant the Corn again," they sang. "When the boys come to smile at us we will send them on their way."

Corn thought, "I am the single most important plant in America." This was true: everything in America and eventually the whole planet would somehow involve Corn. For those who need independent verification, simply Google "the importance of Corn." With the quotation marks removed there will be at least 1,250,000 Internet entries. However, if you insist on typing "Corn Is Number One" you will only find one entry, in which Corn is implicated in the case of a constipated dog who is discussed in a veterinary forum.

Meanwhile, Corn looked down and saw something interesting. A tubular thing came out of the ground and unfolded its green wings. But instead of flying away, it sent out a long green feeler and started to climb onto Corn.

"What are you doing! You're going to strangle me; get off! Can't you stand on your own!" cried the Corn.

"No," said the Bean, "this is what I do." It continued to make its way up by wrapping itself around and around, hugging onto Corn. "And furthermore, it is for your own good that you support me. I can do lots of good tricks. I can take the air and turn it into nitrogen for your roots. I can turn you into a complete protein. I can make you famous:

there will be a song called 'Beans and Corn Bread' on TV. Yeah, you need me. I have more surprises after this," said Bean.

Corn was not a hugger, but that was the situation.

Then along came Squash. Two blunt shiny green sprouts split into more and more leaves, and the leaves grew huge and floppy on long prickly vines. Squash spread out all over like a blanket or shawl around the Corn and Bean plants. Broad and humble and ground hugging and patient and lying low was the Squash.

"Is that all you do?" asked the Bean. The Squash said, "Look, I have both male and female blossoms," and two gigantic yellow flowers burst open, shocking Corn and Bean. They shut up. "And my leaves will keep the ground moist and shady and weed free, so your roots will not dry up in the heat of the Sun, while my itchy vines will discourage the hungry animals, and there are big colorful fruits hiding underneath these leaves."

The spirit of Corn, being a creative and adventurous risk taker, began to feel stifled with this arrangement, always under wraps. Corn wandered off in the cool of the night, wanting to find and collect the dews, which came to the earth on moonbeams. Corn thought, "I am sure that I have magic powers to attract the night mist and fog that >>

drip from my leaves in the morning, which my sisters are always drinking, although it is I who make this happen."

As soon as Corn left, a being known as Chi-Jyawb came and blighted the garden. The spirits of Bean and Squash were crushed beneath its dark, moldy disposition. Chi-Jyawb went after Corn and took her captive in his abode deep beneath the surface of the earth. Corn wept. She wept and sang a germinal song to feel her way out of this mess.

A little animal was listening to the gentle breeze, which picked up the lament from a hole in the ground. The little animal did not immediately comprehend the Corn language, but being moved by the strange silky voice, formulated a response using the highly evolved, complex, sophisticated, yet divinely designed vocabulary of a prairie dog.

Thus alarmed, Sun sent a messenger in search of the Corn spirit because of the germinating tune that lingered in the air. The messenger called to Corn and, shining a light into the black tunnel of Chi-Jyawb, led her back to the garden where her sisters were dying of thirst.

Corn made a promise to the Sun that she would never again leave the garden until the harvest time was over and all seeds were safely stored away. The Sun stationed its messenger to keep watch over the garden from that day forward.

"Who are you, and why are you beaming at us like that?" asked Corn, Squash, and Bean when they saw the stranger.

"I am your new sister the Sunflower, and it is my job to project a positive mental attitude. I will stand to the north, and thus encourage all living things in this beautiful and scientifically sound ecosystem, which is our joint accomplishment."

The pressure was off, because Sunflower could stand with Corn, which would take the heat off Bean and Squash, who could just go and do their things now. So then Sunflower called forth the little animal whose voice she had heard, and gave her a beautiful green shawl with corn-silk tassels and intertwined designs of leaves and vines and flowers that was spontaneously generated from a song, which got all messed up in translation but went something like this:

Manidoominens, Little Spirit Seeds. I am but one in the design.

Of the scroll, of the spiraling vine, flowering tendrils of the scarlet runner a red spark I glimpsed like hope, like the sweet wild strawberry oday-imin on a spear of light in the shade of a forest that signified our origins.

Oday, the poor heart of a human being. Send us light, the "little spirit seeds" are in your hands, dear holy curvilinear path flowering through all time and trespass, five fingers of the hawthorn leaf like a hand to hold this crown of mysteries.

Lead us from all darkness, bead by bead by bead. As it was in the beginning is now and ever shall be, as it is manifest in this greenery this vinery this leafery, the fingers work in your own language: I believe in the Almighty, Creator of heaven and earth: And I believe each and every deed is a bead, is a seed, is a need, is in every one of us, unfurling the vine, still growing.

SERVES 6-8 | *Corn smut, an ingredient Buffalo Bird Woman included in her historic recipes, is available as huitlacoche, a staple in Mexican cuisine that is now fairly easy to find in markets. Richard LaFortune and I made this dish on a bit of a whim. I was hesitant at first. It wasn't just the huitlacoche—corn fungus, also called smut—which I had never used. It was that corn mush doesn't sound tasty. So, think grits or polenta. Then think polenta that went wild one day and turned purple with passion. That's what happens when you put red sumac in blue corn mush. The smut just takes the flavor beyond to a place of vivid yummy-ness. So while you are there, just slap a cooked egg on it (or several small quail eggs) and be blissed. Be blessed.*

Allow each guest to sweeten with agave or maple, or use Maple Sugar and Spice Sprinkle (page 200) at the table.

>   4 cups water
>   1 cup roasted, salted sunflower seeds
>   1 tablespoon olive oil
>   1 cup blue cornmeal
>   1 teaspoon salt
>   6-8 quail eggs
>   butter
>   ½ cup huitlacoche, rinsed and drained
>   1 teaspoon sumac
>   2 teaspoons agave syrup, or substitute maple syrup
>   Maple Sugar and Spice Sprinkle (page 200)

In a large saucepan set over high heat, boil water. In a coffee grinder or food processor, grind sunflower seeds into a meal, adding oil to create a paste. When water is boiling, whisk in cornmeal and continue whisking until it begins to thicken. Reduce heat to low. Stir in sunflower meal and salt and allow to simmer, stirring regularly, until mush becomes very thick. Turn off heat, but leave mush on burner. Fry quail eggs in one mass, in plenty of butter; set aside. Stir huitlacoche into mush. Stir in sumac and agave just before serving. Cut eggs into individual servings and place on top of mush; serve hot. ●

Historian and Red Lake tribal member Brenda Child writes about Ojibwe women and work. A few times a year, I am lucky enough to help feed her and listen to her stories. Food brings good stories. From Brenda I have learned her research shows Ojibwe women were in charge of harvests and that gardens and food belonged to women. Somehow, and for a long time, the larger world has viewed this essential role of American Indian women as a life of drudgery and subservience rather than as a key economic and social power position that suited their lives as mothers and medicine keepers. In my own family history, women of my great-grandmother's generation worked hard to gather plants to heal as well as to sell to patent remedy companies as a means of support for their large and extended families. Our grandfather Patrick Gourneau (also known as Aunishinauby) was a truck farmer whose work with his large garden would no doubt have been described as "providing for his family," although the work was essentially the same as his mother's had been.

Our garden, small and minimally productive as it is, is my realm. But everyone helps out when there's squash to pick or herbs to gather. My role in our immediate family is traditional as well, I think: I go out into the forests of Costco, Trader Joe's, and the farmers markets and gather food items, plan their use, and prep ingredients for recipes. I am lucky to have a husband who not only cooks daily but does all the baking and does it extraordinarily well. So well in fact that we had to start a holiday, Pie Friday, to show off his pie prowess. We did not begin our life together this way—I think I may even have taught him to make a quiche—but now the oven is his territory and he is Pie King of our place.

All of the pie and cake recipes in this book were thoughtfully, imaginatively, and lovingly created by John E. Burke, who married me more than twenty years ago. I am still feeling lucky today. My sister-in-law Mary Burke, who trained with a French pastry chef, bakes all her own bread and hasn't bought a loaf in decades. Mary created the recipe for Mandaamin-Manoomin Bread. It is not that I can't bake; it is just that those Burkes have taken to that role with fervor, and it seems a fine division of labor.

MANDAAMIN-MANOOMIN BREAD

MAKES 2 LOAVES | *At some point in my Ojibwe language lessons, I had a flash of insight about anadama bread, which I had loved when I lived in New England. Although the name is usually explained through a joke about a weary husband tired of the same old fare hollering, "Anna, dammit," I just did not buy the story. First of all, it is terribly sexist. Second of all, they also call it "Indian" bread, and a main ingredient is cornmeal. Since New England tribes spoke a related language, I just bet* anadama *must be related to the Anishinaabemowin word for corn,* mandaamin.

For years, I hankered after anadama bread, which I do not often see in Minnesota. So I asked my sister-in-law Mary Burke to try her very capable hand at a version more suited to this region by adding manoomin and using maple in place of molasses. Her recipe is perfect: golden, chewy, dense, nutty, and slightly sweet. It can hold a hefty sandwich, is perfect with soup, and, if you can manage not to eat it all fresh, toasts extraordinarily well. I've used it for Manoomin Corn Bread Stuffing (page 37) as well as in any other recipes that involved bread and been thrilled with the results. Freezes beautifully, too.

1¼ cups boiling water

1 cup cornmeal

2 tablespoons butter

1 cup cooked manoomin

1 cup warm water (about 100 degrees)

6 tablespoons maple syrup

1¾ teaspoons salt

2 teaspoons yeast

3 cups all-purpose flour

1½ cups whole wheat flour   >>

Pour boiling water into a large bowl and gradually whisk in cornmeal. Stir in butter and allow to cool to lukewarm. While cornmeal is cooling, place manoomin in a food processor or blender. Process until broken down into small bits but not into mush. To cooled cornmeal mixture, add warm water, maple syrup, salt, and yeast and mix well. Stir in manoomin. Add flours a cup or so at a time, mixing to form a fairly dense dough. Knead dough for 8 to 10 minutes, adding as little flour as possible to prevent sticking. Give the dough a light poke with a fingertip; it should spring back a bit when ready (it will feel somewhat less "alive" than an all-wheat dough). Form dough into a ball and place in a large bowl. Cover with plastic wrap and leave to rise until double, about 2 hours.

Grease two 9x5–inch bread pans. Punch dough down and divide in half. Form each half into a loaf and place in pans. Allow to rise until approximately double, about 1 hour. Preheat oven to 350 degrees. Bake loaves 30 to 35 minutes or until done, checking after about 25 minutes and draping loaves with aluminum foil if the tops look too brown. Allow to cool at least 1 hour before slicing. •

POLENTA-STUFFED PATTYPANS

SERVES 4-6 | *Space aliens have landed in their little ships! No wait, that's a pattypan squash. They come in yellow, green, and white and are perfect for stuffing.*

This dish includes two commonly used indigenous foods: cornmeal and squash. Both the fruits of squash and the blossoms are used in indigenous cooking. Squash plants have two kinds of blossoms, one that will yield fruit and one that will not. Indigenous gardeners collected the infertile blossoms and dried them for thickening soups and stews. They can also be eaten raw and taste pleasantly sweet, like lettuce.

If you have lots of pattypan squash, let your kids make space alien ships from them using green cherry or pear tomato Martians with black-eyed peas for a single eye. When they are done playing with their food, you can clean and cook the squash thusly.

6 medium pattypan squash, various colors if possible, rinsed

4 cups water or stock, plus more for pan

½ cup minced red, yellow, and orange bell peppers

1 clove garlic, minced

1 cup polenta meal (not quick-cooking)

1 tablespoon butter or flavored oil

salt and black pepper

squash or zucchini blossoms, optional

½ cup herb-flavored soft cheese or cream cheese, optional

Preheat oven to 375 degrees. Cut a little lid from the top of each squash and scoop out ¼ to ½ cup space depending on size of squash and whether it has seeds. Don't pierce the skin. You could also cut off the tops and microwave the squash briefly first.

In a large saucepan set over medium-high heat, bring stock to a boil, reduce heat, and simmer peppers and garlic for 5 minutes. Gradually stir in polenta, whisking constantly, until all the stock is absorbed. Reduce heat to low, and cook until creamy, stirring regularly. Remove from heat, stir in butter or oil, and season with salt and pepper to taste.

Stuff squash with polenta, top with "lid" slightly askew, and place in a 9x13–inch baking dish. Add a small amount of stock or water to the pan to prevent sticking and burning. Bake, covered, 30 to 50 minutes, depending upon the size and thickness of your squash. Squash are done when fork tender.

If using flowers for garnish, remove and discard threadlike pistils from blossoms; rinse blossoms. Fill with cheese for serving. You could also fill blossoms with any extra stuffing mixture, dip in egg whites and bread crumbs, and bake 10 minutes or until crisp.

Over the top: Mound each stuffed pattypan squash with herb-flavored soft cheese or cream cheese, replace lid at a jaunty angle, microwave for a few seconds to wilt pickles, and return to oven until cheese oozes from beneath the little hats. ●

SERVES 6 | *The first time I saw this dish made was in Las Cruces, New Mexico. It was also the first time I ever thought about indigenous relationships to plants on an intellectual level. Our guest teacher was Pueblo and was deeply knowledgeable about plants. He gathered the students around him and shucked corn while telling us about the sugars in corn, the way corn pollinated, cross-pollination, male and female roles in corn keeping, and how philosophy and technology are shared through cooking. Meanwhile, he was also heating a pan and adding butter. Soon he was cutting an ear of white corn, all the while speaking gently. Kernels and corn milk fell into the browning butter, sizzling and giving off a caramel scent. He then cut a green squash into cubes as tiny as the corn and tossed it all together. He asked how many of us liked green chili. We were in New Mexico, a few miles from Hatch, the green chili capital of the United States: we all loved green chili. He finished the dish with diced green chili, and we sampled a heavenly summer succotash.*

The two sisters, corn and squash, are good in any weather, but when joined by that brother from the south, green chili, the sisters sing a fine reunion song. Serve as a side to fish or with beans and rice. Two Sisters Succotash is also good in a tortilla with cheese or on corn bread, but I have been known to eat it right out of the pan.

> 1 tablespoon butter, or substitute extra-virgin olive oil
> 1 small onion, cut into pieces the size of corn kernels
> 2 ears fresh sweet corn, husks removed
> 2 zucchini, cut into pieces the size of corn kernels
> 1 hot green chili, seeded, cored, and diced, or substitute
>   green bell pepper, seeded, cored, and diced
> fresh oregano or herbs for garnish, optional

In a skillet set over high heat, melt butter. When butter begins to brown, reduce heat to medium, add onion, and stir. Cut corn from cob directly into the pan, taking care to get as much of the milk (corn juice) as you can from the cob. Stir. Add zucchini, and cook, stirring, until onion is translucent, corn begins to brown, and zucchini is bright green but cooked through. Add green chili, and stir. Garnish with a small amount of fresh herbs (if using). Remove from heat and let rest briefly before serving. •

SERVES 4-6 | *This dish is adapted from a recipe in* Blue Corn and Chocolate *by Elisabeth Rozin, who sought to indigenize the crab soup found on old-school Chinese restaurant menus. I've changed it a bit from Rozin's recipe, and I offer it here as further proof that the Bering Strait was never a one-way street.*

1–2 tablespoons toasted sesame oil, divided
1 tablespoon grated fresh ginger
4 cloves garlic, minced
4 green onions, white parts chopped, half the green tops chopped and reserved
2 cups corn, thawed if frozen
5 cups stock
¼ cup rice wine or mirin, optional
1 teaspoon soy sauce, or use fish sauce
1 large egg
½ cup coconut milk, or use half-and-half
white pepper
1 cup flaked smoked whitefish

In a skillet set over medium-high heat, warm 1 tablespoon sesame oil and cook ginger, garlic, and chopped white green onion pieces until just fragrant. Reduce heat to medium, add corn, and stir well, adding more sesame oil as needed to prevent sticking. Cook 5 to 10 minutes, stirring occasionally, or until corn is heated through. Add stock, rice wine (if using), and soy sauce, and allow to simmer on low for 10 minutes to blend flavors.

In a small bowl, beat egg lightly and set aside. Increase heat to high until mixture boils, then use a fork to slowly drop in egg strands, breaking up strands as they rise to the top of the pot. Stir and reduce heat to low. When the soup is no longer boiling, stir in coconut milk, white pepper, and any remaining sesame oil. Serve into soup bowls, add whitefish, and garnish with onion greens. Serve immediately.

Variation: Use dried sweet corn soaked overnight and simmered until very soft. •

MAKES 8 OR MORE CUPS | *If you grow lots of your own corn (or buy it in quantity), you can preserve it and increase its nutrition by making your own hominy. In the Upper Midwest, the Oneida people are known for their corn soup.*

The process of making hominy is ancient, but we borrowed the updated instructions from Dream of Wild Health Cookbook. *Oneida corn soup is traditionally made with this hominy along with beans and meat simmered together in stock.*

> 8 cups dried corn
> 1 cup sifted wood ash, or 3 heaping tablespoons baking soda, dissolved in water

Place corn in a large enamel or stainless-steel stockpot. Add water to cover the corn, and heat to a boil. Add wood ash or baking soda water, reducing heat to prevent boiling over. Boil for approximately 3 hours, stirring occasionally. Add water as needed to cover the corn. When the corn turns bright orange and then yellow, remove it from the heat.

Drain the corn and immediately rinse it in cold water. Use your hands to rub the kernels, loosening the hulls. Rinse several times to remove the wood ash. Return corn to pot, cover with water, and bring to a boil again. Drain and rinse the corn again, loosening and removing hulls. Return corn to pot, cover with water, and simmer 1½ hours, until corn is tender and doubled in size. Corn is now ready to be canned or frozen for future use. •

GWEN WESTERMAN WASICUNA *Sisseton-Wahpeton Dakota*

professor, artist, author | My husband Glenn Wasicuna was raised in Sioux Valley, Manitoba, among his extended Dakota family. When he was young, their community dried corn the "old way" by braiding ears and leaving them in the sun. He remembers wearing heavy gloves and twisting the dried kernels that fell easily from the cobs. His mother kept a coffee can of dried corn near the stove and would add a handful to soups whenever she cooked. Now we dry corn in that same way and keep it near the stove for soups.

feast-maker | One of my earliest childhood memories was going next door to borrow the proverbial "cup of sugar" from our neighbor. I guess that's where I got my first smell and taste of Grandma Armstrong's venison or wild rice soup. Those kinds of memories tend to stay with you and pop up at unexpected times. When I started cooking for groups and family feasts, I remembered her using hominy or Indian corn in soups. It made a huge difference in the taste, so people started asking for hominy soup more and more.

MANDAAMIN-MANOOMIN NABOOB—HOMINY SOUP

SERVES A CROWD. *To complete the meal, Robin Thompson says this soup is always best served with fresh, hot fry bread.*

> 10 cups stock, plus more as needed
> 2 (15-ounce) cans white hominy, drained, or 3 cups cooked hominy (Native Harvest brand)
> 2 cups cooked manoomin
> 2 cups diced or shredded cooked partridge, or substitute turkey
> 1 cup diced onion
> 1 cup diced celery
> 1 cup diced carrots or cubed butternut squash
> salt and black pepper

In a large stockpot set over medium heat, combine stock, hominy, manoomin, partridge, onion, and celery. Simmer for at least 2 hours. Add carrots and cook until tender. Season with salt and pepper to taste. ●

TIFFANY MIDGE *Dakota/Sioux*

author and editor | Winter stew used dried ingredients, things traditionally put up for winter: wild turnips, dried bison (really sawdusty), dried corn. Reconstituted, these ingredients really leave a lot to be desired, let me tell you. It's like rubber bands and toenails, but my relatives loved it, tasted like home to them. It was like, "Uh-oh, Grandma's making that soup again, try and be appreciative!" She'd pack the dried corn, meat, and turnips in her suitcase, and travel across most of three states by train just to make it for us.

DRIED CORN AND JERKY CASSEROLE

SERVES 6 | *One of my favorite books about indigenous foods is* Blue Corn and Chocolate, *from which this recipe is adapted. While Elisabeth Rozin's casserole is like a frittata, mine is closer to a midwestern hot dish, including a sweet potato chip topping. The two ingredients that make this a decidedly indigenous food are hominy and jerky, which, it turns out, are not as chewy as the stew components in Tiffany Midge's hilarious childhood memory.*

Cookbook author Beth Dooley gives the excellent advice to treat hominy the way you would treat dried beans. I soak hominy overnight and simmer the corn long and slow before using it in recipes.

1½ cups dried hominy

4–5 juniper berries, crushed

  3 large eggs

  1 cup half-and-half or light cream

  1 teaspoon salt

cracked black pepper

  1 cup minced fish, venison, elk, or bison jerky

  1 tablespoon dry mustard

  3 green onions, chopped

  2 tablespoons garlic chives, chopped

½ cup thinly sliced winter or summer squash

butter

1 cup crumbled sweet potato chips

hot sauce

Soak dried hominy overnight in water to cover. Drain and cover with fresh water to about 2 inches above the corn. Cook 2 to 3 hours in a slow cooker with juniper berries, until corn is soft and smells lovely.

Preheat oven to 350 degrees. Grease a 1½- to 2-quart baking dish and set aside. In a mixing bowl, whisk eggs with half-and-half, and add salt and pepper. Stir in hominy and jerky, then mustard, green onions, and garlic chives. Mix well.

Turn mixture into prepared pan. Place the shaved squash atop the mixture, taking care that the slices do not sink. Dot with butter. Bake 30 to 40 minutes, until slightly puffed, firm, and golden. Sprinkle with sweet potato chips. Return dish to oven 2 to 3 minutes, just long enough to crisp chips, taking care not to let them burn. Or just sprinkle the chips on before serving. Pass hot sauce at the table. ●

SAVING THE SACRED SEEDS

Meskwaki tribe member Jerry Young Bear is trying to preserve the genetic purity of his tribe's corn. "Corn has significant value to the Meskwaki people in our culture, tradition, religious ceremonies, and as a major food source," he says. "We want to take care of our corn to make sure it is viable for future generations."

The sacredness of Meskwaki corn is expressed in the story of how the tribe received it. Two tribe members were hunting in a forest when they met a beautiful woman. They thought she was hungry so they gave her deer venison to eat. She thanked them for their kindness and told them to return to the same place in one year and they would receive a gift. After a year, the hunters and other tribe members returned to the place. They found sacred corn at the spot where the woman's right hand had been, sacred beans where her left hand had been, and tobacco at the place where she had been sitting.

The Meskwaki have been growing Tama Flint corn ever since, says Young Bear. —*"Meskwaki Native Americans Aim to Preserve Genetic Heritage of Flint Corn," Ken Roseboro,* Iowa Source Magazine

Grandpa Pat Gourneau with freshly harvested corn, Rita Gourneau (Erdrich), and Gladys Gourneau (Poitra), 1943

 CORN BREAD DUMPLINGS

SERVES A CROWD | *There was almost a bidding war when cookbook author Debbie Miller posted the listing for* Tribal Cooking: Traditional Stories and Favorite Recipes, *published in 1996 by the Nutrition Project of the Great Lakes Intertribal Council, Inc. Rather than competing in the auction, I just paid the asking price so I could offer you this recipe by Julie Williams (Stockbridge-Munsee) from those bright pink, photocopied pages.*

Julie Williams's original recipe made a massive quantity of dumplings and suggested, "Cold dumplings can be eaten as bread, slice and eat cold or reheat." I think they are best placed sliced side down in a brothy soup. The water you cook the dumplings in will become a kind of corn broth that can be reserved as a good basis for bean chili.

1 teaspoon salt

4 cups white corn flour or masa harina, divided

1 (15-ounce) can kidney or pinto beans, rinsed and drained

½ cup pumpkin puree

2 tablespoons chopped fresh or dried cranberries

Fill a large stockpot nearly full with water, bring to a boil, and add salt. In a large mixing bowl, combine 3¾ cups corn flour, beans, pumpkin, and cranberries, stirring into a sticky dumpling mixture. Stir in up to ¼ cup remaining corn flour if dumplings are too sticky. Divide dough into 12 to 15 oblong dumplings, using two spoons to form each dumpling between them. Drop into boiling water. They will sink. Boil until the dumpling rises to the surface, about 5 minutes. Remove dumplings as they rise; drain and set on a plate. Add a warm dumpling to hot soup or eat as a side dish, with butter and salt. ●

DUMPLINGS AND HUSK BREADS

The popularity of dumplings in tribal communities was a bit of a mystery to me, until I began reading about indigenous cooking and learned how long such a meal has sustained us. In their excellent book, *Native Cooking of the Americas*, Beverly Cox and Martin Jacobs tell us that one of the earliest forms of corn-based food was "made of cornmeal mixed with boiling water to form a moldable dough. In some areas, culinary ashes were added as a leavening agent and flavoring. The dough was then wrapped in corn husks or grape leaves and baked in the ashes around the edges of the campfire."

I am sure the dumpling developed at the same time. Think about it: it takes a lot of time and energy to make an open-fire oven, but excellent technology for boiling water has existed for millennia in North America. Skin pots, birch-bark containers, clay pots filled with water—all could be brought to boiling quickly with the addition of a super-hot stone. European and early-American cookware also favored the boil, hence many old-time dishes are soups, stews, or chowders, often with dumplings. If you wanted something rib-sticking fast, your choice was obvious: boil your bread and make a dumpling.

However, the dough described in the following recipe could easily be cooked in corn husks, which are sold for tamale making. Follow package directions for soaking and filling husks, but do not tie small packages. Instead, make larger oblong loaves rolled into the husks and tied with additional husk material. Tribes to the south of us call this shuck bread.

SERVES 6 | *Long ago I had an Italian corn cake that I have dreamt of ever since. Something golden, yet light. John Burke and I worked and reworked this recipe, and now it is our favorite cake. You could double the recipe and make a layer cake, as our daughter has demanded. It is perfect with raspberries.*

- ¾ cup all-purpose flour
- ¼ cup whole wheat flour
- ½ cup fine-ground yellow cornmeal or masa harina
- 1½ teaspoons baking powder
- 8 tablespoons (1 stick) unsalted butter, softened
- ½ cup granulated sugar
- ¼ cup maple sugar
- 2 large eggs, at room temperature
- ½ cup vanilla- or honey-flavored yogurt
- seeds scraped from 1 vanilla bean or 1 teaspoon vanilla extract
- Raspberry-Mint Bubbles (page 213) or fresh fruit or jam

Preheat oven to 350 degrees. Grease and flour a 9-inch cake pan; set aside. In a large bowl, sift together flours, cornmeal, and baking powder. Using a standing mixer, combine butter and sugars and beat until fluffy, about 5 minutes. Beat in eggs, one at a time. Add yogurt and vanilla seeds, and mix until just smooth. Do not overbeat; batter should be thick, almost like custard. Add to dry ingredients, stirring with a large spoon.

Pour batter into prepared pan. Bake 25 minutes or until lightly golden and a pasta noodle or wooden pick inserted into center comes out dry. Set on a rack for 10 minutes, then invert to continue cooling. You might need to run a butter knife inside the cake pan to allow the sides to release. Serve with Raspberry-Mint Bubbles or any fresh fruit and jam. ●

SUNSEED CORNMEAL COOKIES

MAKES 1 DOZEN COOKIES | *These pretty cookies are sophisticated and not too sweet, a bit like a cornmeal scone, if there were such a thing. They get better after a day or more and keep very well. Try topping them with a dollop of bergamot jelly, available from Native Harvest (nativeharvest.com).*

¼ cup minced dried cranberries

1 mint tea bag or 1 tablespoon loose wild mint or bee balm/bergamot tea

½ cup boiling water

1½ cups whole wheat flour, or use white whole wheat for a lighter color

1 cup cornmeal

¼ teaspoon salt

⅛ teaspoon white pepper

3 egg yolks

½ cup honey

8 tablespoons (1 stick) butter, melted, or substitute Earth Balance sunflower spread

⅓ cup roasted, unsalted sunflower seeds

Preheat oven to 375 degrees. Lightly grease a cookie sheet with butter or cover with Silpat liner or parchment paper. In a small bowl, cover the cranberries and the tea with the boiling water. Let sit for an hour.

In a large bowl, combine the flour, cornmeal, salt, and pepper; set aside. In a small bowl, whisk the egg yolks with the honey, then slowly add in the melted butter, whisking steadily. Drain the cranberries and add them and the sunflower seeds to the dry mix, but don't stir. Add the egg mix to the dry ingredients, stirring to incorporate into a soft dough.

Scoop dough a tablespoon at a time onto prepared cookie sheet. Bake 12 to 15 minutes, until the tops begin to turn golden.

director, Ethnobotany Project | Scott Shoemaker cares for the Science Museum of Minnesota's collection of American Indian seeds. He explains the close relationship the Miami have with corn:

> Stories, places, our language, and our corn teach the Miami people many things about what it is to be nahi-mihtohseeniaki—proper human beings—who can tend these gifts to help us to grow as a community of individuals stronger in heart, mind, and body. If we take care of these things, they will take care of us. We, the myaamiaki or mihtohseeniaki, are the original people of what is now the state of Indiana. It was in our homeland that, according to our oral tradition, a spirit gave miincipi—corn—to the Miami people during a time of great famine and community suffering. Being nahi-mihtohseeniaki is having a responsibility toward the corn and the spirit of the corn, to treat it properly, so that we may continue to feed ourselves as a people and thrive as a nation.

The Miami were dispossessed of their land in Indiana, and many were forced to leave the Great Lakes area for life on the plains. Scott links indigenous language and the Miami relationship to corn to cultural survival:

> Miami people, whether in Indiana, Kansas, or Oklahoma, had to endure efforts to dismantle the fabric that held us together. This was not a fertile and nurturing environment for our community or for our language. Once again, we were starving, in several meanings of the word. While the death of our last fluent speakers led "experts" to declare our language as a "dead" or "extinct language," a label that persists, this is not necessarily an assumption shared by the Miami people. It was, rather, a period of dormancy for our language, for our corn, and for our knowledge, yet the Miami people did not disappear and survived the best they could. We as a community were ready again to plant the seeds for the rebirth of our corn and our language.

Miami elders Lora Marks Sider and Mildred Walker cared for the last corn farmed around Peru, Indiana, near where Scott grew up. He witnessed a revival that included corn:

> We began to see the connections of the physical and mental health of our community and the revival of our language. With an enormous field before us as we began our efforts to combat these issues and revive our language, we started a small crop with a handful of seeds, planting these within individual community members. These individuals helped to foster community-wide enthusiasm and

support. In the 1990s, our communities began the next part of that cycle: the sprouting. As we began to learn to grow our corn again and began to relearn our language, we have nourished our bodies, hearts, and minds. Since then, we have grown several crops of corn and have tried several different activities, materials, and programs to help our community relearn our language. Both have been learning processes in themselves, all successes in their own ways. The Miami people have reawakened our language and our corn from their dormancies and replanted them in our homeland of Indiana and removed land in northeastern Oklahoma, and more importantly have replanted and reawakened them in our hearts and minds so that we can be in a place once again to properly take care of them.

ahkawaapamankwike, ahkawaapamelankwiki-kati—if we take care of them, they will take care of us.

POPCORN WITH SWEET-HOT SUMAC SEASONING

SERVES A CROWD | *Most books on indigenous foods include a recipe for popcorn. Historians agree that it was popcorn served at the colonial feast, not corn on the cob as the Thanksgiving myth generally suggests. Popcorn was also a traditional treat for many tribes and the basis of a particular type of flour ground from popped kernels. Popcorn is one of my all-time favorite foods and most certainly the single largest part of my diet, at least by volume. Snacking on popcorn is a family habit, shared by my sisters and instilled by our mother, who popped corn many nights of the week when we were young. For me, it is the ultimate comfort food.*

A few years ago, my husband started using zatar to season popcorn, the key ingredient of zatar being sumac. He has adapted his recipe to spread the obsession. We often eat spicy popcorn as a meal along with a cup of soup or salad.

1 clove garlic, crushed

4 tablespoons sunflower oil, divided

2 teaspoons sumac

1 tablespoon maple syrup

3 tablespoons Tabasco (classic red for hottest; chipotle or green for milder)

1 cup unpopped popcorn

grated Parmesan cheese, optional

In microwaveable cup, stir garlic into 3 tablespoons oil. Microwave on high for 30 seconds (it'll make some noise). Using a fork, beat in sumac, then maple, then Tabasco. Set aside.

In a large pan set over medium-high heat, warm remaining 1 tablespoon oil and pop the corn, covering with a lid. Pour popped corn into a very large bowl; drizzle sauce over hot popcorn while stirring and tossing popcorn with a large serving spoon. Sprinkle with grated Parmesan (if using). Serve in bowls or use a ladle so folks can spoon handfuls without making a mess. ●

Native Harvest
www.nativeharvest.com
607 Main Avenue
Callaway, MN 56521
888-274-8318; 218-375-4602

Native Harvest hominy is made from flint corn grown by Anishinaabe gardeners for centuries. Native Harvest works to "continue, revive, and protect native seeds, heritage crops, naturally grown fruits, animals, wild plants, traditions and knowledge of our indigenous and land-based communities; for the purpose of maintaining and continuing our culture and resisting the global, industrialized food system" as well as rejecting genetically modified foods. Native Harvest's catalog is extensive: bison meat products, maple products, jams and jellies, teas, and more are sold at its site, which supports White Earth Land Recovery Project.

Other sources for corn products grown and prepared by indigenous farmers include:

Bineshii Wild Rice & Goods *(yellow and white hominy; cornbread mix)*
www.bineshiiwildrice.com

Lakota Foods *(popcorn)*
www.lakotafoods.com

Native Seeds/SEARCH *(parched corn; blue corn flour)*
shop.nativeseeds.org

Oneida Nation *(white corn hominy)*
exploreoneida.com/attractions/oneida-market/
Available at Oneida Foods Market in Green Bay, Wisconsin

And, with a broad array of options:

Mobile Farmers Market
mobilefarmersmarket.localfoodmarketplace.com
2890 Terra Court, Unit 29
Sun Prairie, WI 53590
608-280-1267

Mobile Farmers Market offers an online marketplace of tribally grown, produced, and harvested food.

BERRIES ...

MAPLE COFFEE

Maple syrup and sugar are more than simply foodstuffs to Anishinaabe and other indigenous peoples of the Upper Midwest. Maple remains essential as the first harvest of spring, the lifesaving gift of the creator, the blessed substance that once broke the fast of winter's starvation. Maple sap is also an icon in Ojibwe stories, connecting to women and our roles as life-bringers and protectors of the waters of the earth. The importance of maple shows in the name of the first month of spring in the Ojibwe calendar, called Iskigamiige-giizis or Maple Sugar Moon.

Maple sugar, traditionally stored in birch-bark cones, is used to season meat, vegetables, manoomin, and berries all year long. Smoky, grainy, subtle, or strong—varied like wines—real Ojibwe maple syrup (zhiiwaagamizigan) or sugar cakes (ziiga'iganan) borrow their taste from the bark containers and the wood fires used to cook down the sap. Me, I like my maple dark and smoky, like my manoomin or my coffee. In fact, one of the enormous treats of working a sugar bush, or maple sap processing camp, is making coffee from maple water. Adding a teaspoon of maple sugar to a cup of coffee gives a similar, though not quite the same, subtly refreshing sappiness.

You can get granulated maple sugar in bulk at food co-ops or order it from a number of Native stores online. Perhaps it goes without saying, but all the recipes in this book are created for 100 percent pure maple products. Don't confuse maple sugar with commercially available maple sugar candies, which can have additives such as gums. If you don't have friends who give you maple sugar, it may seem a bit of a luxury, but think of it as a treat that lasts. I use it a lot, yet I go through a mere two to three cups a year, which makes it a reasonable purchase. Although salt occurs naturally in the Upper Midwest and people have always used salt when available, the long-held preference was to season meals with maple sugar. Studies have shown pure maple products to have remarkable antioxidant content as well as vitamins and minerals—unlike most sweeteners. Even more interestingly, the type of antioxidant is of the same class found in berries, the other main seasoning of indigenous foods in the Great Lakes and prairie areas nearby.

In keeping with my sense of indigenous foods traditions that long favored maple and seasonal, many of the recipes in previous sections feature berries and maple syrup or sugar as seasonings, often combined. The recipes that follow create a seasoning palette to accompany other meals in the form of dressings, mixes to keep in a shaker, even cooking sauces. These recipes also bring the sweetness of indigenous fruits and maple forward as desserts while also using their tartness to complement savory meals.

ZINZIIBAKWAD

Margaret Noodin, Anishinaabe, Lake Superior

Gabe biboon ishkwa gii iski-gamizigeyaang
All year after we go to sugar bush

Gabe biboon ishkwa gii ombi-gamizigeyaang
All year after we boil the sap down

Ininatigaboo minogame
Sap tastes good

Zinzibakadoo minopagwad
Sugar tastes good

Tkaagame minogaame
Cool water tastes good

Mitigoog minopigoziwag
Trees taste good

Photo by Ivy Vainio.

Patricia Northrup processing maple at her family sugarbush, 2012. Photo by Ivy Vainio.

 ## MAPLE SUGAR AND SPICE SPRINKLE

MAKES ¼ CUP | *Picture a table with the usual salt and pepper shaker, then add a third shaker for maple sugar and spice. You might find yourself using this condiment on everything from fish to grilled foods to squash, hash browns, ravioli, manoomin, corn on the cob, and popcorn. Try Maple Sugar and Spice Sprinkle on Pumpkin Bangs (page 96). I mean it.*

> 2 tablespoons maple sugar
> 1 tablespoon sumac
> ½ teaspoon smoked paprika
> ⅛ teaspoon smoked salt
> 2 juniper berries, cracked

Stir together all ingredients and store in a spice shaker. •

MAPLE-BLUEBERRY WILD RICE COFFEE CAKE

SERVES 8–10 | *You can make your own gift basket of indigenous foods at Northland Visions in Minneapolis, which is owned by an Ojibwe family of artists. Their pancake mix is 33 percent wild rice flour, which makes for a nicely nutty product. Here we adapted the mix for a special coffee cake loaded with maple and berries.*

> 1 (16-ounce) package Northland Native American Products
> Wild Rice Pancake Mix
> 1 teaspoon ground allspice
> ½ teaspoon ground cinnamon
> ¼ cup packed brown sugar
> ⅓ cup melted butter
> 1¾ cups buttermilk, or 1½ cups milk
> 2 large eggs beaten with 2 tablespoons water
> ½ cup maple syrup
> 3½ cups blueberries, fresh or frozen
> 2 tablespoons maple sugar, or substitute brown sugar
> ⅓ cup minced dried cranberries, or substitute zest of 1 lemon
> 1 tablespoon cranberry juice, or substitute lemon juice

Preheat oven to 350 degrees. Grease a 9x13–inch cake pan with butter, taking care to coat the corners of the pan. In a large bowl, stir together pancake mix, allspice, cinnamon, and brown sugar. Add melted butter, buttermilk, egg mixture, and maple syrup to dry ingredients. Mix gently, until moist throughout; do not overbeat. Mixture should be sticky and lumpy—the consistency of muffin batter. Transfer mixture to pan: it should need to be scraped into pan. Gently push mixture into an even layer with a spatula. Layer blueberries on top of mixture and sprinkle with maple sugar. Bake 25 to 30 minutes, until top is browned and berries bubbly. Remove cake from oven and sprinkle chopped cranberries and juice over the hot cake. Serve hot or cold. Better the next day.

Over the top: Make Maple-Berry Whipped Cream by whipping 1 cup heavy cream with 2 tablespoons maple and 1 teaspoon Chambord raspberry liqueur or 1 teaspoon cranberry juice. ●

MAKES 1 SCANT CUP | *There's a very light maple syrup I am lucky enough to get from friends who have their own sugar bush. Others might think of it as syrup that did not set up and even soured a bit, but I think of it as maple wine. Further thinned with a splash of vinegar, this maple wine is great for deglazing a pan of onions and garlic. And apparently indigenous people have been letting the last of the maple sap sour for a long time. Early-twentieth-century ethnobotanist Huron Smith wrote of Ojibwe use of "'cîwa'bo' made from souring maple sap," which he said was used to flavor cucumber that was also sprinkled with maple sugar.*

Zhiiwaaboo is often translated as "vinegar," but really the word means "sour water." Maple wine or sour water, either way, both supply the bright, acid element that complements the earthy tastes of indigenous foods perfectly. But unless you have kind friends who tap their own maple trees, it's not likely you will get your hands on maple zhiiwaaboo. Thankfully, forager and cook Brett Laidlaw, author of Trout Caviar, *suggests making a maple-vinegar reduction as a "rustic condiment" that he had hoped would be like balsamic. His results sound much more like the maple wine I love. I suggest you try the Laidlaw formula of two parts vinegar to two parts maple, using Grade B maple syrup. And call it zhiiwaaboo. Let's see if we can get that handle to catch on.*

Use zhiiwaaboo to deglaze skillets, in dressings and marinades, and as a light glaze on roasted vegetables, game birds, or fish. Or use it to season manoomin for salads. Laidlaw uses his reduction sauce on ice cream and baked apples. Just for fun, try it on sliced cucumbers, then add a sprinkle of maple sugar. Or use it as Huron Smith saw it used: "The vinegar, made from the last run of sap in the maple tree, is used to cook the leaves of dandelion for a dish of greens."

> ½ cup maple syrup
> ½ cup vinegar (Laidlaw uses apple cider vinegar)

In a small saucepan set over medium-high heat, stir together maple syrup and vinegar and bring to a boil. Simmer, stirring occasionally, until mixture reduces by half. Remove from heat and allow to cool. Store in a tightly covered glass container in the refrigerator. ●

VIOLETS DUSTED WITH MAPLE SUGAR

MAKES 2 CUPS | *Springtime means violets. Their scent is clean as rainwater and slightly sweet. Violets taste like tender lettuce and are terrific in a salad. In our yard, violets bloom just before the lawn is long enough to mow, so we pick the blossoms and even eat the tender green leaves, then we mow and never get another full crop. Our lawn is chemical free and so are our neighbors', so we know the blossoms are safe. We don't pick from the boulevard—too much pollution and dog walking there—and we don't pick near the foundation of the house, where lead from paint could be an issue. Tell a pack of little kids you'll give them a quarter per full paper plate, and you'll get all the violets you need in no time.*

Unlike the classic candied violet that uses egg whites and gum and changes the flower's texture, I suggest this simple process that also takes less time.

Violets Dusted with Maple Sugar make a sweet decoration for Golden Corn Cake (page 190) or a garnish for fruit salad.

2 cups violet flowers, rinsed and spun
   or allowed to dry on a towel
water
1 tablespoon maple sugar,
   or substitute confectioners' sugar

Place blossoms in a freezer bag. Sprinkle a drop of water into bag. Add maple sugar and gently shake the bag to distribute. Place in freezer and use whenever you wish for up to a month. •

SERVES 8 | *Maple has half the calories of honey and nearly half that of molasses. If you are going to indulge yourself or loved ones, why not make a sweet that has maple's nutrition and packs in fiber from indigenous nuts as well? Another John Burke creation, this dessert is so pretty it gets* oohs *and* aahs *when guests arrive. We have friends who eat pie as a first course, so we put it front and center on the table instead of revealing it after the meal. This pie also suits our gluten-free friends, while proving a profound tribute to pure maple. It is the perfect once-a-year dessert.*

For crust:
1½ cups pecans, black walnuts, or pine nuts,
    or substitute almonds or walnuts
3 tablespoons sugar
2 tablespoons butter, melted

For custard:
⅛ teaspoon salt
⅓ cup cornstarch
1½ cups warm water
1 cup maple syrup
4 egg yolks
1 tablespoon butter

Preheat oven to 400 degrees. In food processor, grind nuts fine, to the consistency of bread crumbs. In a bowl, stir together nuts, sugar, and melted butter. Press mixture into a 9-inch pie plate, covering bottom and sides evenly. Bake for 8 to 10 minutes, until golden. Set aside to cool while you make the custard.

In a saucepan, combine salt with cornstarch. Add water and maple, whisking until smooth. Over medium heat, bring mixture to a boil, stirring frequently. Remove from heat.

Whisk egg yolks in a dish. Temper the eggs by whisking in a tablespoon of maple mixture, then another, then a third. Whisk yolk mixture into pan slowly, then return to medium heat. Stir continuously until it thickens; do not bring it to a boil. Remove from heat and stir in the butter until completely incorporated. Pour into crust. Allow to set at least 30 minutes before serving. ●

HICKORY NUT–MAPLE TOFFEE

MAKES ENOUGH TO FILL 2 QUART BAGS | *Beautiful Ojibwe beadwork, tiny colored glass beads worked into bright patterns of leaf and vine, often on the luxurious contrast of deep black velvet—it was Ojibwe beadwork that taught me how important nuts are to indigenous cooking. In a museum long ago, I first noticed a beadwork pattern that included the usual grapes, berries, flowers, and leaves and something else, something familiar: the particular shape of wild hazelnuts, the nuts we called* puckons *when I was growing up. Soon I was noticing leaves of oak, chestnut, and other nut trees in Ojibwe artwork of all kinds. Clearly we long loved (and honored in art) these hard-to-crack but nutritious treasures.*

Hickory nuts are fairly easy to find in many parts of the Upper Midwest, and Amish farmers often sell the nutmeats picked clean—but at a price. We found "Amish Hickory Nuts" at a food co-op and bought them to make gift offerings of this special toffee.

> 2 cups hickory nuts, toasted,
>   or substitute black walnuts or butternuts
> ¾ cup maple syrup
> ¼ cup packed brown sugar
> ½ cup granulated sugar
> 2 tablespoons water
> 16 tablespoons (2 sticks) butter, melted
> ¼ teaspoon salt

Cover a shallow baking pan or cookie sheet with a Silpat sheet or baking parchment. Spread the nuts in the center of the sheet, in a single layer, close together—you do not need to fill the whole sheet. In a saucepan, stir together the other ingredients and cook over medium-high heat until temperature reaches 300 degrees on candy thermometer. Pour over nuts, starting at center; it doesn't spread far!

Allow to harden for 2 minutes, then score top with a knife, making roughly 2x2–inch squares. Allow to harden where no extra humidity will interfere, such as a cold oven, for 20 minutes. Using the score lines, cut toffee into small squares. Many will not be perfect. Store in a sealed plastic bag or in aluminum foil in an old candy box in a dry place. If your toffee fails to fully harden, just crumble it and call it "brickle" for ice cream. ●

pparently children the world over are taught that there were only three fruits native to North America: grapes, blueberries, and cranberries. I saw this misinformation all over the Internet and have heard it from my own children's mouths. The USDA lists thirty-four varieties of berries as native to the area before 1600. How did everyone miss such vast diversity? I can understand folks not knowing about buffalo berries, dewberries, or saskatoons (Juneberries), but blackberries, strawberries, raspberries? Do we really have to give Europe sole credit for them? In fact, our Anishinaabe sacred stories mention the "heart berry" or strawberry, and the berry is prominent in Haudenosaunee cosmology as well. Berries remain tremendously important to indigenous people, who have long known them as essential to health and happy eating. Studies today continue to find extraordinary nutrition in wild berries indigenous to the region, which is further cause to be happy.

Berry soup, an unsweetened mash of berries often served with meat, invariably shows up in most literature and cookbooks on indigenous foods of the region. For generations, however, the main way folks have eaten berries is as a dried food. I encourage you to lay in a good supply of dried berries and experiment with them as an accompaniment to savory dishes. Add a little maple, and you get a good sense of what it has been like to eat here for centuries.

Go berry picking. Berry bushes often do have thorns, but I never think of them as forbidding in any way. In fact, berry bushes mean peace to me: I remember crawling into the raspberry bushes, to that cool center, to sheltering shade away from mosquitoes and neighbor boys. Sometimes I would sing to myself, enjoying the snacks I found hanging right over my head, and once I fell asleep in a neighbor's patch, which I had entered through the parking lot next door. Raspberries have always been a huge treat for me. Raspberries-Juneberries-strawberries-blueberries-gooseberries-currants-cranberries: I love them all and see that love as proof of my bear nature.

WOJAPI/WOJABI—THICK BERRIES

*Many tribes of the region made a thick berry sauce such as wojapi, sometimes re-
ferred to as berry soup. Where maple was available, the dish was probably sweetened,
but elsewhere it was not. Wojapi goes with both sweet and savory foods and was
often served with meat—a little like cranberry relish. Wojapi is expected at all gatherings and events in North and South Dakota and in parts of Minnesota, too. I think
it best if made from Juneberries that you have gathered with your family, but frozen
berries are also excellent. Arguments over the real way to make this dish abound—
some folks even use cans of blueberry pie filling! As a peace offering, I've included two
recipes. The second is the maple-sweetened variety with its Dakota spelling,* wojabi.

DENISE LAJIMODIERE'S WOJAPI (MAKE 3 CUPS)

Serve with Pumpkin Bangs (page 96).

2 cups Juneberries, fresh or frozen, or substitute blueberries
1 cup sugar
2 tablespoons cornstarch dissolved in ¼ cup cold water

In a heavy saucepan set over medium-high heat, stir together berries, enough
water to cover, and sugar. Bring to a boil. When berries are boiling, slowly stir
in the cornstarch mixture. When thickened and a gorgeous shiny purple, remove from heat.

WOJABI (MAKES 4–5 CUPS)

Adapted from Dream of Wild Health Cookbook. *More thickener may be
needed if using frozen berries.*

4 cups blueberries or Juneberries, fresh or frozen (see head note)
1 tablespoon cornstarch or arrowroot dissolved in
   ¼ cup cold water
maple syrup

To a heavy saucepan set over low heat, add berries and enough water so they
will not stick to the bottom of the pan but do not float. Simmer over low heat.
Stir occasionally and watch carefully so that the berries do not scorch. When
the berries are soft and heated through, stir in cornstarch or arrowroot mixture.
Sweeten to taste with maple syrup.

SERVES 6 | *An Oneida woman told me about her wedding, where the guests were served a salad of strawberries and white corn. My imagination went wild. In my mind this salad manifested innocence and delight. It is the food of lovers' picnics or breakfast-in-bed brunches. When I finally tried my hand at it, I used the best oil I had, sunflower oil from Driftless Organics in Wisconsin (driftlessorganics.com). I do not know how the Oneida cook made her salad, but these results made us all happy. This salad is summer on the tongue, excellent with Wild Black Bean Burgers (page 46) and Ferdinand the Bison Burger Gets Loose (page 88).*

3–4 ears very fresh white sweet corn,
or use 1 (11-ounce) can white sweet corn, drained

1 pint fresh strawberries (organic and chemical free
really do taste better), hulled and sliced

½ cup fresh basil, minced

2 tablespoons gourmet sunflower oil,
or substitute extra-virgin olive oil

¼ cup white balsamic vinegar, or use rice wine or other mild,
clear vinegar

1 tablespoon poppy seeds

1 teaspoon white pepper, or use extra-fine ground black pepper

Into a large bowl, cut kernels from cobs, tossing to break apart. Stir in strawberries and basil. In a small bowl, whisk oil, balsamic, poppy seeds, and pepper until well combined. Toss corn, strawberries, and basil with dressing and serve immediately. •

WILD RASPBERRIES AND BLACKBERRIES AND THEIR RELATIVES *(Rubus* spp.)

There are at least twenty-five species of the genus *Rubus* indigenous to various parts of Canada. Most of these have edible berries of the raspberry or blackberry type, which were eaten by indigenous peoples. —Traditional Plant Foods of Canadian Indigenous Peoples, *Food and Agriculture Organization of the United Nations Agriculture and Consumer Protection*

SWEET AND SOUR GOOSEBERRY QUINOA

SERVES 6 | *Yes, I am the one who eats the gooseberries raw off the bush before they turn red. I like the pucker. But I never thought to turn these raw beauties loose on a grain until, looking at the abundance my mom had picked, a picture of gooseberries on a mound of quinoa leapt to mind. Gooseberries' swirly inner structure pairs visually with quinoa, which might be what gave me the idea to combine the two.*

Although quinoa is grown in South America, and some say our northern trend toward it has caused indigenous people there to suffer shortages, it is the closest comparable thing to wild grains of the pigweed family eaten long ago in North America. The resulting dish has the sweet and sour thing down to a pop and would be an excellent side to venison or salmon. We eat it with morsels of chubby smoked lake trout and make noises like happy bears.

- 3 cups cooked quinoa, cooled, or substitute couscous in a real pinch
- 2 tablespoons maple syrup
- 1 cup gooseberries or currants (if frozen, thaw in 1 tablespoon maple syrup)
- ¼ cup dried sweetened cranberries, more if gooseberries are very tart
- 3 green onions, chopped
- 1 tablespoon balsamic vinegar
- 1½ tablespoons minced fresh mint
- 1 teaspoon sumac
- 1 teaspoon toasted sesame oil
- 1 medium or 2 small sunchokes, peeled and minced
- wild hickory or hazelnuts, toasted, optional
- 5 ounces smoked lake trout or other fish, optional

In a medium bowl, combine quinoa, maple syrup, gooseberries, cranberries, onions, balsamic, mint, sumac, sesame oil, and sunchokes, tossing to mix. Garnish with hickory or hazelnuts if serving as a side. If serving as a meal, top each serving with a small amount of smoked lake trout—it really does not need much more to make a wonderful lunch. ●

GOOSEBERRY-CRANBERRY CHUTNEY

MAKES ABOUT 3 CUPS | *"An aboriginal Menomini dish was spikenard root, wild onion, wild gooseberry and sugar. This is described as being very fine," wrote ethnobotanist Huron Smith in 1924. What others find delicious is sometimes curious. I've read that spikenard root is not unlike a parsnip. Can't quite get my mind around sweet and sour mash of any kind, but gooseberries and currants work perfectly in a chutney. The color will be a lovely red, not unlike cranberry relish. Serve this chutney on baked or broiled fish and meat or with couscous or rice dishes. It is also quite tasty with squash.*

> 2 cups gooseberries
> ½ cup cranberries
> 1 red onion, chopped medium
> 1 teaspoon ground allspice
> 1 tablespoon grated fresh ginger
> 1 teaspoon red pepper flakes
> ¼ cup maple syrup
> ¼ cup water

In a heavy saucepan, stir together all ingredients and bring to a boil, stirring occasionally. Reduce heat and simmer until berries have burst and sauce has thickened. •

MOM'S GOOSEBERRY-RASPBERRY JAM

MAKES 6 (HALF-PINT) JARS | *"We can because we can can." —*Old Family Saying

Mom's preserves are always so pretty. She has a basement room lined with glimmering jars of ruby red, amber, and amethyst like a dragon's horde of treasured fruit. Chokecherry jelly, candied crab apples, wild grape jam, plum butter, Juneberries, and deeply colored gems of mixed fruit. They are all so, so good, but gooseberry-raspberry is the best.

Jam goes on Gullet/Bannik (page 110)—which you serve with hot tea or iced tea. Say no more.

> 4 cups medium-ripe gooseberries
> 1 cup water
> 1 cup raspberries
> 1 cup applesauce
> 5 cups sugar
> 6 sterilized half-pint jars with lids and rings

In a heavy saucepan set over medium-high heat, cook gooseberries in water until tender. Mash the gooseberries in the pan. Stir in raspberries, applesauce, and sugar. Bring to a boil and stir until the mixture thickens, perhaps 15 to 20 minutes. Keep testing as it cooks by spooning a bit onto a cold plate. When it gets somewhat thick, it is done. While hot, pour into sterilized jars and seal (see instructions, page 163). •

WHAT GATHERS

Heid E. Erdrich, Ojibwe, Turtle Mountain Band

Twisting stems weave
green to red against leaves
raindrop-shaped and tender,
shelter for blue-black berries.

We taste pure purple. We gather.
We touch our tongues to juice
we've asked to grow for us.

We children in our northern gardens
gather dark sweetness of saskatoons,
indigenous fruit that taught Ojibwe
beadwork patterns of vine and leaf
—winter's longing, worked by hand,
reminder of a hot day to come,
promise bright against threat.

Doubtless that was part of it:
what was gathering long ago,
the rush of other, the great change,
foods, woods, bison, prairie,
gods, songs, goods,
all about to alter.

We touch our tongues to summer.
What gathers now we do not know—
some low rumble on the globe's edge.

We gather. Nail tips and lips
stained, we do as our blood asks.
These berries the same berries
our ancestors plucked,
rolling a thumb against the curved edge,
teasing ripeness, readiness,
old ladies joking: Find me a man
can handle a woman like that!

Swoon in July sun, in sensual acts,
the fruit asks. We do as it wishes,
    we gather,
chilled still by long winter—
always just behind us, always just ahead.

RASPBERRY-MINT BUBBLES

SERVES 6 | *Did I mention how I love raspberries? In the winter when our resident rabbit comes to trim my berry bushes, I sit at the window admiring his ability to survive the cold and I wish him no ill. But in the summer, when I cannot get enough raspberries, you can hear me in the garden mumbling about snaring me a waboose and making me a stew.*

Raspberries really do not need much to make a dessert or a marvelous topping for a special cake. But I wanted to do raspberries proud, so I let my imagination roll around awhile, like a berry on the tongue. Tapioca is another indigenous cousin, from the cassava plant, whose roots make the starch manufactured into "pearls" and used for pudding and bubble tea drinks. Tossed in with raspberries, tapioca bubbles make a party out of a few simple ingredients. Serve beside Golden Corn Cake (page 190) or layered with yogurt in a fancy little parfait dish.

¼ cup large tapioca pearls (not the quick-cooking kind)

2 cups water, plus more as needed

2 cups raspberries, fresh or frozen

¼ cup chopped fresh mint

½ cup cranberry-raspberry juice, or other 100 percent juice raspberry drink

1 tablespoon poppy seeds

1 cup honey- or raspberry-flavored yogurt

In a medium saucepan set over medium heat, combine tapioca pearls and water. Stir. Simmer 12 to 15 minutes, stirring frequently. Remove from heat, cover, and let sit 15 minutes. Drain and rinse tapioca bubbles.

In a large bowl, combine tapioca, raspberries, mint, juice, and poppy seeds. If you are using frozen raspberries, something interesting happens: the pearls turn from translucent to white and freeze. Let the whole thing thaw a bit if you do not like the effect. Spoon over sweetened, flavored yogurt. ●

WILD GRAPE PBJ COOKIES

MAKES ABOUT 2 DOZEN COOKIES | *Indigenous cookbooks from the American South invariably include a recipe for peanut soup. Peanuts are a cousin food from Paraguay that arrived here, it is thought, by way of European trade. But we know peanuts came looking for grapes. Long before their arrival, and before anyone conceived of the peanut butter and jelly sandwich, the Upper Midwest was rich with indigenous grapes. Wild grapes may seem sour and seedy to our contemporary tastes, but grapes were long eaten fresh, out of hand as a special treat. Grapes are a favorite element in Anishinaabe beadwork patterns, which shows the people's affection for the fruit. Wild grapes amble along power poles and through brush piles in small towns and reservations all over the Upper Midwest. But city dwellers suffer no shortage of wild grapes: we put up an arbor we found at a yard sale and, I am not kidding, a wild grape plant just started growing on it the next year. My sister Angie has been known to do a little urban foraging to make her scrumptious Alley Grape Jam.*

Several Native-owned food companies make and sell wild grape jam, which is gone in a flash once you open a jar but lingers a bit longer when you make these cookies.

½ cup sunflower butter sticks or regular shortening (Earth Balance)
½ cup smooth peanut butter
½ cup granulated sugar
½ cup packed brown sugar
1 large egg
1¼ cups all-purpose flour
½ teaspoon baking powder
¾ teaspoon baking soda
¼ teaspoon salt
 wild grape jelly or other wild berry jam

In a large mixing bowl, stir together shortening, peanut butter, sugars, and egg, mixing thoroughly. In a separate bowl, stir together flour, baking powder, baking soda, and salt, then stir into shortening mixture. Chill dough for 30 minutes.

Preheat oven 375 degrees. Remove dough from refrigerator and roll into 1¼-inch balls. Place dough balls 3 inches apart on greased baking sheet. Flatten each ball by gently pressing your thumb in center. Bake 10 to 12 minutes, until golden. Remove from oven and place 1 teaspoon wild grape jelly into thumbprint on each cookie. Remove each cookie to a cooling rack. Allow to cool before serving.

Wild Grape PBJ Cookies get better a day or two after they are made. Don't try to eat them fresh out of the oven like some bear did, or molten jelly will burn your paws! ●

BERRY-MAPLE DRESSING

MAKES ABOUT 2 CUPS | *Use this dressing for salads or as the basis for marinades. It's terrific on Four Esteemed Manoomin Ways salads (pages 25–28).*

> 2 tablespoons raspberry or other indigenous fruit jam, warmed
> 1 tablespoon maple syrup
> ⅓ cup raspberry vinegar, or substitute other fruit vinegar or balsamic vinegar
> ½ teaspoon dried tarragon, or use mountain mint
> 1 teaspoon minced chives, or substitute ramp greens
> ¼ teaspoon salt
> ¼ teaspoon black pepper
> 1 cup organic sunflower oil, or substitute extra-virgin olive oil

In a small bowl, whisk together jam, maple, vinegar, herbs, salt, and pepper. Whisking constantly, slowly pour in oil until thoroughly mixed. ●

musician | Next to a photo showing a mass of glistening red cranberries, Wade Fernandez wrote, "pickin' piakemenan . . . today in the bog . . . Our ancestors used them long before Ocean Spray's ancestors ever set sight on a cranberry. They are native to North America. My dad used to pick them when he was a kid with his mom on the reservation. I wasn't sure that they still grew up here until a few years ago."

Later I asked Wade if he had a favorite cranberry recipe, and he replied, "I just love them cooked with honey, maple syrup, and wild rice, and sometimes I just freeze them and eat them raw all winter."

BERRY KICK KETCHUP AND BBQ SAUCE

MAKES ABOUT 3 CUPS | *Ground cherries (also called husk tomatoes) are much like the related tomatillos, but they grow wild in prairie regions. Their little paper jackets make them interesting to children—which is probably why I liked to pick them when I was young. They are ripe when they turn golden; do not eat them green. The flavor is said to be a cross between tomatillo, tomato, and pineapple. My mom always made jam from her ground cherries, but I was interested in their savory profile, so we experimented with making a ketchup that can also serve as a barbecue sauce.*

Use as ketchup with burgers and hot dogs or as a barbecue sauce or kebob dip. Berry Kick Ketchup and BBQ Sauce is especially good on baked fish.

> oil for frying
> 1 red onion, chopped
> 2 cloves garlic, crushed
> 1 teaspoon dried bergamot, or substitute mint
> 1 teaspoon dried thyme
> 1 tablespoon curry powder
> 4 juniper berries, crushed
> 1 tablespoon white vinegar
> 1 cup water

2 cups chopped ripe ground cherries, or substitute 1 cup chopped tomatillos, 1 cup yellow cherry tomatoes, halved, and ¼ cup crushed pineapple, drained

½ cup Juneberries, or substitute wild or regular blueberries

1 (6-ounce) can tomato paste

¼ cup honey, or substitute agave syrup

1 teaspoon hot sauce (Sriracha), plus more to taste

In a medium saucepan set over medium-high heat, warm oil and cook onions until just translucent. Reduce heat to low, add garlic and spices (bergamot through juniper), and stir. Add vinegar and water. Stir in chopped ground cherries and Juneberries, and simmer 20 to 30 minutes until thickened, stirring often. Skins of fruit will be obvious, but do not skim them. Turn off heat and allow mixture to cool for 10 minutes.

Using a blender, briefly puree sauce for a few seconds, until skins are incorporated. Return mixture to saucepan; stir in tomato paste, honey, and hot sauce. Cook on high 2 to 3 minutes, stirring constantly, until the color has deepened. Cool and store in a glass container with a tight lid. ✺

HONEY BUZZ SALAD SPLASH

MAKES ABOUT 1 CUP | *There's something about tart fruit juices meeting sweet fruits that makes the mouth buzz pleasantly. Although honey was not part of the area's indigenous diet in the deep past, it has been a tradition here for a long, long time now.*

This recipe makes something less rich than a salad dressing and more exciting than a squeeze of lime. Use Honey Buzz Salad Splash on Honey Buzz Melon Salad (page 164), on Strawberry and White Corn Salad (page 208), or on lightly mashed berries to serve on shortcakes or Golden Corn Cake (page 190).

¾ cup pure cranberry juice, or another 100 percent berry juice

¼ cup honey, plus more to taste

1 tablespoon poppy seeds

hot sauce to taste

Combine all ingredients, whisking to incorporate the honey. Test and adjust to taste. ✺

GARLIC-ROASTED CRANBERRIES

SERVES 8–10 | *This recipe creates a kind of condiment to be added to roasted squash or other cooked vegetables, placed on top of a Brie-type cheese, served as a relish, or even spread on hearty bread. It might seem like an extra step, but if you were to add the cranberries to the vegetables during roasting, they would turn hard and possibly burn. Follow this technique and you wind up with three important items: roasted garlic to mash with vegetables, roasted cranberries that have sucked up garlic and herb flavors, and garlic-rosemary oil to use in dressings, on mashed potatoes, or on anything else. I'd eat my thumb if you put garlic-roasted cranberry on it.*

1 large bulb garlic
3 tablespoons olive oil, plus more for baking dish and drizzling
½ cup dried cranberries
1 sprig fresh rosemary, plus additional leaves for garnish
sea salt

Preheat oven to 375 degrees. Strip the first layer of papery husk from the garlic bulb, exposing the cloves still in their peels. Trim off any dirt or root matter on the bottom. Grease a small baking dish or large ramekin with olive oil. Put garlic bulb in center, flat side down. Surround with cranberries, and tuck rosemary sprig securely into bulb. Drizzle the 3 tablespoons olive oil over the garlic, berries, and rosemary, so the bulb is sitting in a pool of oil. Roast until garlic is softened and berries plump up, about 25 to 30 minutes. Remove from oven and allow to cool. When garlic has cooled enough to handle, remove peels or squeeze garlic from peels into a small bowl. Drain oil from cranberries. Reserve extra oil. Discard rosemary. Lightly mash garlic mix in roasted cranberries and add a little oil if the condiment looks too dry. Garnish with a few leaves of fresh rosemary, sprinkle with salt to taste, and use as described above. If you have leftover oil, use it to make a salad dressing. ●

SERVES 8 | *There's a tradition in many indigenous cultures that elders be considered grandparents, whether related to you or not. We had two "grandmas" who were not our grandmothers and, in our case, not even from our tribe. Our Dakota elder was a widow we called Grandma Farmen, who made the most wonderful pies and sold them for a little income. Once or twice my mother let me help in the kitchen. I learned Grandma Farmen's recipe for lemon meringue pie and taught it to my husband. He took it to the indigenous side using cranberries to create a glistening, light red custard that can be capped with snowy meringue and garnished with fresh or dried cranberries. Any way you present this pie, it is a delightful surprise and a sudden favorite.*

   1¾ cups sugar, divided
   ⅓ cup cornstarch
     salt
   1½ cups warm water
   ¾ cup pure cranberry juice
   1 teaspoon grated fresh cranberries, optional
   4 large eggs, separated
   1 tablespoon butter
   1 (9-inch) pie shell, baked and cooled

Preheat oven to 400 degrees. In saucepan, mix together 1¼ cups sugar, cornstarch, and ⅛ teaspoon salt. Add warm water, cranberry juice, and grated cranberries (if using), whisking until smooth. Over medium heat, bring mixture to a boil, stirring frequently. Remove from heat as soon as it boils.

Whisk egg yolks in a dish. Temper them by whisking in a tablespoon of the hot sugar mixture, then another. Whisk yolk mixture into pan slowly, then return to medium heat. Stir continuously until mixture thickens; do not bring it to a boil. Remove from heat and stir in the butter until completely incorporated. Pour into baked and cooled crust.

In the bowl of a standing mixer, combine egg whites and ¼ teaspoon salt. Beat on high until soft peaks form. Add remaining ½ cup sugar, 2 tablespoons at a time, beating until stiff and glossy peaks form. Top pie with meringue, and bake until golden all over, about 10 minutes. •

LEGREN — DRIED CHOKECHERRY CAKES

Denise Lajimodiere, Ojibwe, Turtle Mountain Band

After the first freeze
go out into the Turtle Mountain
bush to your favorite spot
you keep secret from all your cousins
and pick some chokecherries
when they are sweetest,
you won't have to fight
mosquitoes or ticks.
Have your grandkids help you pick.
Pound the chokecherries
on your Kookum's
flat rock using her oval shaped
pounding rock that fits snug in your hand.
Grind the pits as finely as you can.
Shape the pounded berries into small
"cookies," and lay on an old window screen.
Put on top the lean-to where they will dry
slowly in the North Dakota sun.
Store in a cracker tin.
On Thanksgiving day put a couple cookies
worth in a cast iron skillet
with some water and set over a low fire,
when soft and starts to smell like summer,
add sugar and a pinch of flour to thicken,
stir in some bacon grease and fry it up a little,
put a small amount on all your relatives' plates,
kids too, and tell them they have to eat it, pits and all.

HAU KOLA/HAU KODA (CHOKECHERRY SODA)

SERVES 4 | *Technically the chokecherry is not a berry. I know this, but chokecherries are so important to indigenous cooking and culture in the Northern Plains that it would not feel like an indigenous cookbook without offering a taste of the chokecherry.*

Few people know and enjoy the tremendously tart (often described as astringent) and fragrant chokecherry. Baby Boomers might recall the taste of Smith Brothers Cough Drops with some fondness—chokecherry is one of the ingredients. The easiest way to introduce yourself to the flavor is to buy some chokecherry syrup for pancakes—but don't stop there.

For instance, we were joking about creating a line of sodas with indigenous flavors, like "fry bread and swamp tea" soda. We knew the first soda in the line would have to be made of chokecherry, the official state fruit of North Dakota. That's when Richard LaFortune came up with a name for our first pop, a terrible pun, a play between the English word cola and the Lakota word for friend, kola. We didn't dare leave out our Dakota friends, so we also suggest making a lower-calorie drink with the natural sweetener stevia. Don't forget to toast with Hau Koda ("Hello, Friend")!

Something about the coconut water makes this drink taste very cola like, but it is good with plain fizzy water, too.

> 4 (12-ounce) cans LaCroix coconut-flavored soda water,
>   or substitute plain club soda
> 8 tablespoons chokecherry syrup
> 1 cup ginger tea or strong ginger ale
> 4 tablespoons agave syrup, or substitute stevia to taste
>   (omit if using sweetened ginger ale)

In a large pitcher, combine all ingredients, stirring well. Serve over ice.

Over the top: Why not freeze ice cubes with a Smith Brothers lozenge in each and serve this drink on the rocks, for nostalgia's sake? ●

Spirit Lake Native Products
1032 Spirit Lake Road
Sawyer, MN 55780
218-644-0912

Bruce and Tawny Savage and family operate Spirit Lake Maple Syrup, which sells tradition-
ally harvested maple syrup and maple sugar. Bruce is an enrolled member of the Fond du
Lac Band of Lake Superior Chippewa; Tawny is an enrolled member of the Pyramid Lake
Paiute Tribe. Tours are provided at their sugarbush, located on the Fond du Lac Reserva-
tion, in the spring during the sugaring season. Each year students from local colleges and
grade schools have toured the sugarbush and watched the evaporation process happen in
the sugarhouse. The family also harvests and sells manoomin. Tours of the wild rice plant
are available upon request to small groups: call for more information. Spirit Lake Maple sells
food items at the Duluth Farmers Market and online.

Red Lake Nation Foods
www.redlakenationfoods.com
PO Box 547
15761 High School Drive
Red Lake, MN 56671
888-225-2108; 218-679-2611

Seller of cultivated wild rice and wild rice products, Red Lake Nation Foods has expanded its natural foods line to present hand-harvested wild fruit jellies and jams (wild blueberry, wild grape, and chokecherry!) and a large variety of syrups, including the hard-to-find cranberry and wild plum flavors.

Maple and berry products are also available from:

Birchbark Books and Native Art *(wild grape, chokecherry, wild berry jellies)*
www.birchbarkbooks.com
2115 West 21st Street
Minneapolis, MN 55405
612-374-4023

Native Harvest *(maple syrup; maple sugar; bergamot jelly)*
www.nativeharvest.com

Northland Visions *(hawthorn jelly; chokecherry syrup)*
northlandvisions.com/product-category/food-products/
861 East Hennepin Avenue, Suite 130
Minneapolis, MN 55414
612-872-0390

Northland Visions sells packets of manoomin/wild rice, along with berry syrups and jellies. They offer chokecherry, hawthorn, highbush cranberry, rose hip, and wild plum jellies as well as teas, honey, popcorn, and other indigenous food products. Soups and pancake mixes are also a part of their packaged goods and gift baskets.

... HERBS AND

TEA ···

THE GREAT MILKWEED CAPER

*I*n the languages of many cultural groups, the names of the months translate to read like a menu: Sturgeon Moon, Wild Rice Moon, Corn Moon, Maple Sugar Moon, Berry Moon, and so forth. You could read them as instructions as well: make sugar this month, plant corn this month, harvest manoomin this month. Food, the gifts that sustained people for millennia, is the center of our cultures. Sometimes when we worry about diet, food production, or prices, or even when we strive to create with food and excite our senses, we forget what most indigenous spiritual practice teaches: these foods are living beings upon which we are dependent.

Food is medicine. In researching food traditions of Menominee, Potawatomi, and Ojibwe people, I saw this sentiment expressed repeatedly. I took care to respect or to learn about the sacred nature of each food before I wrote a recipe containing it. However, many foods that are considered powerful healers are also everyday ingredients in traditional indigenous dishes. To some an herb might be medicine and to others a flavoring. For instance, wild sage: Most of the cultural groups in the Upper Midwest burn wild sage for spiritual cleansing and do not eat it. Some drink wild sage in a tea.

In general, leaves, buds, twigs, berries, and other aromatics are used the same way we use other contents of our spice cabinets, a pinch here and a pinch there. Ethnobotanists describe in most cultures the use of "pot herbs," which both flavor foods and provide nutrition. Favorite green herbs include ramps, ostrich fern tips (fiddleheads), wild mint, bergamot (or bee balm), wintergreen leaf, watercress, and nettles. People of the prairie areas traditionally use dried and fresh flowers to thicken and flavor soups and stews. Everyone drinks tea. Teas from twigs, needles, flowers, and leaves are always mentioned in cookbooks from indigenous communities. That makes sense to me, because tea goes great with that other gift from the creator, conversation.

In writing this book I had many conversations with people from many tribes about food. Often those chats would start with a humble comment along the lines of "all food is good" or "we get enough." There are indigenous foodies, but even among chefs, fishermen, and foraging fanatics, the conversation around indigenous foods tends to center on concerns about who gets enough nutritious food and how to bring people back into relationship with their food. Food equity is a real conversation in Indian Country—which includes the urban areas where more than half of all indigenous people now live. Protecting water to sustain our foods is always a part of the conversation, and most discussions end with recognizing food as a gift from the creator.

But none of these conversations about indigenous foods are ever somber. People tell the best stories about food: just ask about food instead of the weather if you really want to get to know people. It really tickled me that every Ho-Chunk person I asked about indigenous foods mentioned milkweed soup or pickled milkweed buds with what I can only describe as an appetized enthusiasm. Milkweed buds are supposed to taste like giant capers—which sounded great to me. However, you won't find a recipe here. My attempts to harvest milkweed required some stealth and a partner in crime. Alas, the Great Milkweed Caper resulted in not a single pickle. I determined that in this section on herbs and tea, I would focus on easily obtainable foods that can be purchased at markets or co-ops or foraged in your own yard.

My own weedy yard was at its peak abundance a few years ago when the author Gary Paul Nabhan came to my sister's bookstore, Birchbark Books in Minneapolis. He is known for championing indigenous foods and food diversity. His influence has contributed to dozens of food-related movements, and his scholarship informs a great deal of current thought in the local foods conversation both in North America and beyond. But I did not know any of that until just before I met him. I had known Dr. Nabhan as a poet and interdisciplinary scholar—one of the few people I'd encountered who engaged the odd marriage of science and poetry. When I learned he had written a book on plant diversity, *Where Our Food Comes From,* and that he spoke regularly on preserving indigenous languages and how doing so saves plant and climate knowledge, he became my hero. When he came to town, there was no way I was not going to his reading.

I did not go empty-handed. We picked Yard Salad.

Yard Salad is an annual event at our house—sometimes semiannual if lots of violets come up. Plants that grow in my yard, aka weeds or what we do not plant but that we can eat, include yellow sorrel, plantain, violets, mulberries, pin cherries (though the birds always get them first), sunflower (volunteers from the neighbor's bird feed), wild daylilies, catnip, horse mint, clover, nettle, waterleaf, lamb's-quarters, wild grapes, dandelions galore, and more. For two years, after an old elm was taken down, we had morels in the spring. All this within a mile of downtown Minneapolis.

In addition, we have planted highbush cranberries, asparagus, strawberries, raspberries, nodding onions, zucchini, tomatoes, cucumbers, and other garden crops in our small and shady yard.

On the evening of Gary Paul Nabhan's reading, my daughter, who is pretty good at finding wild edibles (and even better at spotting four-leaf clovers), picked a salad with me. We washed it and placed it on a bed of wild rice that we had dashed with maple syrup. As we foraged our yard, we looked for something from every continent, and we found it all growing just outside our door. We started with yellow sorrel, the wild kind we called sauerkraut plant when I was a kid. My little girl calls it pickle plant. With the sorrel and the maple syrup, the salad would be a kind of sweet and sour offering. She picked all the tiny pickles from the leaves to use as a garnish. To the sorrel leaves and flowers we added some nasturtium blossoms, a little mint, chive flowers, and I don't recall what all else. When we brought it to Dr. Nabhan, he inspected it, pronounced all continents accounted for, and ate it on the spot, making appreciative sounds that delighted my daughter. Then he read poems and the evening grew lush and lovely around us.

BUFFALO BIRD WOMAN *Mandan-Hidatsa*

Boiled Squash Blossoms: A little water was brought to boil in a clay pot. A handful of blossoms, either fresh or dried, was tossed into the pot and stirred with a stick. They shrunk up quite small, and another handful of blossoms was tossed in. This was continued until a small basketful of the blossoms had been stirred into the pot. Into this a handful of fat was thrown, or a little bone grease was poured in; and the mess was let boil a little longer than meat is boiled, and a little less than fresh squash is boiled. The mess was then ready to eat.

SERVES 6 | *It is a personal disappointment to me that rhubarb is not an indigenous plant. My grandparents loved it, and it was the prime ingredient in the first thing I ever baked: rhubarb bread from my mother's wonderful recipe. Sometimes I stand and stare at plants in my garden until an idea comes to me. One day when I was looking at my rhubarb, it began to look a bit like blushing celery to me. Perhaps I could use it like celery? Finally, I remembered Gary Paul Nabhan's visit and the salad we made, recalling I had put rhubarb in it. I set out to re-create and improve the yard salad that spanned seven continents, but I had no manoomin that day.*

Turns out quinoa and rhubarb go nicely together, and all the fresh yard-foraged herbs wake your mouth right up! Serve with something rich, like Pure White and Deadly—Hot Smoked Fish Spread (page 59) or Mushroom-Nettle Pâté (page 236) and crusty bread. Also good as a side to oven-baked fish such as walleye or salmon.

½ cup fresh sorrel leaves and flowers, or substitute micro greens or sprouts

4 nasturtium leaves, torn into small bits, or substitute 1 tablespoon watercress or arugula

2 cups cooked quinoa, chilled or room temperature, or substitute couscous

¼ cup minced rhubarb

1 tablespoon maple syrup

1 tablespoon chopped fresh wild mint, or substitute other mint

1 teaspoon sumac

salt

Soak greens and flowers in very cold water, then spin or allow to dry on a towel. Combine all ingredients in a serving bowl, toss, test, season with salt to taste, toss again. ●

FLOWER AND MINT SALSA

MAKES ABOUT 4 CUPS | *In 1917, Buffalo Bird Woman described half a dozen ways she used squash blossoms for food. To me blossoms sound tasty, but what is really nostalgia inducing is a dish strewn with fresh flowers and savory mint. I remember being taught to pinch the tips of wild columbine between my teeth to get "the honey," and I have done so ever since childhood. We learned to identify mint by its strong, clean scent and square stem. I enjoyed picking what we called horse mint and nibbling a tiny bit of it, too. Turns out our treat was bee balm or bergamot, also called* oswego *in Anishinaabemowin.*

Another favorite in the Upper Midwest is the naturalized daylily Hemerocallis, which tastes like very sweet lettuce. It is the same plant used in Asian cooking sold as "golden needles" and familiar as an ingredient in lily bud soup or hot-and-sour dishes. We have a lot of them growing in our weedy yard, although I am sure I never planted a one. If you can't beat 'em, eat 'em.

Serve this salsa with tortilla chips or as a side to grilled meats or Wild Black Bean Burgers (page 46).

about 1 cup fresh, edible flower petals: pansies, violets, spiderwort, columbine, dandelion, tiny zucchini or squash blossoms, sunflower petals, chive blossoms, mint flowers

2–4 Hemerocallis daylily blossoms (see Important Note, below)

2 tablespoons chopped chive or wild garlic

½ cup chopped wild mint, mountain mint, or bergamot

1 tablespoon chopped cilantro, optional

¼ cup dried edible flower petals, cleaned of stems or twigs, crumbled: calendula, lavender buds, clover, chrysanthemum, safflower threads, etc.

1 (20-ounce) can crushed pineapple, drained, or use chopped fresh mango or peach

4 cloves minced garlic

¼ cup minced red bell pepper or a mix of bell peppers

1 small hot chili, minced

hot sauce to taste

Soak fresh flowers in very cold water, then spin or allow to dry on a towel. Pluck petals into a large bowl; trim and discard white ends of fresh daylily blossoms. Add herbs (chive through cilantro, if using). Toss to mix. Stir in dried flowers, pineapple, garlic, pepper, and chili. Season with hot sauce and allow to mellow at room temperature for at least 20 minutes, then cover and chill before serving.

Important Note: Make sure you positively identify any flower *before you eat it.* In larger flowers, pull and discard the pistils and stamen before eating. Generally, the petals of edible flowers are tasty, but the area where the stem joins can be bitter. Eat just the blossoms or petals of smaller flowers. Trim daylilies of the white bottoms, leaving only the orange-colored blossom, which can be chopped or torn into small bits. Be absolutely sure that you positively identify any daylily as Hemerocallis before you eat it. Also be sure none of the flowers you choose to eat are chemically treated or growing near where a neighbor, farmer, or other caretaker has used chemicals. Some grocery stores sell edible flowers in the herbs area. The packages I have seen contain pansies for the most part. ●

ROASTED RAMP AND JUNIPER DRESSING

MAKES 1 SCANT CUP | *Ramps, often called wild leeks, have long been a foraged food and a favorite of indigenous cooking. They are like green onions pumped up in both flavor and form. The bulb, stem, and abundant garlicky greens are all edible and distinctly tasty in their own ways. Indigenous cooks eat ramps raw, roasted, and pickled and, like our ancestors, dry them for later use.*

Recently, organic ramps have become available for sale in Wisconsin and parts of Illinois. One Twin Cities co-op describes ramps as "a native wild leek, indigenous to the region with sharp onion-garlic flavor and wild smoky undertones." This dressing plays up those smoky tones and gives sharp greens a talking to so they mellow like a fire laying low.

Try this dressing on bitter, mixed greens salad with ramp tops chopped finely and a crumbled salty cheese (like feta) along with sunchokes sliced very thinly, like radishes. Immediately soak sliced sunchokes in 1 cup water with 3 tablespoons of lemon juice for a few minutes (while you clean and mix your greens) or they will darken.

¼ cup oil from roasted ramps (see page 130)
6 juniper berries, crushed
coarse salt to taste
cracked black pepper to taste
2 tablespoons balsamic or berry vinegar
2 tablespoons maple syrup
1 tablespoon chopped fresh tarragon or mountain mint

To a small bowl, add oil and stir in juniper, salt, and pepper. Add remaining ingredients, stirring well. ●

PAUL DEMAIN *Oneida/Ojibwe, Makwa Doodem*

journalist | When I went up into the Penokee recently, there was nothing but wild onions everywhere. I don't even know what elder told the story, simply in passing, maybe thirty years ago that the Giants of the Penokees had an onion garden there, and that the Ojibwe helped protect it.

RAMP REFRIGERATOR PICKLES

MAKES 1 QUART | *These pickles just make a person glad to be in the world. Nothing you use them in will be ordinary, not egg salad, not tuna fish—all will shine in their glow. So why not use them in a fancy salad of fiddleheads or asparagus or set them next to a luxurious piece of cheese and crusty bread?*

Double this recipe according to your abundance of ramp blessings.

enough ramp bulbs and stems to fill a quart jar
(reserve greens for other recipes)
1 sterilized quart jar with lid and ring
1 cup water
½ cup white vinegar
6 tablespoons sugar
2½ tablespoons coarse salt or pickling salt
1 tablespoon juniper berries
1 tablespoon whole allspice

Prepare ramps by carefully trimming roots and greens. Rinse well, taking care to remove dirt from any splits in stems. In a sterilized jar, pack cleaned ramp stems and bulbs. If you have only a few ramps, don't worry; just let them float. Pack bulb side down.

In a stainless-steel stockpot or nonreactive saucepan, combine water, vinegar, sugar, salt, and spices. Cook on medium-high heat, stirring, until sugar and salt dissolve and the brine comes to a boil. Remove from heat. Pour hot brine over ramps, and seal immediately. Allow jar to cool. Once jar cools, place in refrigerator and promise not to eat them for a week. ✻

RAMP GREENS IN SESAME OIL

MAKES ABOUT 2 CUPS | *Ramps are available fleetingly, so make the most of them. One of the first things I did with ramps was to process the lovely greens into this very simple preserve. Use it in salad dressings, in sauces, or as you would pesto. Many, many months later, I found the last smidgens of this paste, bright green and fresh smelling, in the back of the fridge. I did not eat it, but it proves the staying power of both ramps and sesame oil.*

    2 cups ramp greens, rinsed
    ½ cup toasted sesame oil, some reserved

Using a food processor, process ramp greens with most of the oil to make a paste. Scrape paste into a small glass container, and cover top with sesame oil to preserve. Store in the refrigerator. ●

RAMP KIMCHI FOR NORTHWOODS BIBIMBAP

MAKES ABOUT 3 CUPS | *Once we had made ramp pickles, we wondered what to do with the greens. We had enough to fill a large salad bowl, and they smelled wonderful. I chopped a few in salads, and then it came to me: make kimchi! I am sure our ancestors did not eat kimchi, but I could not resist. For encouragement, I took a look at a wonderful locavore website: hungrytigress.com. However, even though the recipe posted there is dead simple, I was sure it wouldn't work for me, and I took a short cut in the form of sambal olek, the crushed chili and garlic paste available in the Asian section of most grocery stores. We sterilized an empty one-gallon pickle jar (thanks, Costco) and set to work.*

You can eat the kimchi the moment it smells tasty to you, but try to leave some for later: it lasts indefinitely in the refrigerator and gets better as it ages.

10–12 cups ramp greens, rinsed well, coarsely chopped

½ cup sambal olek

1 tablespoon sugar

2 tablespoons toasted sesame oil

1 teaspoon salt

Place chopped greens in large jar. Slather with sambal olek. Add sugar, oil, and salt. Shake the jar to mix everything. Place jar in the refrigerator. Shake the jar once each day for 5 to 7 days. Soon the entire contents will reduce to a wilted, glistening mass at the bottom of the jar and begin to smell really good. Transfer to a smaller, sterilized jar and store in the refrigerator.

NORTHWOODS BIBIMBAP (SERVES 4–6)

Here is one method for a regional bibimbap. You could also add spinach or wild greens cooked in sesame oil, pickled vegetables such as radish, ramps, or onions, and, for a vegetarian version, smoked tofu and morel and shiitake mushrooms fried in toasted sesame oil.

4 cups cooked manoomin or brown rice

¼ cup Ramp Kimchi

1 cup flaked smoked whitefish

½ cup each shredded cucumber, carrots,
   and sunchokes

4 large eggs (or 8 quail eggs),
   fried in sesame oil

¼ cup Famous Dave's BBQ sauce,
   or substitute Korean bibimbap sauce

toasted sesame seeds for garnish, optional

seaweed for garnish, optional

Fill each of 4 bowls with 1 cup manoomin and arrange other ingredients on top, with fried egg and sauce last. Garnish with sesame seeds and/or seaweed if desired. ●

SERVES 10–12 | *The flavor of nettle is savory and rich, much like parsley with hints of basil and tarragon. Nettle makes a great broth and can be bought in bulk in the tea aisle at food co-ops and online from local sources. If you gather your own nettles it would be well worth it to dry some for winter use. In this recipe, adapted from a Moosewood cookbook entry, nettles season a first layer that is decorated with slices of mushroom. We use a pretty morel (fresh or reconstituted dried), but any mushroom will do for this rich spread. Serve on water crackers or crusty bread with Ramp Refrigerator Pickles (page 233), Rez Water Pickles (page 102), and a little mustard.*

1 (12-ounce) package firm tofu
sunflower oil
½ cup chopped walnuts
6 tablespoons roasted, unsalted sunflower seeds
⅔ cup chopped green onions, white parts only, or ramps,
   greens removed
6 cups sliced mushrooms, plus 1 whole mushroom, sliced
2 tablespoons tamari or 1½ tablespoons soy sauce
¼ teaspoon dried tarragon
¼ teaspoon dried thyme
⅛ teaspoon black pepper
⅛ teaspoon paprika
1 cup whole wheat bread crumbs
¼ cup cooked nettles, drained and minced,
   or ¼ cup reconstituted dried nettles, drained

Place unwrapped tofu in a flat-bottomed strainer, put a plate on top of it plus a heavy can or jar, and press for 10 minutes. Grease a loaf pan generously with sunflower oil. Preheat oven to 400 degrees. Bring a saucepan full of water to a boil.

In a food processor, grind walnuts to a coarse meal. Set aside. In food processor, process sunflower seeds with 2 teaspoons sunflower oil until a thick paste forms. Set aside. In a heavy skillet set over medium heat, cook onions in 1 tablespoon sunflower oil until translucent. Add 6 cups sliced mushrooms, toss to mix thoroughly, cover, and cook for 10 minutes, until mushrooms are completely softened and have given up a lot of liquid. Remove cover from skillet, and cook 5 more minutes.

While the mushrooms cook uncovered, prepare the tofu by placing it in the boiling water for 5 minutes. Remove and return to press. Add tamari to mushrooms, stir it in, then add herbs and spices (tarragon through paprika), stir again, reduce heat to low, and let simmer 5 minutes, then turn off heat.

Stir in sunflower seed paste and walnuts, mixing them into the liquid thoroughly. Crumble in the tofu, stir, then add the bread crumbs, stirring again. Working in batches, puree in a food processor until smooth. Arrange slices of reserved mushroom on bottom of prepared loaf pan. Spoon nettles over and between mushroom slices. This will be the top of the pâté, so decorate as you wish. Spoon pâté mixture into loaf pan on top of nettles, cover pan tightly with aluminum foil, and bake 50 minutes. Allow to cool, uncovered, for at least 45 minutes, then turn out of loaf pan onto serving plate. Cool another 30 minutes or more before slicing. ●

TOM WESO *Menominee Nation*

visual artist | During the times when we would go out wild foraging, I ate plenty of dog roses. We ate rosebuds boiled until they were soft. They were vegetables, really, that tasted like roses. Small rose leaves are good in salads. Rose hips are like fruits. We waited until after the first hard frost, when rosehips are soft and sweet, and then ate them—not the seeds inside. You have to cut them open and scrape the seeds out. Fruit are very sweet.

It wasn't that we needed the food so much that it was pleasurable to go out, take a walk, and my small daughter Pemy would jump up ready to go . . . Pemy has a good diet to this day. She's never been one to suck down fast foods. One of the things her mother and I did right is the natural diet. One reason—it was pleasurable for her to eat fresh-picked food.

SERVES 6 | *The flavors of wild greens can seem strong and match well with mellow greens such as mâche, better known as corn salad. This green, long a home gardener's staple, is becoming more available in groceries and food co-ops. I buy mine at Trader Joe's. I've heard folks say that miner's lettuce, a wild green, tastes a bit like corn mâche. You could add any edible greens to this mix, but take the time to pick the violets: they are sweet as springtime and, besides, you are probably out there weeding them, anyhow.*

Serve with Pan-roasted Rabbit (page 80) or Summer Squash and Manoomin Terrine (page 148).

¼ cup young plantain leaves

¼ cup young violet leaves

¼ cup violet blossoms

1 (4-ounce) package mâche, or substitute buttercrunch lettuce

1 tablespoon walnut or sunflower oil, or substitute extra-virgin olive oil

1 tablespoon white balsamic vinegar

½ teaspoon white pepper

Rinse and spin or towel dry wild greens and mâche. Whisk together oil, vinegar, and white pepper. Toss with salad just before serving. •

DANDELION KRAUT

MAKES 4–6 CUPS | *My brother Louis is handy with the fermentation. He's good at wine and beer and such. And, like our grandfather Ludwig, for whom he is named, he makes the kraut. Lately he has gone high end on the low tech: "One needs to have a fermenting crock for the following technique. Without one, using a glass crock with an airlock will work as well to assure the air and other contaminants do not get to the fermenting vegetable matter." His current food of choice for fermentation is the dandelion. I tried to get him to pick mine, but no go.*

While dandelions did not originate in the Upper Midwest, people here took to them pretty quickly. Most of the cookbooks from American Indian communities mention cooking dandelion greens or using tender young leaves in salads. None of them mentioned making dandelion kraut.

4 cups tender dandelion greens
4 cups shredded red cabbage
½ cup pickling salt
1 tablespoon juniper berries
1 tablespoon whole allspice
few tablespoons starter or juice of live kraut, optional
4–6 cups salt water (about a 2 percent solution)

Rinse the dandelion greens well and spin or gently towel dry. Toss the dandelions and cabbage with salt and spices, and let stand for a couple of hours. Toss starter (if using) with the dandelions and cabbage and then place mixture in fermenting crock with any and all juice that has accumulated. Add enough salt water to nearly cover the dandelions and cabbage. Place crock weights over the top of the mixture. If after a few hours the weights are not covered in water, add additional salt water until covered. Cover and seal the fermenting crock and let the lacto fermentation occur for a few weeks. Sample for level of crispness and sour flavor. When you like the taste, the kraut is done. ●

Few cooks continue the tradition of seasoning their food with ashes, so let this be a comeback call. Buffalo Bird Woman made an ash ball seasoning from corn cobs, carefully watching the pit where the cobs were burned until a crust formed, then rolling that crust into balls: "I collected about a quart of ashes; only two kinds were used, cottonwood or elm wood ashes. When I was cooking with such wood and thought of making hominy, I was careful to collect the ashes, raking away the other kinds first."

Such care not only provided a seasoning as vital to improving the taste of foods as salt; it also unlocked nutrition in corn and was a particular contribution indigenous cooks made to the world. As Elisabeth Rozin notes in *Blue Corn and Chocolate,* "The elaborate age-old technology for processing corn with alkaline solutions made from culinary ashes and other substances never traveled beyond the New World; it surely developed here as a sophisticated and essential response to a primary food that would otherwise have been less valuable nutritionally."

In *Foods of the Americas: Native Recipes and Traditions,* Fernando and Marlene Divina describe the use of a flower, coltsfoot, to make ashes: "Found throughout North America, this plant from the daisy family has yellow petals that are used to make a wine and an herbal tea. The ash produced by burning the dry leaves was used to make a salt substitute by many indigenous people of North America. Dried coltsfoot leaves can be bought in health food stores. Simply burn them in a pan, allow the ashes to cool, and crumble for use."

I have used ash from juniper twigs to delicious effect, but identifying the tree is a bit tricky since European Junipers are not edible. Make it easy on yourself and use ash of wood from a maple tree. Oak ash is often suggested as well. Once you use ash in a meal, you will want to fill a shaker and use it regularly. Ash is particularly good in corn dishes and in soups or stews featuring game meats; see Duck and Corn Soup (page 72) and Blue Corn Mush with Smut (page 177).

TEA-INFUSED BISCUITS

MAKES 1 DOZEN SMALL BISCUITS | *Is a biscuit a small version of gullet bread, or is bannik bread a huge biscuit? Either way, these quick breads are favorites of cooks in Indian Country. We've souped them up and tea-d them off by adding some wild herbs. Use this recipe to top Black and Blue Bison Stew (page 87).*

      2 cups all-purpose flour, plus more for work surface
    ½ teaspoon baking powder
   2½ teaspoons baking soda
      1 tablespoon maple sugar
    ½ teaspoon salt
      4 tablespoons (½ stick) butter, softened
      1 bag sage and white mint tea, or 1 teaspoon each dried sage
        and dried mint
    ¼ cup half-and-half or light cream
    ¾ cup buttermilk

Preheat oven to 350 degrees. In a large mixing bowl, sift together dry ingredients, and cut in butter with two forks or a pastry blender until mixture resembles cornmeal. Stir in contents of tea bag. Stir in half-and-half and buttermilk. Work the dough with your fingers until coarse chunks of butter show and a coarse dough forms. Sprinkle flour on a work surface, and roll out the dough to a round about 6 inches wide and ½ inch thick. Use a knife to cut the dough into "puzzle pieces" without removing the pieces. Slide biscuits onto a cookie sheet and bake 10 to 15 minutes, until golden. Serve hot from the oven.

Variation: Use a plastic cap from a beverage bottle to cut very small biscuits to serve with Bison Summer Sausage with Licorice Berries (page 242). •

BISON SUMMER SAUSAGE WITH LICORICE BERRIES

MAKES 12–24 APPETIZER-SIZE SERVINGS | *Deconstructing a summer sausage is a lot like playing with your food. My cooking partner Richard surprised me one day when, instead of placing summer sausage atop a cracker, he removed the casing and performed alchemy. The result looked a bit like tuna tartare and was a huge hit served on tiny biscuits.*

¼ cup dried berries (blueberries, cranberries, strawberries)

1 cup hot, strong, licorice-flavored tea (Victory Tea from Native American Tea Company)

2 fully cooked bison summer sausages in casings

1 tablespoon or more maple syrup

Soak dried berries in hot tea for 15 to 20 minutes. Remove and discard casings from sausage. In a large bowl, mix and "massage" sausage contents with maple syrup until the texture changes and seems slightly whipped. Add more syrup, if needed. Mix in berries. Let sit 10 to 15 minutes. Serve mixture on top of the tiny variation of Tea-infused Biscuits (page 241). •

HERBAL TEAS

Beverages made from steeping herbs and plant matter in water should be called tisanes, officially, but I've never heard anyone refer to them as anything other than tea. I don't know about all Native people, but coffee and tea are always offered in American Indian homes that I visit. Many people have stories of a grandmother serving healing teas and favorite "visiting teas," including Labrador or swamp tea, wintergreen tea, and mint teas including Oswego, made of bee balm or bergamot. Plant leaves make flavorful infusions: strawberry leaf and raspberry leaf seem the most popular throughout the Upper Midwest. Favorite drinks are made from twigs: black birch, chokecherry, wild cherry, and young raspberry canes. Flowers also make tasty drinks that are less in fashion now than they once were: clover tea, goldenrod, and rose hips were common. *The young needles of conifers make up another class of favorite teas: juniper (without berries) and pine tip tea, made with the new growth of white pine. Root teas are most often medicinal teas, with the exception of sassafras, which one reservation community cookbook called a "favorite of old-timers."*

All of these teas are available to order through online sources, including from Native American purveyors. Most teas come with their own instructions and serving suggestions. However, here's a general rule:

1 tablespoon fresh or dried ingredient for every cup of water

For Bon Annee Tea: steep wintergreen leaves in boiling water, strain, and serve hot or cold. If you have fresh wintergreen leaves, you can make a stronger drink by boiling the leaves in water, then placing them in a loosely covered sterilized jar set in the sun for two to four days. Shake the contents regularly, and when the liquid "fizzes" it is time to boil and strain. Wintergreen tastes like old-fashioned teaberry gum, and in fact *teaberry* is the plant's other name. Wintergreen contains the same key ingredient as aspirin, which is why, perhaps, I think of it as a good New Year's Day drink.

For Labrador/Swamp Tea: allow this tea to steep as long as possible. Serve with a teaspoon or more of maple syrup. Labrador tea, most often called *swamp tea,* is a favorite of Ojibwe people and a tea I have enjoyed since I was a teenager. It is quite mild, and I prefer it iced.

Oswego Tea: make this tea of bee balm/bergamot leaves the same way you would make any mint tea. Serve it hot or cold. Some find the taste of Oswego to be stronger than mint and add honey to temper it.

Pine Tip Tea: boil pine tips in a nonreactive pot (you might need to clean it with vinegar later to remove sap), strain, and serve with honey or maple, if you wish. This tea is astringent and invigorating. ●

SERVES 6 | *A traditional drink of folks in the Upper Midwest is sumac lemonade. I've adapted the old "Indian Kool Aid" recipe to make a refreshing drink with the grassy summertime sweetness of clover.*

> 1 cup dried red clover blossoms
> 6 cups water, divided
> 1 tablespoon dried sumac
> ½ cup maple syrup
> cranberry juice, optional

Place clover blossoms and 3 cups water in a large pan and simmer over medium heat, stirring occasionally, for 15 minutes. Strain, discarding blossoms. Add remaining 3 cups of water, dried sumac, and maple, and bring to a simmer, stirring until maple dissolves. Chill and serve over ice. For a more tart drink, add ¼ cup pure cranberry juice per serving. ●

Native American Tea Company
www.nativeamericantea.com
421 South Lincoln Street
Aberdeen, SD 57401
888-291-8517; 605-226-2006

Just a few tea blends make up the whole of the product line for Native American Herbal Tea, but these teas are iconic in their flavors and packaging—which features American Indian art. Victory Tea contains wild cherry bark, rose hips, mint, and licorice root—all favorite herbs of indigenous cooks in many cultures. Good Medicine Tea is a minty tea with strong tones from ginseng, licorice, and edible flowers.

The company means to pay it forward, too: "Native American Herbal Tea, Inc. donates 5% of profits and royalties after taxes toward scholarships at Sitting Bull College. SBC is a fully accredited, four-year tribal college with a strong emphasis on entrepreneurship education. It is located on Sitting Bull's Lakota Sioux Standing Rock Sioux Reservation at Ft. Yates, North Dakota and has branch campuses at McLaughlin and Mobridge, South Dakota."

While this popular line of teas is available from many indigenous foods sellers, you can also order directly from Native American Herbal Tea's website.

Other purveyors of indigenous herbs, spices, and teas include:

Native Harvest (*raspberry and strawberry leaf tea*)
www.nativeharvest.com

Native Seeds/SEARCH (*wild Mexican oregano; red chili*)
www.nativeseeds.org

··· GOOD SEEDS ···

Good seeds are the essential bit of something good about to grow. I try to keep that in mind. At times in creating this book the conversation around indigenous foods was a disheartening struggle. How to find hope in a time of climate change, a time of a new and constant push for mining in a race for energy and mineral sources—essentially a new land grab—and under the constant threat of genetically modified organisms contaminating indigenous foods?

Dedicated individuals and relentless organizations are making sure we have an indigenous food heritage to share with everyone. Often I hear of these efforts from people who are already benefitting from the classes, camps, conferences, and cook-offs happening in Indian Country. And although many are unaware that indigenous people are trying to guard the safety of our foods for everyone, sometimes I find a news item and see a little of our story trickling into the mainstream and I am profoundly glad. Often I am inspired by the efforts of elders sharing their food knowledge with children and students. I think of these folks and their work as "Good Seeds," and it is in their honor that I wrote this book. Some of the Good Seeds I want to acknowledge include

- *Decolonizing Diet Project at Northern Michigan University*
- *Manoomin restoration efforts in Michigan*
- *Tribal gardens at the Red Cliff Reservation in Wisconsin and elsewhere*
- *Meskwaki Food Sovereignty Initiative canning classes in Iowa*
- *White Earth Tribal and Community College website list of local foods*
- *Dream of Wild Health indigenous foods community cooking classes*
- *Lac Courte Oreilles Ojibwe Harvest Camp in the Penokee Hills of Wisconsin*
- *Indigenous Corn Restoration Project in Minnesota, Wisconsin, and North Dakota*
- *Anne Kuyper Community Garden at United Tribes Technical College*
- *Mashkiikii Gitigan, the Medicine Garden, at the 24th Street Urban Farm, Minneapolis*
- *White Earth Farmers Market at Mahnomen, Minnesota*

Good Seeds come to me in other forms as well. This year my family is part of a pilot program Indigenous Foods Community Shared Agriculture (CSA) weekly "share" that we pick up at a local farmers market. Nothing could have given me more hope than those first deliveries of lamb's-quarters and manoomin and black beans, all organically grown with the help of Native American youth.

Finally, a brief conversation with my mother became one of my treasured Good Seeds. Mom described to me a time in the 1940s when the weather was erratic and there were no Juneberries on our home reservation in North Dakota. This memory of my mother's may seem like a little bit of information, but, having been shocked by the loss of berries in 2011, to me it means that the plants have adjusted to climate change in the past and they may be able to adjust now. Not a little thing at all. A seed is not a little thing—a seed is everything.

In the spirit of the Good Seeds,

Heid E. Erdrich
July 2013

··· ACKNOWLEDGMENTS ···

Miigwech manidoog. I offer this first acknowledgment to the spirit of our relatives, corn and manoomin, and to all the good foods that deserve our unending thanks and our protection.

Thanks to my family members who helped in harvesting and cooking foods in this book: Rita Erdrich, Ralph Louis Erdrich, Dolores Manson, Gladys Poitra, Denise Lajimodiere, Mary Burke, Pallas Erdrich; my brothers Ralph David Erdrich and Louis Erdrich; and most importantly my sisters and fellow indigenous foods enthusiasts who helped me in all ways, Angie Erdrich, Lise Erdrich, and Louise Erdrich.

To those who contributed recipes, comments, information, assistance, and interviews to this book, I am deeply grateful and in awe of your work and knowledge. Miigwech to Austin Bartold, Brenda Child, Pauline Danforth, Paul DeMain, Wade

Fernandez, Ben Gessner, Leslie Harper, Biskakone Greg Johnson, Ron Libertus, Doug and Rachel Limon, Tiffany Midge, Montana Pecore, Lois Red Elk, Marty Reinhardt, Bob Rice, Scott Shoemaker, Robin Thompson, Deb Wallwork, Tom Weso, Gwen Westerman Wasicuna, Diane Wilson, and Odia Wood-Krueger. For photos, Angie Erdrich and Ivy Vainio.

Recipes require ingredients, and I thank those who supplied them. For manoomin, miigwech to Madonna Youngbear. Thanks to Uncle Ron Manson for fish. For maple syrup, miigwech to Pat and Jim Northrup. For chokecherry, wild turnip, and poetry, miigwech to Denise Lajimodiere. For butternut squash, thank you to Howard Burke. For his beautiful Dakota corn, thank you to nephew Aaron Erdrich.

For bravely and regularly sitting down to tastings and giving feedback, my particular thanks to Dan, Persia, Big S2, and Jonathan Thunder. Apichigo miigwech to Mike Zimmerman and Margaret Noodin for songs and food talk. The world owes a debt of gratitude to Jim Denomie and Bruce White for liking my husband's pies and inspiring him to keep inventing lusciousness.

On a cold, clear day my sister Angie, her husband Sandeep, and their kids opened their home and, along with other fine people, ate in front of Kate Sommers's camera. I send my warm gratitude to Kate and our Sister's Potluck models Richard LaFortune, Megan Treinen, Kate Beane, Hinhan Cetanhotanka, Stuart Wayne Perkins, Jr., and Denise Lajimodiere. Thank you Hema, Kiizh, Saheli, and Shivani for being beautiful and for having some wild nail polish on that day.

For encouraging me, cooking alongside me, inspiring me, and conspiring with me, my profound thanks to Richard LaFortune and Helen Miller before him.

And my deepest thanks to Shannon Pennefeather for extraordinary patience, keen editorial skills, and generosity. Thanks to Ann Regan and to all of the folks at Minnesota Historical Society Press who helped me get through this life-altering process mistakenly referred to as "writing a cookbook."

I especially thank my niece, the artist Aza Erdrich, for her beautiful illustrations and her kindness in putting so much time into this project.

Ultimate thanks to John, Jules, and Eliza. The dining room table is finally clear of my notes and books. You have been stalwarts. Let's eat!

··· RESOURCES ···

ORGANIZATIONS

First Nations Native Foods Systems Resource Center

www.nativefoodsystems.org

"We recognize that accessing healthy food is a challenge for many Native American children and families. Without access to healthy food, a nutritious diet and good health are out of reach. To increase access to healthy food, First Nations supports tribes and Native communities as they build sustainable food systems that improve health, strengthen food security and increase the control over Native agriculture and food systems."

Great Lakes Indian Fish and Wildlife Commission (GLIFWC)

glifwc.org

"Formed in 1984, GLIFWC represents eleven Ojibwe tribes in Minnesota, Wisconsin, and Michigan who reserved hunting, fishing, and gathering rights in the 1837, 1842, and 1854 Treaties with the United States government."

Mazopiya Natural Food Market

www.mazopiya.com

"Mazopiya is a community oriented natural food market that focuses on clean organic foods and carries local products whenever possible, including produce from the Shakopee Mdewakanton Dakota Community's organic garden . . . In the Dakota language, 'Mazopiya' means 'a store, a place where things are put away and kept.'" Mazopiya offers catering services and cooking classes and publishes Wiconi Magazine.

Meskwaki Food Sovereignty Initiative

www.facebook.com/pages/Meskwaki-Food-Sovereignty-Initiative/338806802877345

The Meskwaki Food Sovereignty Initiative is a program of the Sac and Fox Tribe of the Mississippi in Iowa. MFSI works with the Meskwaki people to redefine our agriculture system to be focused around traditional, healthy, and sustainable foods. The program provides workshops, strategic planning, and other educational opportunities and resources to community members to provide support and opportunities as the Meskwaki redefine and reclaim their food system. This work is integrated with school gardens, community gardens, and the Meskwaki Community Farm, a forty-acre organic workers cooperative farm.

Native Wild Rice Coalition

www.nativewildricecoalition.com

"The Native Wild Rice Coalition will sustain, restore, and protect native wild rice communities in the Great Lakes Region and promote understanding of the cultural and natural values of wild rice." This organization lists sources for hand-harvested wild rice by state.

Penokee Hills Education Project

www.miningimpactcoalition.org

"The Penokee Hills Education Project is an education and outreach project of the Mining Impact Coalition and is focused on issues related to the proposed development of iron mining in northern Wisconsin."

Protect Our Manoomin

www.protectourmanoomin.org

"Protect Our Manoomin strongly opposes changes in environmental laws that affect the natural wild rice stands and ecosystem in northern Minnesota. These changes are culturally and ecologically irresponsible. Therefore, we are resolved, as a group of Anishinaabeg, non-Anishinaabeg, and non-Native, to resist any changes that endanger our manoomin. We will protect our manoomin for the present generation to the Seventh Generation . . . and beyond."

Save the Wild U.P.

www.savethewildup.org

"Save the Wild U.P.'s mission is to protect Michigan's Upper Peninsula's (UP) unique way of life, wildlife, landscape, and freshwater resources. Through public awareness and education we strive to protect the Upper Peninsula from unsustainable development, degradation and dangerous contamination."

White Earth Land Recovery Project (WELRP)

www.welrp.org

Founded and directed by indigenous activist Winona LaDuke, this organization initiated the Anishinaabe Seed Library, which saves and grows seeds important to Anishinaabe people. WELRP programs include food sovereignty–building resources, symposiums, and conferences for indigenous farmers and slow food events.

HELPFUL TOOLS

American Indian Health and Diet Project: lists of indigenous foods

www.aihd.ku.edu

Buy Fresh Buy Local Iowa

www.bfbliowa.org

Buy Fresh Buy Local Northeastern Iowa

www.iowafreshfood.com

Decolonizing Diet Project at Northern Michigan University

decolonizingdietproject.blogspot.com

The Northern Michigan University Center for Native American Studies implemented the Decolonizing Diet Project from March 2012 through March 2013. The DDP blog holds resources associated with the project, including recipes and spreadsheets of indigenous foods.

Local Harvest

www.localharvest.org

Find farmers markets, family farms, and other sources of sustainably grown food in your area or shop Local Harvest online.

Michigan Land Use Institute: local food directory

www.mlui.org

Native American manoomin sellers

www.manoomin.com/Distributors.html

North Dakota Local Foods Directory

www.nd.gov/ndda/files/resource/2013_Local_Foods_DirectoryWeb.pdf

Seed Savers Exchange

www.seedsavers.org

Slow Food USA

www.slowfoodusa.org

White Earth Tribal and Community College Extension Service: list for local foods

www.wetccextension.org

Wisconsin Local Food

www.wisconsinlocalfood.com

About tribal fishing:
www.lakesuperiorwhitefish.com

About Red Lake Nation efforts to reestablish walleye and other fish:
www.returnoftheredlakewalleye.com

About the food sovereignty movement:
view the film *Regaining Food Sovereignty: Neyaab Nimamoomin Mewinzha Gaa-inajigeyang* at www.ienearth.org

About indigenous seed saving and plants in the Upper Midwest: visit Jijak Foundation, Gun Lake Band of Pottawatomi Indians, www.jijak.org

About harvesting manoomin and to sample manoomin treats: attend the Wild Rice Festival in Roseville, Minnesota, www.wildricefestival.org

About indigenous resources in Michigan:
www.lifewaysinstitute.org

About wild foods of the Upper Midwest:
visit Standish Price Wild Food Interpretive Trail, www.foragersharvest.com

About Lac Courte Oreilles Ojibwe Harvest Camp in the Penokee Hills of Wisconsin, which hosts LCO members and guests inventorying resources, blazing trails, doing archaeology, and harvesting: www.lco-nsn.gov/mining.php

About Sustainable Agriculture Research and Education (SARE) growing indigenous corn varieties in a number of sites on reservation and nontribal lands in northern Minnesota, Wisconsin, and North Dakota, with the assistance of North Dakota State University: mysare.sare.org/mySARE/ProjectReport.aspx?do=viewRept&pn=LNC08-301&y=2010&t=0

READ MORE

Cox, Beverly, and Martin Jacobs. *Body Mind and Spirit: Native Cooking of the Americas*. Phoenix, AZ: Native Peoples Magazine, 2004.

Cox, Beverly, and Martin Jacobs. *Spirit of the Harvest: North American Indian Cooking*. New York: Stewart, Tabori and Chang, 1991.

Divina, Fernando, Marlene Divina, and the Smithsonian National Museum of the American Indian. *Foods of the Americas: Native Recipes and Traditions*. Berkeley, CA: Ten Speed Press, 2010.

Foushee, Lea, and Renee Gurneau. *Sacred Water, Water for Life*. Lake Elmo, MN: North American Water Office, 2010.

Laidlaw, Brett. *Trout Caviar: Recipes from a Northern Forager*. St. Paul: Minnesota Historical Society Press, 2011.

Nabhan, Gary Paul. *Renewing America's Food Traditions*. White River Junction, VT: Chelsea Green Publishing Company, 2008.

Peta Wakan Tipi. *Dream of Wild Health Cookbook*. Scandia, MN: Peta Wakan Tipi, 2012.

Rozin, Elisabeth. *Blue Corn and Chocolate*. New York: Alfred A. Knopf, Inc., 1992.

··· INDEX ···